*For Patrick and Ciaran*

# Contents

# The Academic Quality Handbook

Enhancing Higher Education
in Universities and Further
Education Colleges

Patrick McGhee

First published in Great Britain and the United States by Kogan Page Limited in 2003

120 Pentonville Road
London N1 9JN
UK
www.kogan-page.co.uk

22883 Quicksilver Drive
Sterling VA 20166-2012
USA

© Patrick McGhee 2003

**British Library Cataloguing in Publication Data**

A CIP record for this book is available from the British Library.

ISBN 0 7494 3661 1 (paperback)

**Library of Congress Cataloging-in-Publication Data**

McGhee, Patrick, 1962-
  The academic quality handbook : assuring and enhancing learning in higher education / Patrick McGhee.
    p. cm.
Includes bibliographical references and index.
  ISSBN 0-7494-3662-X (hardback) -- ISBN 0-7494-3661-1 (pbk.)
  1. Education, Higher--Great Britain--Evaluation--Handbooks, manuals, etc. 2. Quality assurance--Great Britain--Handbooks, manuals, etc. 1 Title.
  LB2331.65.G7M35 2003
  378.1'01--dc21
                    2003002786

Typeset by Saxon Graphics Ltd, Derby
Printed and bound in Great Britain by Bell & Bain Ltd, Glasgow

# Preface

This book is intended as an introduction to the management of quality assurance and enhancement in higher education particularly in England. The text focuses on the relationship between institutional quality assurance and the auditing authority of the Quality Assurance Agency for Higher Education, the QAA.

Although drawing heavily upon the 'quality infrastructure' agenda of The Framework for Higher Education Qualifications (FHEQ), subject benchmark statements (SBSs), the QAA Code of Practice and the arrangements for institutional audit, the book seeks to look beyond this infrastructure to the fundamental features of robust quality assurance processes and effective quality enhancement arrangements.

The book is designed to be practical, accessible and a resource for staff development. Although it is not designed as a scholarly analysis of quality as a theoretical concept, or a review of empirical data relating to implementing quality initiatives, recent research and analyses are drawn on where relevant.

This book is intended for anyone with an interest in quality assurance in education, but will be particularly useful for course leaders, Departmental heads, administrators, educational developers, quality unit staff and senior managers looking to review and develop practice, systems and policies. I hope that this book will also be useful to those with an interest in staff development as it is designed to stimulate reflection and research into institutional practices, personal views on quality and the future of enhancement. This book would be particularly useful as a common discussion point for course teams, departments or new staff cohorts.

Quality assurance is a rapidly developing area. Some chapters and articles published as late as summer of 2002 still operate on the assumption that the primary methodology for review of provision by the QAA would be what was known as 'academic review'. This has been largely abandoned in favour of an institutional audit arrangement focused supposedly on a lighter touch and the promotion of enhancement. The arrangements for institutional audit published by the QAA in Spring 2002 now appear to be stable until 2006. But, as was seen in the implementation of comprehensive subject review the nuances and emphasis can change over time. In order to ensure that this text stays as relevant as possible in the current climate and to facilitate discussion and access to additional resources, a Web site has been established for this book. It can be found at: www.academicquality.com.

If you have comments about this book or suggestions for improvement for any subsequent editions please visit the Web site and e-mail me.

I am grateful to various people who have helped me develop my ideas on quality over the past few years including Peter Marsh, Paul Birkett, Helen Marshall, Daniel Lamont, Angela Murphy, Pam Houghton, Bob Millington, John Shaw, Kevin Ellard and Elizabeth Fish. I am grateful to Jonathan at Kogan Page who initially commissioned the book and made sure it got started and Stephen Jones who made sure it got finished. As always I am grateful to Ciaran, Patrick and Marianne who put up with me while I wrote it.

# Introduction

A handbook on quality for higher education (or indeed on quality for anything else) might read something like this:

Chapter 1: Quality assurance (QA)
Write down what you are trying to do and check periodically that you are doing it.

Chapter 2: Quality enhancement (QE)
Write down what those who use your systems say about their experience and amend the systems accordingly.

However, as is often the case in quality matters the statements raise more questions than answers. What is involved in writing down what you are trying to do? What are the headings for this 'doing'? What is involved in 'checking periodically'? What systems? What experience? What kind of amendments? Who takes responsibility for doing all these things?
   Crucially there might also need to be a third chapter:

Chapter 3: Audit
Make sure you keep records as you go to prove to outsiders that you are following the advice of Chapters 1 and 2.

It is important that we do not lose sight of this third dimension. Universities, while constitutionally autonomous from government in the UK, are hugely dependent on public funding and therefore are subject to a heavy burden of accountability and audit. However, while audit is an important aspect of quality assurance (QA), it should not be allowed to become the motivation for it. Effective management of quality, understood as the effectiveness of a programme of learning given the needs of the student in the context of a defined set of learning outcomes, involves bringing assurance, enhancement and audit systems together while recognizing their different functions and rationale.
   In many respects, managing academic quality, particularly quality enhancement, is essentially an exercise in change management, and as such requires strategy, leadership, and sensitivity to local cultures and histories. This is no easy task when perceptions of quality at the start of a new century in the context of the inspectorial comprehensive subject review methodology are often expressed in terms of administrative burden, centralism, the dismantling of consensus, erosion of professional authority, short-termism and disempowerment.

## QUALITY ASSURANCE (QA) AND QUALITY ENHANCEMENT (QE)

QA and QE cannot be separated from one another. We cannot fully understand the nature of QE unless we recognize that it is often about ensuring that innovation, development, progress and change are not compromising the core aims and standards of a learning programme. Equally we cannot fully understand QA without considering how the setting, monitoring and review of academic standards if done effectively should automatically highlight opportunities for development and improvement.

However, there is another sense in which QA and QE are tightly related. While, in principle, a focus on QA can promote QE, it can if mismanaged also undermine it. For example, in formalizing learning outcomes for complex, extended and dynamic learning opportunities such as a research project, work placement or languages year abroad, there is a risk that the opportunities for development of the student's relationship with the learning opportunity are diminished. Learning outcomes are necessary to ensure that students have a framework for learning, but where such frameworks prematurely foreclose the learning that is possible, or valued, then there is clearly the risk that the learning experience is severely, and unnecessarily, diminished.

Additionally, there is a general principle that QE should not be attempted until QA is secure. No-one should be sailing to uncharted waters if the ship is not seaworthy, whatever the potential treasures over the horizon. In the case of new courses there is often a need for two or three full cycles of monitoring before significant enhancements can be confidently pursued. Similarly, in the development of placement learning it is essential that the foundations of trust, company buy-in and reciprocal confidence are established before the provision is substantially developed.

## INTERNATIONAL AND SECTORAL COMPARISONS

The role of value for money in public services and the perceived need to ensure that quality standards are protected in the context of widening participation is not limited to the UK. Smeby and Stensaker (1999) have reviewed the quality systems used in Sweden, Norway, Denmark and Finland and concluded that systems are closely allied to government general strategies and aims for higher education rather than to any particular philosophy for what is good academic quality. However, the relationship between government policy and quality systems, and the implications for university autonomy are not straightforward. Akoojee (2002) for example has argued that in the case of higher education in South Africa, QA systems *should* reflect broader sociopolitical goals – in the South African case, the goals of social redress, justice and equity. Despite the influence of political rather than pedagogical agenda there is evidence that counter to expectations higher education in Europe, while not convergent in terms of organizational structure, is increasingly convergent in terms of QA systems (Rakic, 2001). Since Rakic's review this process has accelerated with for example the QAA qualification descriptors (Chapter 1) being adopted as the core proposal by the post-Bologna conference of European Ministers for Higher Education (van der Wende and Westerheijden, 2002).

Looking across to other regulated sectors it is clear that the challenges and dilemmas facing higher education are not unique in the context of public expectations of standards and quality. Huitema, Jeliazkova and Westerheijden (2002) argue that quality managers in higher education face policy choices similar to those faced by managers of environmental quality. Using Fischer's (1995) framework of policy deliberation, they argue that both sectors face challenges from external stakeholders based around technical verification, situational validation, problem formulation and ideological argumentation.

The relationship between public and private sector provision is one that currently does not significantly affect higher education institutions (HEIs) in the UK. However, in the context of collaborative provision with overseas partner organizations (POs) it is important to recognize the role of QA as a regulatory resource. For example, Mehrez and Mizrahi (2000) have highlighted the tensions that occur when government policy incorporates significant private non-university provision but government is reluctant to intervene to monitor threshold standards, either with new institutions or in relation to their impact on standards in the established institutions. In the Israeli context they report that between 1989 and 1994 the total number of students increased by 26,000, representing a 40 per cent increase of which 11,000 of the students were in non-university institutions – a rise in that sector of 130 per cent. They suggest that extending educational opportunities to meet student demand connected to fluctuations in the employment market reinforces the instrumentality of degrees such that variations in academic quality become a much more marginal concern for student customers, who value the degree purely in terms of its impact on promotion or salary.

In addition to the rapidly changing economic and regulatory environment in which universities must exist in the 21st century is the unravelling of many of the cultural and ideological constructions on which the very idea of a university is founded in Western thought. Established HEIs were largely developed in the context of rationalist, scientific and modernist society, and as the certainties of those foundations dissolve with the dawning of a postmodern, 'chaotic', distributed knowledge society, universities must re-examine their role in broader economic and social terms (Scott, 2002; Smith and Webster, 1997). (See also Chapters 5 and 16).

## QUALITY CULTURES AND SERVICE

As stated earlier in many respects managing academic quality is essentially an exercise in change management, and requires strategy, leadership, and sensitivity to local cultures and histories. In particular strategic leadership is required to protect and enhance standards while *reducing* administrative burden, centralism, the dismantling of consensus, erosion of professional authority, short-termism and disempowerment.

Consideration of some of these dynamics makes it clear why highly structured approaches to modelling the quality landscape can only take us so far. Newby (1999) has argued that the fundamental distinction in QA systems is between purpose (threshold focus or enhancement focus) and source of judgement (external or internal). In this framework QAA institutional audit would clearly fall into the threshold-external category, in-house staff development into the internal-enhancement category and so on. Within this context internal enhancement procedures would include adoption of some form of total quality management (TQM) or related approach. Newby argues that such formal internal enhancement schemes have failed in higher education because of management culture, academic cultures and the legacy of past quality initiatives. In terms of management culture the shift from democratic academic management structures to line management systems coupled with a focus on costs and revenues has militated against the devolution of authority and empowerment which TQM-type initiatives entail. In terms of academic culture, the complexity and ambiguity of the student as customer allied to academic commitment to the discipline rather than the institution makes any simple focus on customer service problematic. In terms of quality legacy the focus in academia is on the credibility of the inputs, argues Newby, not on the experience of the student.

There is much in this analysis but there are other factors. In the chaotic postmodern university, there is not only a distrust of systems, there is an absolute distrust of total systems. The whole discourse of TQM 'customer', 'service' and its assumptions of employee commitment to the corporate goals can be incompatible with the academic discourse of 'learning', 'collegiality', 'development' and 'professionalism'. In the UK it should also not be underestimated that the perceived 'Americaness' of TQM and related systems is another piece of baggage which limits its credibility. Nevertheless, commitment to the ideas of flexibility, improvement and responsibility are widespread in most UK university departments but they are just not seen as part of an overall quality architecture. Conceptions of 'service' are also a locus for dispute. In the academic collegiate discourse 'service' – understood as good quality teaching, academic counselling and feedback in the sense of a student-centred orientation – is a central category. However, 'service' perceived as 'the customer is always right' mentality coupled with inane 'have a nice day' pleasantries is clearly outside the world view of most academics. Additionally, the greater a *quantitative* approach to TQM is pursued with a discourse of key performance indicators, customer response time and service satisfaction ratings, the less likely academic acceptance will be given. By contrast the commitment to a *discursive* model of quality focusing on narratives of personal, curricular and disciplinary development and transformation is likely to be more persuasive.

It is recognized in the private sector that excellence through service quality is not the same as excellence through product quality. Service is essentially a complex, interpersonal transaction rather than a manufactured object and as such needs to be managed in a different way. However, some of the major strategies employed by service-focused organizations are arguably not easily transferable into higher education. The first strategy is training and this provides no problems of principle in higher education given the broad culture of learning and development. However, the second strategy is empowerment and this in the context of detailed QA regimes is perceived as problematic. Effective service delivery requires employees who are empowered to do whatever is required to ensure that customers are satisfied, and the employees need to know that their decisions will not be overturned by management, and that within reason, they will not be disciplined for any suboptimal resolution. It is interesting to reflect upon whether academics are empowered in this particular customer solutions way. It is clear that in universities academics have significant autonomy over time, the expression of ideas, the design and delivery of the curriculum and so on. However, most of these are contingent on the agreement or review of peers and not all of these relate to the everyday problems that students have with their learning or their relationship to a bureaucratic organization. Academics have discretion over such matters as whether or not to accept an essay that has arrived after the deadline or to penalize a student for non-attendance at a laboratory class (though of course there are signs that the boundaries of this autonomy are being renegotiated through managerial and administrative interventions). Ultimately, the central issue for academic life in particular and for public sector service in general is that the greater the degree of empowerment of front-line employees who interact in significant ways with clients, the greater the danger of case-by-case inconsistency and overall lack of transparency. Academics just cannot give a student a dispensation from class, or a higher mark than is justified or exemption from a pre-requisite module on the grounds of customer satisfaction – that would be ridiculous. But that is not the issue, which is rather how far do institutions go in supporting students with on-the-spot decisions about access to library resources, additional tuition, additional feedback or guidance? Institutional managers or quality monitors will have no problem with academics spontaneously giving more of their *own* time on the spot to help a student, but there is much less scope for academics (or anyone else) to cut through procedures and exercise discretion in relation to *institutional* resources. From the point of view of customer service this is a very impoverished notion of empowerment indeed, and not one likely to change in the foreseeable future. Thus customer-orientated models of service and hence of quality may have limited applications in higher education at least in academic contexts.

## THE FUTURE OF QUALITY

Pond (2002), writing about the challenges facing traditional US institutions in the light of distributed learning made possible through the Internet, has argued that there is a fundamental mismatch between traditional accrediting paradigms and new educational realities. He suggests that the private sector rather than the government will establish 'consumer-based' means for judging quality, with the possibility of an Amazon or eBay for learning programmes. Alternatively, he proposes, alliances of universities, private providers, learners, professional organizations and businesses will develop their own quality regimes. Finally, he suggests the possibility of an accreditation of learner (outcome) achievement rather than recognition of (course) credit or the status of the instructional institution. Despite Pond's assertions to the contrary it seems difficult to see how any 'post-accreditation' consortium could manage QA as distinct from customer preference. However, the shift from campus-based traditional programmes to distributed and assembled learning packages may accelerate the move towards threshold standard accreditation underwritten by universities in conjunction with coordinating public agencies and customer service-based differentiation managed by private sector bodies. Clearly this trend is already more prevalent with the demise of points-based comprehensive subject review and newspaper league tables awarding points for the quality of sporting and social facilities. Additionally, the 2003 White Paper, which makes provision for a Guide to Higher Education produced by HEFCE in collaboration with the National Union of Students, takes us further down the path of customer defined quality challenging standards-defined quality.

It is difficult to see how some of the disputes around the appropriate balance between autonomy and accountability, between QA and QE can be resolved in any meaningful way. As noted by Scott (2002) the resolution and closure of controversies is becoming increasingly difficult in the postmodern age and when faced with multiple inspection and quality regimes universities may retreat into excessive instrumentalism and relativism.

## THE ORGANIZATION OF THIS BOOK

This book is organized into two parts. The first, entitled 'The quality infrastructure', reviews the framework for higher education qualifications, subject benchmark statements, institutional audit and QE. It provides the basis for the second part, 'Managing quality in the context of the QAA Code of Practice', which examines through the various relevant sections of the Code of Practice the issues, risks and opportunities for good practice inherent in a comprehensive approach to quality in higher education. A directory of Web addresses and contact details of key quality organizations is attached as an appendix and are available on the Web site.

Throughout the book there are **reflective practice points**, designed to stimulate further consideration of the material in the context of the reader's own professional practice. These may be useful discussion points for course teams or departmental groups. Occasionally there are **good practice points** which highlight examples of good practice which may, or may not, be useful in specific institutional contexts. Boxes in the text highlight key points or examples of particular policies or initiatives. At the end of each chapter is a list of the **key issues in QA** and **key issues in QE** for the area reviewed. These are presented as summaries of some of the main points raised in the text and as an input to further thinking about activities or developments that may be effective in the particular context in which the reader is operating. They are not intended to be prescriptive but it should be clear from the text why they are effective in the right context. Finally at the end of each chapter is a set of reflective practice points encouraging reflection on broader issues, often across two or more sets of related issues.

## A NOTE ON HIGHER EDUCATION IN FURTHER EDUCATION COLLEGES (FECs)

The focus of this book is on higher education but recognizes that 11 per cent of higher education is delivered by the FE sector in collaboration with HE partners. The emergence of Foundation degrees in the 2003 Government White Paper as a key mechanism to widen participation raises further the profile of quality assurance of franchised sub-degree provision. While there are many explicit references in the book to FE delivery issues affected by QAA codes and benchmarks, it should be remembered that institutional audit and academic review typically involve review of all HE provision wherever it is delivered and as such the general discussions here on Subject Benchmark Statements, managing assessment, course validation and review, and monitoring are equally relevant to FE and HE providers.

# Part 1
# The quality
# infrastructure

# 1 The Framework for Higher Education Qualifications (FHEQ)

The definitive framework for qualifications that applies to courses and programmes of study in higher education in England, Wales and Northern Ireland is that published by the QAA in January 2001: the Framework for Higher Education Qualifications (FHEQ). The framework for Scotland is slightly different, reflecting historical traditions in naming awards, particularly the MA, which refers to under-graduate degrees of four years' duration.

The National Committee of Inquiry into Higher Education (NCIHE, 1997 – the Dearing report) and the Scottish equivalent (the Garrick report) both recommended the establishment of a qualifications framework.

> Students need to be clear about the requirements of the programmes to which they are committed, and about the levels of achievement expected of them. Employers want higher education to be more explicit about what they can expect from candidates for jobs, whether they have worked at sub-degree, degree, or postgraduate level. Existing arrangements for safeguarding standards are insufficiently clear to carry conviction with those who perceive present quality and standards to be unsatisfactory. We believe there is much to be gained by greater explicitness and clarity about standards and the levels of achievement required for different awards. (NCIHE, 1997: S10.2)

The aims of the FHEQ are to promote transparency and consistency in awards and facilitate greater public understanding of the distinctions between different levels of award. It attempts to do this by providing a structure for understanding higher education and making the outcomes of individual awards more explicit. Additionally, the existence of a framework in principle supports public confidence in awards across the UK and enables comparability with qualification schemes across Europe and beyond. Some specific issues addressed by the FHEQ include the idea that postgraduate programmes should in some way 'build on' undergraduate programmes (in terms of curricular challenge and skill development) rather than simply 'follow on' from them. The FHEQ is an outcomes-based qualifications framework, which defines qualifications in terms of the end product rather than inputs, processes or increments in learning. The FHEQ is expected to be in place in relevant HEIs by the start of the academic year 2003–04.

The descriptors for each award comprise two parts: a statement of outcomes (what students need to achieve for the award) and a statement of skills and abilities that a typical student should be able to demonstrate if he or she possesses such an award. This outcomes-based approach means that the framework provides a context for subject benchmark statements (SBSs – see Chapter 2) which in turn inform programme specifications. It is in this way that the QAA seeks to develop a quality infrastructure for the higher education sector nationally.

The FHEQ is distinguished from a credit framework. The former is a statement of the characteristics of achievement at different levels; the latter is a statement of how units of learning effort build up through credit accumulation into an award associated with a programme of study. The FHEQ does not seek to directly map skills or knowledge highlighted in SBSs onto qualifications, nor was it intended to. It can be noted however that we see here the significance of the lack of articulation between learning outcomes and degree classification, something which remains an unresolved issue in the quality infrastructure (see Jackson, 2002). The FHEQ does reflect this issue indirectly when it states: 'The outcomes associated with a qualification should be understood in an holistic way, and their achievement should be demonstrated directly.'

## REFLECTIVE PRACTICE POINT

Consider the distinctions either across or within SBSs between a threshold and a typical/modal level of achievement. Which of these two levels seems to map most closely on to the level of skills and attainment outlined in the qualifications framework for the honours award? Why might there be a discrepancy here?

The framework overall has five levels as follows: Certificate (C) level, Intermediate (I) level, Honours (H) level, Masters (M) level and a Doctoral (D) level. Each of these levels has a corresponding set of specifications about what level of knowledge and skills should be associated with successful completion of awards validated at that level.

The system still leaves some anomalies. The Oxbridge MA system, which involves BA (Hons) graduates receiving an MA four years after graduation without the inconvenience of any further study, remains unaltered. A note in the FHEQ helpfully 'clarifies' the situation 'the MAs granted by the Universities of Oxford and Cambridge are not academic qualifications'.

The full descriptor for each level is made up of:

- a statement of the learning outcomes students for the award would be expected to be able to demonstrate;
- what holders of the qualification would 'typically' be able to do;
- the qualities and transferable skills an award holder would normally possess.

It is worth looking at the full descriptor for the level H, the honours degree award. (See Box 1.1.)

---

**Box 1.1**

*Descriptor for a qualification at level H (honours)*

**Bachelors degree with Honours**
Honours degrees are awarded to students who have demonstrated:

- a systematic understanding of key aspects of their field of study, including acquisition of coherent and detailed knowledge, at least some of which is at, or informed by, the forefront of defined aspects of a discipline;
- an ability to deploy accurately established techniques of analysis and enquiry within a discipline;
- conceptual understanding that enables the student:
  - to devise and sustain arguments, and/or to solve problems, using ideas and techniques, some of which are at the forefront of a discipline;
  - to describe and comment upon particular aspects of current research, or equivalent advanced scholarship, in the discipline.
- an appreciation of the uncertainty, ambiguity and limits of knowledge;
- the ability to manage their own learning, and to make use of scholarly reviews and primary sources (eg refereed research articles and/or original materials appropriate to the discipline).

Typically, holders of the qualification will be able to:

- apply the methods and techniques that they have learned to review, consolidate, extend and apply their knowledge and understanding, and to initiate and carry out projects;

---

- critically evaluate arguments, assumptions, abstract concepts and data (that may be incomplete), to make judgements, and to frame appropriate questions to achieve a solution – or identify a range of solutions – to a problem;
- communicate information, ideas, problems, and solutions to both specialist and non-specialist audiences.

They will also have:

- qualities and transferable skills necessary for employment requiring:
  - the exercise of initiative and personal responsibility;
  - decision making in complex and unpredictable contexts;
  - the learning ability needed to undertake appropriate further training of a professional or equivalent nature.

## REFLECTIVE PRACTICE POINTS

What issues does the existence of the FHEQ raise for managing academic quality at the institutional level?

Who is responsible for revising your university's regulatory framework in the light of the FHEQ?

Who is responsible for ensuring that for validation and review panel chairs are briefed, for example, on the principle that awards need to be defined in terms of positive achievement?

To what extent would you say your validation and review process explicitly checks that new or revised honours programmes have programme specifications that are at least consistent with the level H descriptor?

What mechanisms are there in your institution for revising programmes not due for review in terms of the implications of the FHEQ?

The FHEQ provides an overview of the relationship between different qualifications (particularly in relation to progression) and other parts of the quality infrastructure of external reference points. It is essential to consider the FHEQ in the context of specific detailed statements identified in the detailed SBSs when constructing programme specifications for a given programme. Together these give an overall framework for the knowledge, understanding and skills that need to be delivered and assessed in specific courses.

Consider the Certificate level descriptor in the FHEQ. To what extent does this map on to any advice given to module writers at your institution? In your experience are there students failing their year 1 (or equivalent) programme who meet this specification? Are there students who pass year 1 who do not meet this specification? How many students each year leave with a Certificate in Higher Education? What are the criteria at your institution for this award?

## USE OF THE FHEQ

The FHEQ is an important part of institutional audit. It should be noted however that the link to review/audit in the original publication refers to the now downgraded 'academic review' methodology. Paragraph 82 in the *Handbook for Academic Review* very much gives an impression of policing of an external standard while the comparable paragraph in the *Handbook for Institutional Audit* (para 55) presents a more developmental approach. Nevertheless, where programmes have outcomes that do not clearly map on to the descriptors specified in the FHEQ for the level of the programme award, the HEI will have the burden of proof to justify its use of the award: 'Claims that those outcomes can be achieved from volumes of learning that are significantly below those found necessary by institutions generally, are likely to be tested by reviewers with particular thoroughness.' It would be interesting if an institution were able to show that students were achieving the aims of the award with a significantly lower volume of study, possibly in the context of a postgraduate programme with a demanding entry requirement. For the issue is not as the example in the *Academic Review Handbook* might suggest (para 82) that outcomes of an allegedly postgraduate programme would be all at the undergraduate level, but rather that students would have demonstrated postgraduate outcomes possibly very clearly but only over a limited range of modules.

## GOOD PRACTICE POINT

Assuming an institution has confidence that its programme specifications map on to the relevant descriptors, and in the case of undergraduate programmes (and some foundation degree programmes) that they also map on to the relevant subject benchmark, there is scope for being more explicit and consistent in the writing of student references after graduation. Indeed it might even be possible for a template for a given course to be produced which lays out the skills and achievements implied by the award of the degree. This would free up time for referees to discuss students' interpersonal skills, interests and extracurricular activities and contributions.

## IMPLEMENTING THE PRECEPTS OF THE FHEQ

In order to clarify the key expectations of the FHEQ and to identify an agenda for good practice, the QAA specify three precepts which institutions are expected to have considered in the construction of their award schemes. These cover award, positioning and naming of qualifications. The small number of precepts here, in what can be a complex topic, compared to areas of the Code of Practice, reflects the concern of the QAA not to be seen as too prescriptive in the area of awards.

### *Awarding qualifications*

*Precept: Qualifications should be awarded to mark the achievement of positively defined outcomes, not as compensation for failure at a higher level, or by default.*

The aim of this precept is to stop the practice of awarding pass or ordinary degrees in the case of students registered for an undergraduate honours degree who have performed poorly in courses or modules associated with the honours element of the programme. This 'catch all' category has traditionally been characterized by failure to achieve sufficient credit to secure the full award. The principle here is that failure in pursuit of award X does not rule out giving award Y, providing the outcomes for award Y have been defined and achieved. Since many universities did not have outcomes specification for pass degrees (because it was never an award for which any student was *enrolled*) this stipulation has led to the need for the formal declaration of what knowledge and skills a pass degree involves.

For awards in general the FHEQ seeks to ensure that there is no backdoor to a qualification. Where compensation or condonation is applied it is a requirement that these devices do not operate in such a way that the students are securing an award for which they have not achieved the specified outcomes. This is most obviously an issue when performance in a 'core' (ie compulsory) module is unsatisfactory. Given that essential learning outcomes are likely to be attached to core modules, condoning failure and awarding the target award would be misleading in as much as the student would not have met the outcomes specified for the award. This theoretically would leave degrees of a similar nature diminished and cause confusion amongst stakeholders.

There are however technically anomalous cases that the application of the above principle creates. If condonement is applied to a core module then the degree is being awarded when the candidate will have not in fact achieved at least some of the essential learning outcomes for the degree for which he or she was registered. However, there will be cases where a student has failed a core module, or has in some other way failed to demonstrate an essential learning outcome as noted in the programme specification for the particular award for which he or she is registered, but *nevertheless* has achieved a level of skills and knowledge, and capability for employment, which matches or surpasses the FHEQ outcome for an award in general. Clearly, students who by virtue of failing, say, a module on practical programming in a computing degree fail the degree are unlikely to be able to demonstrate that they have 'developed analytical techniques and problem-solving skills that can be applied in many types of employment' in some other manner. However, if the degree is in database computing and the students have failed a compulsory module or modules in practical database applications, then while they would inevitably fail the degree for which they have enrolled, they may very well have demonstrated that they have achieved the programme specification outcomes for a general computing degree (where limited database skills while lamentable is not terminal). The FHEQ does not address this issue nor was it designed to. The deeper issue is that the FHEQ, and the principles promoted for its application, reinforce the assumption that students can only be awarded the degrees for which they are registered.

### Positioning qualifications within the FHEQ

*Precept: Institutions should be able to demonstrate that each of their qualifications is allocated to the appropriate level of the framework.*

Addressing this precept involves institutions having considered the *mapping* between programme outcomes (from the programme specification) and qualification descriptors (from the FHEQ); the *volume* of assessed work; and the extent to which the *curricular opportunities* provide an opportunity to demonstrate the programme outcomes.

### Mapping

Within the context of the FHEQ it is essential that the programme outcomes for a particular type of award can be articulated with the framework descriptors for that award. Thus a programme specification for a BSc (Hons) Psychology must contain programme outcomes that map on to the framework descriptors for level H awards. While in principle this need not cause difficulty there are a number of considerations that need to be borne in mind.

---

### Mapping programme specifications on to FHEQ descriptors

Issues include:

- Honours awards should be given to students who have demonstrated 'the ability to manage their own learning, and to make use of scholarly reviews and primary sources (eg refereed research articles and/or original materials appropriate to the discipline)' (FHEQ, Annex 1). Most programmes will show how this is achieved by their graduates through an honours dissertation, thesis, portfolio or other 'independent study' module. Wherever such sustained independent original work with primary sources or materials is lacking as an explicit module, it is essential that the way in which students do in fact show these skills and have them assessed is carefully thought through and demonstrable. The programme specification must be clear about the level of independence expected of the student and where this will be demonstrated. It must not be the case that students can avoid such demonstration within the curricular structure of the programme if the programme specification says it is essential for the award.

- Honours awards, according to the FHEQ, indicate that students have 'demonstrated qualities and transferable skills necessary for employment requiring: the exercise of initiative and personal responsibility; decision-making in complex and unpredictable contexts; and the learning ability needed to undertake appropriate further training of a professional or equivalent nature.'

    The statement of personal and transferable skills is understandably predicated albeit loosely on skills relevant to employment and presupposes that students do not possess these skills prior to completion of their degree. However, over 130,000 part-time students achieved degrees in 2000–01, a significant percentage of whom would have been concurrently or recently in full-time employment. The FHEQ promotes a focus on developing a capability for work but that may not be a priority for all students. It is unfortunate that the FHEQ does not include the skills needs of those who are already experienced in work and have already developed transferable skills.

### Volume of assessed study

The precept here is attempting to ensure that an award cannot simply require students to show the skills or knowledge relevant to the award in a superficial or narrow sense. In practice this means that an award has to do more than just have, say, one piece of work that enables a student to demonstrate 'an appreciation of the uncertainty, ambiguity and limits of knowledge'. This is something perhaps which needs to be demonstrated consistently across a wide range of assessment events. There are no hard and fast rules here about how many times assessment occurs or what weighting of assessment might be involved; the issue for institutions here is, as always, that they are able to present a coherent justification for the arrangements of the provision they offer.

*Curricular opportunities*

If a programme of study in terms of its curricular structure – as defined by module content and the organization of compulsory and optional modules – does not enable a student to demonstrate the knowledge or skills implied by the programme specification, and in turn therefore the qualification descriptor, then clearly there is something profoundly misconceived and deficient about the programme. However, attention must also be paid to the possibility of students being able to avoid certain modules for whatever reason and as a consequence not being required to demonstrate certain skills.

A further important idea here is 'all students'. This may be particularly relevant in areas of collaborative production and performance where not all students will be able to take on, say, the role of director. Such subtleties may be revealed in the delivery of the programme rather than the details of the syllabus and can often need careful scrutiny.

## Naming qualifications

The QAA advice is that degree titles such as 'honours', 'masters' and 'Doctor' are used for awards only when those awards 'meet in full the expectations of the qualification descriptors at levels H, M or D respectively'.

Much is made in the FHEQ of public understanding of the achievements implied by different awards within higher education. But in truth the relations amongst levels, credit, awards and outcomes are not immediately transparent to the casual observer and any attempt to provide an accurate and accessible account is fraught with difficulty. In fact the FHEQ, in its attempt to clarify different types of post-degree awards, introduces a further complication through an additional distinction between postgraduate and graduate awards. 'Postgraduate' is obviously the more established term and is now fixed to mean programmes which *build on* undergraduate degrees and of course are characterized by qualification descriptors from level M. 'Graduate' awards now relate to courses which while requiring a degree to enter do not build on the degree level competence but offer re-training opportunities (such as conversion courses).

## QA ISSUES WITH THE FHEQ

The major threats to QA in this area are likely to be:

- incomplete incorporation of the framework within the QAA timeframe;

- lag between reform of institutional primary regulations on the one hand and the secondary or supporting policies on the other (such as policies on approval, monitoring and review);
- lack of transparency between the intended learning outcomes achieved in joint or combined programmes and the qualifications framework for honours degrees;
- lack of articulation between year 1 or stage 1 intended learning outcomes modules and the descriptor for a Certificate in Higher Education;
- failure to make provision for the demonstration of independent learning in programmes which lack a compulsory or honours dissertation element;
- failure to make provision within regulations for students who fail to make the honours degree classification criteria;
- in the context of the need to provide accurate, reliable and complete information on first destinations, failure to check whether graduates are going on to graduate or postgraduate study.

---

### Reflecting on the FHEQ

To what extent do you believe that relocating some conversion programmes previously at postgraduate level M to level H, and reclassifying them as graduate rather than postgraduate awards, would lead to a dumbing down or marginalization of such awards?

Do you agree that Oxford and Cambridge should be exempt from the level M descriptor on the ground that these are 'not academic awards'? Does your institution have any plans to introduce non-academic awards of this kind?

To what extent do you feel that the FHEQ has successfully addressed Dearing's concern that 'existing arrangements for safeguarding standards are insufficiently clear to carry conviction with those who perceive present quality and standards to be unsatisfactory' (NCIHE, 1997). What else could be done to promote public understanding and confidence of the higher education qualifications architecture in the UK? Is the promotion of this public understanding and confidence the same as for UK audiences as it is for overseas audiences?

What percentage of graduates in your department or in your university currently meet the level H descriptor in the FHEQ? What percentage does the QAA assume meet the descriptor? If your two figures are not the same, how would you explain the discrepancy? In what way might this discrepancy arise during institutional audit?

Which undergraduate programmes you are familiar with in your institution best exemplify the articulation between programme specification, the FHEQ level H descriptor and the relevant SBS? How would you construct a case study in preparation for institutional audit to demonstrate the effectiveness of the process underpinning this outcome? Are there any programmes with which you are familiar which fail to integrate the external reference points with internal practice? How would you explain why this has come about? How would you explain it to an auditor?

# 2 Benchmarking academic standards: the subject benchmark statements (SBSs)

'37. Not everything that is valuable can be separately tested, measured or quantified.'

(Philosophy Subject Benchmark Statement)

The QAA has published 47 benchmark statements (22 in April 2000 and a further 25 in March 2002). In addition there are Department of Health/NHS benchmarks, a benchmark for Masters programmes in business and management, a benchmark for Masters of Engineering programmes and there is also a benchmark for Initial Teacher Training in Scotland. Finally, there is generic benchmark for foundation degrees. The benchmarks were put together by working groups which drew their membership from academic and professional bodies. The statements are seen as evolutionary and will be reviewed from 2003 onwards. As has been noted several times, different disciplines already had benchmark statements of one kind or another. In particular, professional and statutory bodies (PSBs) have, with varying degrees of specificity and with differing levels of policing, issued general curriculum specifications for many years. Houghton (2002) has provided a detailed analysis of how the benchmark statement for engineering was used at his institution alongside the statements from the UK Engineering Council, the UK Engineering Professors' Conference and the US Accreditation Board for Engineering and Technology – and the difficulties this presented. It is interesting to compare on the one hand the experience of Houghton, a practitioner, with the demanding and sometimes contradictory advice on the status of the SBSs, with the reassuring declarations of Laugharne (2002) on behalf of the QAA on the other. To some extent the different perceptions can be explained by reference to the different approach implied by the guidance contained in the academic review methodology of 2000 (which was never implemented in higher education), where the function of benchmarks was for the first time fully articulated, with the more conciliatory and 'lighter touch' approach implied by the institutional audit methodology which replaced it in 2002.

SBSs express expectations in relation to curriculum, skills and standards. In terms of curriculum they lay down a 'broad framework' (rather than any detailed syllabus) for the subject knowledge that an undergraduate degree should contain. In terms of skills, expectations are provided on variously the cognitive, subject and transferable skills that graduates in any given discipline area might be expected to possess. In terms of standards, expectations are expressed as 'threshold' and/or 'typical' student's achievement. Threshold means third class honours degrees and typical means upper second. In some cases reference is made in the standards section to 'levels of excellence' meaning first class degrees. As noted by Jackson (2002) QAA benchmarks only incorporate one of three potential elements of any benchmark. They do involve a reference point against which similar programmes can be compared but they do not include a criterion (ie a dimension or indicator) against which or along which something could be measured, nor gradations of distinction which would mark out the poor, the good, the excellent or the exceptional.

## AIMS AND FUNCTION

The aim of the benchmarks is to provide a common point of reference for achievement of academic standards. However, while the aim of the overall quality infrastructure of the FHEQ, the Code of Practice and the programme specification system is to provide a context for the broad comparability of academic standards across the sector, the aim of the SBS system is also clearly developmental. The SBS system serves to make both entire academic communities and institutional programme teams more explicit about what they judge to be key elements of the undergraduate curriculum and to engage in discussion about the boundaries, definitions and priorities that such explicitness renders more conspicuous.

It was clear from the outset of the development of SBSs from the pilot programmes organized by the QAA, which covered law, history and chemistry, that there would be differences in perception of what SBSs were for and how they might be used. Law focused on the threshold and typical standard, history focused on the typical graduate and the chemistry group focused on progression to a professional qualification.

SBSs are designed to be used to inform programme design by providing a common point of departure for new courses. The SBSs are intended to offer 'variety and flexibility in the design of programmes and encourage innovation within an agreed overall framework' according to the preamble to benchmarks. SBSs also provide an overarching context to support HEIs' own evaluation of the articulation between programme specifications, module learning outcomes, assessment activity and student achievement. Crucially, and most controversially, SBSs are used for external review but are, according to the QAA, not designed to be used as a 'crude checklist'. Rather they are intended as one reference point alongside programme specification and internal self-evaluations of the provision in any given area. Interestingly, the preamble for the second batch of SBSs in March 2002 dropped the reference found in the April 2000 batch to SBSs being used in conjunction with 'primary data' to arrive at judgements. This reflects the radical reform of the review methodology which had been carried out in the interim and which emphasized a lighter touch. Additionally, specific concerns had been expressed about external reviewers using SBSs as a means of making absolute judgements on the 'primary data' of student work rather than the relative judgements against HEIs' own aims, thereby subverting university autonomy. This is reflected in some of the detailed content of the SBSs themselves. In the sociology benchmark for example it is stated that: 'The benchmark statements have a double function: they enable the perform-ance of individual students to be benchmarked in relation to specific learning outcomes; and they provide a framework within which whole programmes can be reviewed' (Sociology SBS: 5).

However, in response to the uncertainty expressed across the sector in relation to the role of SBSs in institutional audit, the QAA has attempted to spell out how it intends the SBSs to be used by auditors and how they should not be used. As made clear by Laugharne, writing on behalf of the QAA, an SBS 'has more to do with a prompt for self-critical reflection than it has to do with providing hard criteria for judging stan-dards' (2002:136). A benchmark, he argues, is more like a map laying out possible routes than like an itinerary laying out a specific necessary route. Some have seen the introduction of SBSs as the beginning of a national curriculum for higher education, policed through the institutional audit methodology. However, Laugharne rejects this interpretation: 'The QAA's position on this is unequivocal. Benchmark information will not be used by auditors as a checklist of prescribed curricular content and speci-fied standards against which to make judgements' (2002:137).

To what extent do SBSs actually provide a basis for reviewing threshold or typical standards though? The problem here is that even when assessments map on to learn-ing outcomes there is limited transparency between the achievement of certain knowledge, understanding or skills and the course or module grade awarded. There is further inconsistency between institutions on the relationship between the grade profile across a range of courses or modules and the degree classification awarded. The relationship between awards and specific learning outcomes is mediated through complex degree classification algorithms that vary from university to university. In other words, a student profile demonstrating the threshold standard in one institution may receive a pass degree, and a third class degree in another. Similarly, it is possible that a student profile would achieve the subject knowledge and skills associated with the typical profile and get a lower second in one university but an upper second in another.

The SBSs are presented as the necessary and sufficient conditions for the confirmation of any given award. Students need to do no more than is specified and there are no other ways in which such an award could be achieved. However, in practice it is not always clear how an institution could easily demonstrate how skills and subject knowledge obtained (or not) within the context of a module correlates with the management of, say, the lower and upper second borderline. In some respects the problem is that the benchmark statements are written as *categorical* statements (students will have or will not have such and such a skill) while degree classification is ultimately determined by statements of the *extent* to which a student is able to demonstrate that he or she possesses that skill. Jackson has referred to this as the 'unresolved issue of the assessment model' (2002:148). As Jackson notes, when there are 30 or more subject and generic skills which students are expected to achieve, the compensation and averaging systems used by most universities render the relationship between achievement and credit problematic. Houghton (2002) has proposed that students should be required to demonstrate 80 per cent of the threshold standard (rather than fully meeting it). However, this does not deal with the large number of 80+ per cent scores that would be required and still assumes the dismantling of the degree classification system.

The SBSs define the difference between threshold and typical (or 'modal') performance very broadly and their application requires the exercise of subjective judgement. A common distinction is that threshold students will 'recognize' or 'describe' patterns or differences while typical students will be able to 'account for', 'analyse' and explain these patterns or differences.

The benchmarks have been seen as a move towards a national curriculum for higher education, if not in terms of content or subject knowledge then in terms of the general skills students need to possess. However, there may be in some areas at least significant differences in what skills are expected.

---

### Key skills?

The benchmarks for English literature and philosophy provide a vaguely amusing illustration of interdisciplinary differences on what counts as 'key skills'.

The benchmark for English literature says:
'a key subject specific skill which students should acquire is:
rhetorical skills of effective communication and argument, both oral and written';

But the benchmark for philosophy says:

'General skills

vii. Ability to recognize methodological errors, rhetorical devices, unexamined conventional wisdom, unnoticed assumptions, vagueness and superficiality.'

Where this leaves the wretched joint honours student of English and philosophy, who must simultaneously demonstrate a fluency in rhetorical argumentation alongside a healthy cynicism for that very activity, is unclear.

## QA ISSUES WITH SBSs

The main point of departure for considering the relationship between SBSs and QA is to recognize that the requirement is not for adherence to, but engagement with, the benchmark. There is thus no problem in principle if after discussion and debate a programme team submits for validation a course in history that in some non-trivial ways does not adhere to the content of the history benchmark statement. There would need to be good reasons for this and given that the benchmarks emerged from discussions with a reasonable cross-section of the history academic community it could be considered as something of a departure from sectoral practice. In that sense a deficiency in QA would not arise simply because a programme did not adhere slavishly to its specification. Much more serious would be the case where the deliberations at the point of validation or review failed to draw upon the benchmark statement. Conceivably a programme which adhered precisely to an SBS but for which there was no evidence that there had been any sensible discussion about the advantages of that specification, would be viewed as more derelict in QA terms.

Of course a programme which slipped over time through a lack of monitoring, or a lack of resources, or through a failure to manage the academic specialisms in relation to staff turnover, would not be consistent with the notion of QA systems at all. Some institutions, mindful of limiting the bureaucratic burden and keen to promote curricular reform and innovation, have established fast-track approval schemes for minor changes to the content of programmes. While these always make a statement to the effect that the net effect of minor changes must not alter the overall character of the programme, this is a very difficult area to monitor. There is a need therefore to make sure that provision does not slip out of the well-intentioned framework of the programme specification or the relevant benchmark statement through oversight rather than through conscious and planned deviation.

# QE ISSUES WITH SBSs

There are several areas of effective practice which relate to the use of benchmark statements:

- In the process of approval, panels need to be aware that the SBSs are designed to be used flexibly: they are not detailed curricula which providers deviate from at their peril.
- Where internal approval and review arrangements enable fast-track or minor changes outside of a full validation or review event, it is important that the implications for the coverage of the curriculum as implied by the relevant SBS are considered.
- In programmes where some skills are delivered alongside the main curriculum it is important that the opportunities for skills development are not diminished without proper review and reflection on the implications. This is important because many SBSs state that students should be given the opportunity to acquire certain general skills. An example of this is ICT skills for students on non-scientific programmes.
- In the development of combined or interdisciplinary programmes, even though there is likely to be no existing SBS, it is useful to explicitly draw on the relevant SBSs to construct a frame of reference that is anchored in the SBS scheme. An example of how this can work is effectively given in the communication, media, film and cultural studies SBS which essentially offers a modular knowledge and skill specification from which providers can select what is useful and relevant.
- For genuinely innovative or radical provision a group of developers could write their own SBS using the same principles and structures of those already published.
- All SBSs will be reviewed and amended from 2003 onwards. Institutions should take the opportunity to ensure that academics working with the benchmarks are supported in the discussions and representations on how the SBS can be improved.
- Assuming the general thrust of any given SBS is welcomed by a department, it might consider building up its own standards around the 'threshold' and 'typical' standards for what would essentially be the lower second and first class threshold. This would enable full articulation across a wider spectrum of performance and achievement with assessment strategies.
- Assuming there is broad convergence at least between the SBS and a given departmental programme, much of what is included in the SBS can serve as a useful teaching resource. In the process of review of provision, students can be asked about what they perceive as the differences between their current programme and the programme implied by the SBS. This is useful in identifying the relative proximity between the documented curriculum and the SBS on the one hand, and the student experience of the curriculum and the SBS on the other. It is particularly useful for identifying the extent to which students genuinely feel they have opportunities for the development of specific transferable skills.
- Although almost all SBSs refer to the difference between the expectation of single honours programmes in the areas and joint programmes (where the discipline is only studied for 50 per cent of the student's overall programme), few actually attempt to address what might be expected of a student under these programmes. It is worthwhile therefore for institutions to lay down general guidelines regarding how 'minor', 'subsidiary', 'major' or 'joint'

elements might relate to SBSs. It should be noted that some institutions still permit triple minor programmes where students study three areas each for 33 per cent of their time. This and other atypical arrangements characteristic of modular schemes make some sort of institution-wide strategy advisable. Jackson (2002:149–50) also provides a comprehensive analysis on the developmental opportunities offered by benchmarks.

---

## Reflecting on subject benchmarking

Do you consider the different approaches to SBSs by different drafting groups to be a positive or negative feature of the system?

The subject benchmarks will be reviewed between from 2003 onwards. What would be the key recommendations you would make in relation to the 1) a subject area with which you are particularly familiar; and 2) the subject benchmarks in general.

There have been claims that the subject benchmark system is the beginning of a 'national curriculum for skills'. Having read some of the benchmark statements do you find this claim convincing? What might be the advantages or disadvantages if a 'national curriculum for skills' were to emerge?

How well do the threshold standards within subject benchmarks articulate with the level descriptor for level H in the FHEQ?

Read Houghton's (2002) account of trying to produce a programme specification in the context of the FHEQ, professional body demands and the subject benchmark for engineering. To what extent does this account match your experience or other colleagues' at your institution or across your discipline generally?

<table>
<tr><td>3</td><td># Institutional audit</td></tr>
</table>

'The mission of the Agency is to promote public confidence that the quality of provision and standards of awards in higher education are being safeguarded and enhanced.'

*(Handbook for Institutional Audit*: p 1)

The institutional audit process is intended to combine scrutiny of internal QA systems at an institutional level with investigations of how those systems operate at the level of the discipline and the level of the programme. In this context a discipline is a defined area of academic study and programme is defined as 'the full diet of modules, options, and other structured learning opportunities, individual research study, and associated learner support, which together comprise a pathway that leads to an award' (*Handbook for Institutional Audit*, p 1).

## AIMS AND OBJECTIVES OF INSTITUTIONAL AUDIT

### *Aims*

'The aims of institutional audit are to meet the public interest in knowing that institutions in England are: providing higher education, awards and qualifications of both an acceptable quality and an appropriate academic standard; and (where relevant) exercising their legal powers to award degrees in a proper manner' (*Handbook for Institutional Audit*, p 2, para 9). It is clear from this description that the focus of audit is on ensuring that QA systems are in place and are working effectively.

### *Objectives*

The objectives of the audit are declared to be enhancement (of teaching quality), validating information on standards, taking remedial measures, and supporting financial accountability. Specifically:

- to contribute, in conjunction with other mechanisms, to the promotion and enhancement of high quality in teaching and learning;
- to ensure that students, employers and others can have ready access to easily understood, reliable and meaningful public information about the extent to which institutions are individually offering programmes of study, awards and qualifications that meet general national expectations in respect of academic standards and quality;
- to ensure that if the quality of higher education programmes or the standards of awards are found to be weak or seriously deficient, the process forms a basis for ensuring rapid action to improve them;
- to provide a means of securing accountability for the use of public funds received by institutions.

The scope of the institutional audit process covers three areas: the extent to which institutions have systems which adhere to the Code of Practice, the effectiveness of these systems in practice in programmes, and to validate the information published by the institution: in other words, Code, Courses and Cooke – (the Cooke report, HEFCE 02 / 15). More formally, Annex I of the Handbook lays out the reference documents relevant to the institutional audit process.

It should be noted that the first objective identifies enhancement as of primary importance. This should not distract attention from the principal focus of institutional audit, which is to ensure that HEIs have effective QA processes which underpin appropriate academic standards.

## MEANING AND CONSEQUENCES OF AUDIT OUTCOMES

The outcome of the institutional audit is a report containing judgements in two areas: the degree of confidence that can be placed in the HEI's management of quality and the degree of reliability of the information the HEI publishes about its operations. Thus the assessment is not just of the intrinsic merits of the provision itself, but also about the credibility of the institution's statements about such merits. It is rather like a health club being assessed on its advertising claims as well as for how close its customers actually get to achieving their fitness plans. It should be noted that the QAA does not seek to specify, metaphorically speaking, how much fitter anyone should actually get. That is, so to speak, a matter for each health club to determine on the basis of its own mission.

**Table 3.1** Sections, coverage and key points of the *Handbook for Institutional Audit*

| Section of the *Handbook for Institutional Audit* | Summary of Points Covered | Key Points |
| --- | --- | --- |
| Introduction | Outlines English audit system and its schedule, background and process. Introduces distinction between discipline and programme | The method only covers England. Key role for students |
| Aims and objectives of institutional audit (IA) | Declares aims of IA to be reassurance to public of English HEI quality and standards, and that HEIs are properly exercising their legal powers to award degrees. Declares objectives to be to enhance provision, inform public, reform deficiencies and support accountability for funding | All institutions will have been involved in an audit by the end of 2005

Aims are about QA but the objectives are a mix of QA, QE and public transparency and accountability |
| The IA process in summary | Defines the relevant scope, evidence and outcome judgements of IA and the role of auditors, institutions and students in the process | Centrality of external reference points and new focus on student voice and the QA of teaching staff. Summary of information and judgements |
| How the process works | Outlines the preparations, analysis, visit system, judgements and follow-up of the audit process | Process begins around 10 months before audit visit. Role of specialist advisers outlined |
| Annex A: Outline of the IA process | Provides detailed schedule from 40 weeks before audit visit to 20 weeks after audit visit | Digest of QAA information on HEI shared with that HEI at A–40 (weeks), Preliminary visit at A–36, Briefing visit at A–5 |
| Annex B: Guidelines for producing institutional self-evaluation documents | Details the function, length, style, content and structure of SED and its status | SED is around 40 pages long. It serves to orientate auditors and frame an agenda, but is itself an example of HEIs' quality procedures, confidence and maturity |
| Annex C: Guidelines for producing self-evaluation documents (SEDs) for discipline audit trails (DATs) | Details the purpose, content and structure of SEDs for DATs when these are required | 3,000 words long |
| Annex D: Written submissions from students | Details the format length and content of the student submission | Role of Students' Union is central. Particular focus on accuracy of information for students, feedback to students on academic performance, learning support and participation in quality management. Option for confidential submission by students |

**Table 3.1** *continued*

| Section of the *Handbook for Institutional Audit* | Summary of Points Covered | Key Points |
|---|---|---|
| Annex E: Information | Details role of Cooke information in audit, including full specification of information required for auditors and for publication | Cooke report (HEFCE 02/15) defines information required but additional information required for audit such as SEDs, SU submission, DAT information, and external body reports |
| Annex F: Selection and training of auditors, audit secretaries and specialist advisers | Details roles of audit personnel, their qualities, training and experience | Auditors will do up to three audits over two years |
| Annex G: Criteria for confidence judgements, and the relationship between confidence judgements, recommendations and follow-up action | Details the criteria for judgements of 'broad confidence', 'limited confidence' and 'no confidence' and the specific consequences of each for further reports and inspections by the QAA | Decision logic for 'no confidence' is particularly complex. Follow-up reflects outcomes |
| Annex H: Indicative report structure | Details the headings for the final audit report | Additional subsections will be added where appropriate. There is no structure for sections on DAT or thematic enquires |
| Annex I: Reference documents relevant to the institutional audit process | Definitive statement of reference documents for audit: HEFCE/QAA reference documents and discipline categorization | Two key documents are HEFCE 02/15 and HEFCE 00/54, rather than QAA documents |
| Annex J: The QAA's operational principles and process standards | Outlines the underlying principles which guide the work of the QAA in IA | Principles are: inclusiveness, openness, accountability, timeliness, comparability and relevance |

## Judgements in the report from the institutional audit

The report makes judgements in two areas:

the confidence in:

- the soundness of the institution's present and likely future management of the quality of its programmes;
- the academic standards of its awards;

the reliance that can reasonably be placed on the:

- accuracy;
- integrity;
- completeness;
- frankness;

of the information that an institution publishes about the quality of its programmes and the standards of its awards.

The degree of externality used by the HEI will be a key factor in arriving at these judgements in relation to quality. This will include the role of external examiners, external panel members in approval and review, and to a lesser extent, the role of employers and other stakeholders in curriculum design, placement management, distance learning materials review and staff development planning and delivery.

In addition to the judgements on the confidence in standards and reliability of information provided, the report makes recommendations with three levels of urgency:

- 'essential' recommendations on urgent corrective action to protect quality and standards;
- 'advisable' recommendations on less urgent corrective actions to remove potential risks to quality and standards;
- 'desirable' recommendations on actions which would enhance quality or safeguard standards.

Different kinds of summary judgements imply a different balance of recommendations. Judgements of 'broad confidence' imply no essential recommendations.

## DISCIPLINE AUDIT TRAILS (DATS)

One of the key elements of an institutional audit is the DAT. This is designed to maintain some kind of engagement with the chalk face after the dissolution of the comprehensive subject review methodology which dug very deeply into discipline quality management.DATs also provide the framework for 'developmental' engagements at HEIs not subject to full audit in 2002–04.

### Function of DATs

The *Handbook for Institutional Audit* offers five reasons why a discipline might be chosen for a DAT. Each of these reveals a different function for DATs. This is not to

**Table 3.2** Overview of audit judgements and their implications

| Judgement | Meaning | Type of Recommendations | Follow-up |
| --- | --- | --- | --- |
| Broad confidence | There can be confidence in the HEIs capacity to 'find and fix' any quality risks. Information given to the public is sound | Some desirable and advisable, none essential | Brief report after one year, brief visit after three to check progress and note plans |
| Limited confidence | HEI sometimes fails to find or fix problems. May be reservations on the accuracy of public information | Several desirable and advisable, some essential | Action Plan within three months. Audit not signed off until implemented (18 months' time limit)<br><br>Brief visit after three years |
| No confidence | Substantial evidence of serious and fundamental weaknesses in capacity to find and fix risks. Public information may be inaccurate or misleading | Significant number of essential recommendations as well as several advisable and desirable ones | Action plan within three months plus quarterly progress reports. Short visit after 18 months. Audit not signed off until satisfactory implementation<br><br>Brief visit after three years |

say that for every institutional audit there would be at least one DAT under each heading, indeed this would be unlikely given the time and resources available (the Handbook suggests that around 25 per cent of auditor time will be spent on DATs). The five reasons why a discipline might be chosen for a DAT are:

- A DAT offers a recent illustration of institutional processes for assuring the quality of programmes and the standards of awards (for example in relation to the nature of approval, monitoring and review – thus serving the function of providing information on QA).
- A DAT enables auditors to look more closely at what appear to be particularly interesting or innovative features of provision (serving the function of reviewing the management of enhancement).
- A DAT is useful where there is a lack of clarity in the institutional self-evaluation document (SED) about particular aspects of the QA arrangements, which might be better illustrated for the team through examination of a particular discipline (serving an illustrative function) – though if there is a lack of clarity this might suggest the institution is unclear about its policy in this area and so there is inevitably an underlying QA assessment function.
- Where a discipline has been identified in the past as a possible weakness, a DAT serves the function of assessing QA and academic standards.

- When taken together with the other disciplines selected, a DAT enables the audit team to sample an appropriate range of the institution's provision (serving the audit function of inspecting a representative range of provision).

(Based on the *Handbook for Institutional Audit,* para 42.)

The 'trail' involves five elements: A short SED, illustrative documentation, meetings with staff, students and external stakeholders, evaluation on published information about the provision and the consideration of external reference points (Code of Practice, benchmarks, the FHEQ). Additionally, and exceptionally, the audit team may call on specialist reviewers to assess particular discipline-specific issues. In extreme circumstances the specialist reviewers may recommend that a full review be carried out under the arrangements specified in the *Handbook for Academic Review.*

## GOOD PRACTICE POINT

### Externality and monitoring

Externality is a key issue in the demonstration that an institution is not inward looking or defensive but prepared to introduce peer review to its operations around QA and QE. One area where traditionally direct external participation is not common but could be developed is in programme *monitoring*, ie the discussion of annual course or departmental reports on programme quality and delivery. While external examiners' reports are always incorporated into such reviews, few universities involve external peers in the overall review of a programme where student evaluations, achievement, progression statistics and resource needs analysis are brought together. If an institution is not currently incorporating external participation in the monitoring process a pilot in one or two areas would allow it to determine whether such an arrangement would be useful across the institution. Additionally, in the context of externality and monitoring it is surprising how few institutions still do not routinely send the external examiner a copy of the annual monitoring report for the programme he or she examines.

### Issues for DATs

### Identification

Identification of potential audit trails is made by the assistant director but the final decision on which trails to pursue is left to the audit team. The institution will know at A–14 (14 weeks before the audit visit) which DATs will be pursued. Institutions have seven weeks to prepare a SED for each area. The assistant director will have been seeking to identify potential DATs at A–32. To ensure balanced and transparent audits HEIs will want to clarify at an early stage the rationale for the selection of each DAT considered separately and the set of DATs as a group.

## Comparison with subject review

The scrutiny involved in discipline level audits will differ not only in volume compared to the old comprehensive subject review methodology (only 25 per cent of two auditors will be devoted to it) but it will also be different in kind. There is no observation of teaching, only limited consideration of student work, and no 'aspect meetings'. However, there is scrutiny of a discipline level SED, considerable review of statistical data and external examiner reports to be submitted and analysed. While the SED, like the SED under subject review, is considered a useful document, it is interesting that the two sources of data regularly found to provide little illumination under subject review – progression statistics and external examiner reports – are retained and foregrounded in the institutional audit methodology.

## Preparation

Theoretically, DATs should involve limited amounts of preparation. The SED will in some cases simply be the most recent monitoring report for the discipline area or some synthesis of relevant programmes. Some institutions have effectively adopted the headings of the SED as the format for the annual monitoring reports produced by disciplines (see the *Handbook for Institutional Audit*, Annex C). Institutions will probably want to take the opportunity of updating the most recent monitoring report to highlight what action has been taken to address any quality issues. There is no scope for institutions to submit SEDs which are less self-critical than the monitoring report for the same area since clearly the monitoring report will need to be available to the auditors no matter what. However, the SED does provide the opportunity to stand back from the monitoring procedure itself and as such is probably the more effective option from the point of view of the institution.

---

**Box 3.1**

*Duplication of effort vs metastatement: monitoring reports vs new SED*

Although the *Handbook for Institutional Audit* states that 'The Discipline SED should normally take the form of a recent... internal review report... covering the area of the discipline audit trail' (Annex C, p 20) it is in fact worthwhile preparing a separate SED. One of the major political dynamics in the reform of the comprehensive subject review methodology was the reduction in bureaucracy through alignment of QAA requirements with the internal procedures of institutions and the reduction of scrutiny of individual departments. Nevertheless, tactically institutions are probably wise to resist the temptation to simply submit the most recent annual monitoring report rather than a separate SED. Although this may involve slight duplication of effort the SED will draw heavily in terms of content from the monitoring report.

However, the SED will *allow commentary on the effectiveness of annual monitoring itself*. Given the different types of rationale for DATs it is worthwhile for departments to adduce clear evidence that the monitoring system works – evidence and arguments which can be difficult to introduce as part of a particular monitoring report (even if the headings for monitoring reports have been amended to reflect new QAA categories). Additionally, and perhaps decisively, it will just statistically be the case that most SEDs will be required more than three months after the submission of an annual monitoring report and as such there is a need to update the state of play on areas of concern or threats to quality. So the SED serves not just as an opportunity to submit a metastatement about the effectiveness of monitoring procedures but also, more prosaically, allows commentary on the effectiveness of the most recent monitoring statement for that area.

## Content of the SED

Since auditors will no doubt expect a rapid prioritization of support for areas identified as subject to a DAT, circumspect HEIs will no doubt want to review carefully the progress made on the previous year's annual monitoring report. Annex C recommends that SEDs should be balanced, concise, accessible and with appropriate measures of analysis and description. It should be remembered that where an additional SED is being provided auditors will also have access to monitoring reports so the SED is an opportunity to demonstrate that the monitoring systems work (see Box 3.1, on page 36).

Illustrative documentation for the DAT may include student handbooks and assessment materials, however the information defined in HEFCE 02/15, the Cooke data, will be expected to be easily assembled and available. Given that auditors are required to assess the relationship between the programmes and the FHEQ, subject benchmarks and the Code of Practice, there is in principle a considerable amount of information which is going to be required. There are as we know 175 precepts in the Code of Practice across all sections and each of these is accompanied by three or four guidance notes. To assess the extent to which a programme is adhering to the Code of Practice alone will take considerable work and documentation. It should be remembered that ultimately the burden of proof in an academic institutional audit demonstrating articulation or compliance with the 'external quality reference points' lies squarely with the institution, not the auditors. Unlike subject review, where points were deducted for inadequacies in the provision only where reviewers were able to produce evidence for these inadequacies, the issue here is the ability of the institution to *demonstrate* that it is maintaining standards, driving QA and enhancing quality. More generally, one of the fundamental assumptions of institutional audit is the centrality of information about quality matters which is available to HEIs in order that they can reassure themselves that they are discharging their quality responsibilities appropriately. If information does not exist and they are unable to reassure themselves, how can they expect external agencies to be reassured?

The unpublished information set which will be assumed to be routinely available will include information on:

- institutional context (including the learning and teaching strategy);
- statistical data on student admission, progression and completion;
- internal procedures for assuring academic quality and standards;
- arrangements and outcomes of programme approval, monitoring and review;
- assessment procedures and outcomes (including outcomes of reviews of assessment strategies);
- student satisfaction data, and information available to approval and review teams.

The *Handbook for Institutional Audit* provides extensive detail on the methodology for the audit process. The Handbook comprises two parts: an initial introductory overview which lays out the aims, scope and procedures for the process and a set of 10 appendices (called Annexes) which each cover key aspects of the process. The Annexes and their function are outlined in Table 3.1.

## CRITERIA FOR CONFIDENCE JUDGEMENTS

As we have noted, audit teams are essentially asked to express a judgement of confidence on quality based on two considerations: the effectiveness of the HEI's management of academic quality; and the level of reliability of the information it publishes about its provisions. As already outlined, the levels of confidence that can be expressed in quality management can be 'broad confidence', 'limited confidence' and 'no confidence'. Justification for each of these decisions has to be very clear, of course, not least because each of these judgements implies different sorts of outcomes for the institution.

'Broad confidence' (*Handbook for Institutional Audit*, p 29) implies that the HEI has rigorous systems and applies these effectively and consistently; is capable of maintaining this in the future, and publishes complete, accurate and reliable information.

The consequence of such a judgement would be that after one year the QAA would require a brief report on how the HEI has responded to the findings of the audit.

'Limited confidence' implies that the systems, or their application, or the HEIs' capacity to maintain quality, or the validity of the information published, is in some way flawed. Specifically, that there may be 'notable weakness either in the management of the institution's structures and procedures or their implementation at discipline level'. As the *Handbook for Institutional Audit* states: 'A judgement of limited confidence indicates that there is evidence that the institution's capacity to manage the quality of its programmes and/or standards of its awards soundly and effectively is limited or is likely to become limited in the future.' Annex G of the Handbook indicates how the term 'limited confidence' should be interpreted. This judgement is not given due to the presence of flawed programmes as such, but rather the possibility that an institution might not have been aware of the difficulties (which would imply deficient monitoring procedures), or that there was failure to address known problems (which would imply a lack of concern, or resources, or competence for the maintenance of academic standards). Confidence may also be limited if independent external academics are not effectively involved in assessment or validation and review. Further, confidence may be limited where there are 'reservations' about published information.

---

### Implementation of institutional level structures and procedures outside the discipline

It is interesting to note that the principle of effective application of quality systems is discussed in Annex G purely in terms of their application at *discipline* level. This should not necessarily be understood as simply meaning that where local departments fail to implement central systems, policies or decisions, there is a problem. It also refers to the failure of application of systems which are well-designed but which are poorly applied across the HEI's operations – as may be revealed through thematic enquiries or through examination of how central systems (such as academic board, quality unit or central officers) operate in practice. Thus the audit is not necessarily limited to how central policies are implemented in local departmental actions, but covers the broad link between documented policy and actual operations. Nevertheless, much of the significant academic activity occurs in departments, so implementation at departmental level will weigh heavily with auditors.

A judgement of 'no confidence' implies that there is 'substantial evidence of serious and fundamental weaknesses in the institution's capacity both at institutional and discipline level to secure and maintain the quality of its programmes and standards of its awards.' Thus this implies that there are likely to be flaws *both* in terms of central management and discipline standards. The judgement will be accompanied by a significant number of essential recommendations. The consequence of such a damning judgement is that within three months of the publication of the report the HEI will be required to produce an action plan indicating how the parlous condition of its academic standards will be turned around. This will be followed by the indignity of quarterly reports to the QAA. The QAA will carry out a follow-up visit 18 months later to check progress. If there appears to be insufficient progress the audit itself will not be signed off and the next audit will be brought forward (presumably with time set aside for auditors to meet the new Vice Chancellor).

The evidence section for a 'no confidence' judgement needs some detailed unpacking. (See Box 3.2.)

---

### Box 3.2

*The complex logic of 'no confidence' judgements*

The underlying decision logic of Annex G is not transparent. The following is the basic argument:

If **both**
One or more of:
1.   (Deficient institutional procedures)
or
2.   (Deficient management of institutional procedures)

Is true, **and** one or more of:
3.   (Quality or standards are at immediate risk)
or
4.   (Quality or standards are likely to be at risk in the future)

Is true,
**OR** if:
5.   (The information made available to the public cannot be relied upon *and* can be shown to be inaccurate *and/or* misleading) is true, then a judgement of No Confidence is warranted.

The overall judgement of confidence therefore involves consideration of several different elements but the relationship between consideration of each of these elements in isolation and the overall, summative, judgement is not transparent.

The three sets of criteria do not articulate well with each other. 'Broad confidence' criteria refer to quality mechanisms being applied 'effectively and consistently', in 'limited confidence' they are applied 'soundly and effectively'. The criteria for 'no confidence' refers to a failure to 'secure and maintain' quality.

The attempt to separate these elements of audit analytically is helpful in viewing the coherence of institutional quality. However, separation of the various elements leads to curious possibilities. For example, a poor set of procedures cannot be effectively managed, except in the sense that the deficiencies of the systems are not in fact adhered to. As another example, theoretically, an institution might state that there need not be an external representative on approval or review panels but in practice disciplines routinely ensure that external representatives are in fact present. Similarly, it is conceivable that an institution could have rigorous mechanisms which are effectively implemented, but the validity of the information provided to the public about the provision is misleading. This could be because the information published overstated the level, say, of resources or pass rates – even though the actual level of resources or pass rates was acceptable in the context of the institution's aims, strategy and provision.

---

### Reflecting on institutional audit

What are the differences between DATs and comprehensive subject review methodology? What are the implications for how institutions might manage the DATs in that context?

To what extent does the institution audit methodology constitute a 'lighter touch' regime?

Who or which office or unit in your institution is responsible for providing documentation for institutional audit? How are responsibilities defined in that area?

How did or does your institution intend to liaise with the Students' Union in the preparation of the student submission to the QAA as part of institutional audit? In what ways if any does this exercise affect relations between the Students' Union and the university?

In what ways do thematic enquiries provide information or support judgements that have a bearing on QE issues emerging from audit?

How might an institution reassure itself prior to institutional audit that the information it publishes is not misleading as distinct from merely being not inaccurate?

How does or will your institution use the final report from the QAA on institutional audit? What are the main 'headlines' likely to be noted by 1) current students; 2) potential UK applicants; 3) parents of younger potential UK applicants; 4) potential overseas applicants; 5) employers; 6) potential academic employees; 7) current academic staff; 8) current support staff; 9) senior managers; 10) other academics in other institutions? To whom is the report most illuminating? To whom will the report be least useful?

What are the differences between DATs serving as part of a full institutional audit and as the framework for developmental engagements? What are the implications for institution-level policies and practices?

What are the differences between 'Academic Review' and 'Developmental Engagements'? Consider the rationale, process and outputs of each.

What might be the challenges in managing, from the institutional point of view, an Academic Review of HE in FE, subjects with poor scores in 1995–2001 or as part of a university title bid? (See 'Arrangements during the transitional period 2002–05 for Higher Education Institutions in England www.qaa.ac.uk/public/inst_audit_hbook/transitional.htm)

Thematic enquiries (TEs) are 'explorations' of cross institution functions and activities related to quality assurance that in the view of the audit team are 'interesting or require checking'. This area is severely underdocumented in the handbook but it can be expected that TEs might involve areas such as assessment, placements, admissions or CEIG – in short, areas covered by a specific section of the Code of Practice.

Alternatively TEs may cover an issue relevant to the HEI such as quality management in the context of organizational restructure, new modular degree structures or expansion of postgraduate provision. The relationship between DATs and TEs is fluid, with evidence from one flowing into the other.

# 4 Information on quality and standards in higher education

In March 2002 HEFCE published the final report of the Task Group on Information on Quality and Standards in Higher Education chaired by Professor Ron Cooke, Vice Chancellor of the University of York. The report (HEFCE 02/15) outlines the information which HEIs need to produce, assess, and in some cases, publish in order to demonstrate to auditors, the public and themselves that they have a clear and robust information base on which to manage quality issues.

Specifically there are three main functions of this statement of expectations on the availability of information about quality and standards: to ensure that universities are able to discharge their responsibilities to monitor and assure programmes delivered in their names; to provide information to external stakeholders such as students and employers; and to enable institutional audits to draw up reliable information about university operations.

The need for HEIs to collect information and demonstrate to the QAA that they are collecting this information is one of the prices the sector has had to pay following the abolition of comprehensive subject review. Given that HEIs have the principal responsibility for managing and assuring academic quality, it is essential that they are able to demonstrate that they have the data that will allow them to carry out that responsibility. If, the argument goes, an institution does not have access to comprehensive, robust and reliable data on its programmes, how can it come to meaningful conclusions about the quality or otherwise of those programmes? The price of institutional autonomy in relation to academic standards is that HEIs are required to have the information required for the effective discharge of that autonomy.

Information needs for the external review of quality is a sore point for most HEIs and their relationship with the QAA. During the period of comprehensive subject review there was a widely shared view amongst HEIs that the information demands of subject reviewers were a major burden on institutions, involving the collation of extensive data sets at short notice according to the agenda of the *Handbook of Subject Review*, and, occasionally, the whims of individual reviewers. The new system from 2002 draws on information supposedly that universities would have or should have anyway and which is in any event assumed to be information normally produced by the HEI for its own internal QA procedures, thus reducing duplication. The QAA and HEFCE distinguish between:

- information which should be available in all HEIs to enable academic quality and standards to be monitored, such as information on student progression and completion;
- information for publication to enable students and employers to make informed judgments about the HEIs' provision, such as summaries of external examiners' reports;
- additional information required for institutional audit purposes to enable external scrutiny and confirmation of the level of confidence that can be placed in the institution, such as SEDs.

## MANAGEMENT INFORMATION

It is expected by HEFCE that in addition to data which is required for publication and for audit, HEIs will be able to supply course leaders, departmental heads and others responsible for the quality of a programme with appropriate management information to enable them to monitor and develop the provision. The effectiveness of management information for quality purposes will be assessed by auditors as part of institutional audit. It is essential therefore that the availability, relevance, timeliness and consistency of this information is reviewed periodically, and that the information needs of academic managers are clearly defined and served by central information services.

## GOOD PRACTICE POINT

Most HEIs provide course leaders and departmental heads with the kind of management data outlined by HEFCE only on an annual basis as part of the input into the annual monitoring arrangements. This snapshot approach, while valuable in that context, does not add a great deal to the embedding of monitoring systems in routine departmental operations. More effective is to provide course managers with quarterly reports which will not only allow better analysis of data (in relation to for example the patterns of withdrawals throughout the academic year) but also enable more rapid response to emerging issues.

Paragraphs 11–12 of the Cooke report (HEFCE 02/15) lay out the different categories of data and what should be done with them. This information is presented in the box that follows.

## 1. Management information which should be available in all HEIs

**Information on the institutional context:** mission statement; corporate plan; QA policies and processes; learning and teaching strategy.

**Information on student admission progression and completion:** student qualifications on entry; Higher Education Statistics Agency (HESA) return on basic demographics; student progression and completion data, first destination survey data.

**Information on the HEI's internal procedures for assuring academic quality and standards**: This is very wide but is categorized and broken down as follows:

- *approval, monitoring and review* data such as: programme specifications, internal reports of major programme reviews;
- *assessment procedures and outcomes data* including assessment strategies and external examiners' reports;
- *student satisfaction data* including views on guidance, the library, IT support, quality of teaching and pastoral support;
- *evidence available to teams undertaking the HEI's own internal reviews of quality* such as teaching and learning effectiveness, peer observation and mentoring programmes and involvement of external peers in reviews.

## 2. Information for publication

*Quantitative data*

- HEFCE – 1) PIs and benchmarks on progression and successful completion for full-time first degree students; 2) FDS (First Destination Survey);
- HESA – 1) student entry; 2) degree class data.

*Qualitative data*

- external examiner's summary for each programme;
- HEI response to externals' reports (optional);
- National Survey of Graduate Feedback;
- HEI survey of its current students;
- HEI learning and teaching strategy (summary);
- response to periodic programme and departmental reviews;
- statement of links with employers.

## 3. Information for institutional audit

- SEDs;
- student submissions to auditors;
- information disciplines selected for DATs;
- external body reports;
- miscellaneous oral and written information acquired during the audit process.

Many institutions were disappointed that the issue of 'value added' experience to students (in terms of progress made in learning since starting the course) was not addressed in the Cooke report. They commented on the need to establish a standard methodology for measuring 'value added' and/or 'distance travelled', and thought that this should be given priority by the HEFCE, but this was not incorporated into the final specification of data.

## External examiner's summary

One of the key areas for publication is a summary of the external examiner's report for each programme. For the most part this will be a set of uncontentious confirmatory statements which will simply assert that the programme has sound and fair assessment procedures, and that the standards are appropriate for the awards (given national benchmarks, the FHEQ and programme specifications) and comparable with those of other HEIs. However, the final paragraph (section 9) invites the external examiner to provide a 200–300 word narrative account which conveys the 'examiner's overview of key characteristics of the programme which he or she considers sufficiently significant in relation to present or future standards to be worth drawing to the attention of external audiences'. Universities will be required to publish this summary and typically make it available on the university Web site. It has been argued that this will sour the relationship between HEIs and their external examiners. However, it is unlikely given the culture of external examining in the UK that this device would be used as the primary mechanism for bringing about quality improvements in a programme. It is more likely that concerns will continue to be raised informally or in other areas of the report with the threat of a formal summary in the background.

While the external examiner system has much to recommend it and most external examiners do a thorough job for compensation below the minimum wage, even its most fervent supporters would have to concede that in too many cases the relationship between external examiner and programme team is far too close. There has also been insufficient monitoring of the effectiveness with which the role is carried out, reflected perhaps in the fact that assessment was found to be deficient in many areas under comprehensive subject review. Forcing external examiners to make a very public statement helps concentrate their mind, and develops the relationship between them and programme teams, for the better.

The Cooke report proposes a standard template for the publication of results of student feedback from HEIs' own institutional surveys. This is designed to incorporate students' views on: academic and tutorial guidance, support and supervision; quality of teaching; range and appropriateness of learning and teaching methods; usefulness and promptness of feedback on assessments; quality of learning resources; suitability of accommodation, equipment and facilities for learning and teaching; and the quality of pastoral support. The template also proposes that the HEI publishes a statement on what it is doing to address issues raised by the student feedback.

The template however is an output template, not a template for the conduct of the survey itself. In particular it lays down no suggestion as to the structure, length, response options or sequencing of items themselves. This leads to the potential problem that students will not be able to compare like with like.

One simple issue is that the further down the scale the term the category 'satisfactory' or 'satisfied' is placed, the more likely respondents are to tick that option or something better. Consider the following two questionnaire items:

*A: How would you rate the quality of academic and tutorial guidance?*

Unsatisfactory        Satisfactory        Good        Very Good        Excellent

*B: How would you rate the quality of academic and tutorial guidance?*

Unacceptable    Poor    Adequate    Satisfactory    Very Satisfactory

It is likely that version A would yield more 'satisfactory' responses or better than B because of differences in the structure of the response scale rather than differences in the student experience. For these and other reasons, HEFCE and QAA now complement HEIs own surveys with an annual national student survey of teaching quality and student experience, published for the first time in autumn 2003.

The information contained in the template for publishing summaries of periodic programme/department reviews is probably of more value to those familiar with the process of approval and review than to students and employers. The template covers information on the conduct of the review, the evidence base (external examiners' reports and student feedback etc), innovation and good practice and a judgment on the quality and standards of the programme (such as whether the intended learning outcomes are being achieved by students) and whether the programme remains current. Alongside these areas HEIs are expected to publish information on any recommendations to address shortcomings or for further enhancement. Of course there is always the danger that institutions will become less thorough in their programme review systems and less open in the statement of findings if these are to be placed in the public domain. The counterbalance to this is the QAA institutional audit, which will, amongst other things, confirm the extent to which confidence can be placed in the information an HEI publishes about its quality and standards.

## REFLECTIVE PRACTICE POINT

**Editorial control**
One issue here might be who has ultimate editorial control over the publication of the periodic review summaries: The chair of the review panel? The head of the quality unit? The head of department of the programme? The programme leader? The external panel member?

Given that publication of core information in the public domain is such a new departure for HEIs, and given the sensitivity of the data, there will undoubtedly be a review of the effectiveness of arrangements for managing information on quality and standards in higher education. It will be interesting to review the extent to which two or more external examiners for different programmes agree with each other. It will also be interesting to see how many external examiners use the summary device not for drawing attention to issues within the local provision but for raising questions about the university's policies on degree classification, the conduct of examination boards and the powers of the external examiner. External examiners who feel more of an affinity with their discipline than with the institution which has hired them will also no doubt be keen to use the summary to shame the HEI into appointing more teaching staff, buying more laboratory equipment and so on. What was designed to be a system for external examiners to communicate directly with the public may well turn out to be a system for them to communicate with the institution, with the world watching.

## QA ISSUES WITH INFORMATION ON QUALITY AND STANDARDS

Bearing in mind that QA is essentially about the systems for ensuring that an institution achieves what it set out to do, the role of data publication in this area is particularly interesting. External stakeholders such as potential applicants and employers, particularly those who are in a position to choose between courses or graduates, may not be as interested in what the information says about the extent to which an institution is achieving its mission, but rather how well the institution is likely to meet their own particular needs. Some of this may be driven by prejudices or stereotypes. A postgraduate applicant from North America may steer clear of institutions with successful widening participation missions because it does not correspond to that person's preconceptions of what an English university is. Equally an undergraduate applicant from a low participation neighbourhood may steer clear of a university with a research mission because of fears that part-time staff do the teaching of busy research professors. Institutions are more than capable of addressing these preconceptions, should they wish, through the contextual information that is published alongside the required information. However, in terms of the quality of the data itself HEFCE lays down clear guidelines and the QAA specifies in detail in the *Handbook for Institutional Audit* the way in which this information will figure in the audits.

### Internet memory and search engines

While it is always good practice to update information or to check information for accuracy even after it has been published – particularly in the context of the World Wide Web where republishing costs very little – it should be recognized that several search engines keep copies of original Web pages even after they have been updated. Changes to Web sites will be traceable through systems such as the Wayback Machine (www.archive.org). A further interesting phenomenon is that unlike the traditional Internet practice of inserting lines of code in Web documents to increase the likelihood of being found, HEIs with negative external examiners' summaries may usher in a new Internet cottage industry – the creation of Web pages that are *difficult* to find. One way of doing this would be to use keywords which had nothing to do with the content at all to ensure that whenever the page was found it would not be found by people actually looking for any information on universities. Perhaps there is a need for a specification not just that HEIs publish data, but that they enable easy access to that data through search engines or links to relevant sites.

Wayback Machine: http://webdev.archive.org/index.php

In terms of the risk to QA the following are likely to be areas for particular attention:

- failure to validate and cross reference information such that there are misleading claims made in terms of the actual delivery of a programme compared to the approved and validated range of options on a programme;
- failure to monitor links to contextual information which is partisan in a manner that makes it look independent or objective – for example 'explanatory' links from external examiners' reports to programme descriptions that are actually taken from promotional material;
- failure to prevent information becoming out of date through poor editorial monitoring or for other reasons;
- failure to provide academic managers with reliable information on student progression, particularly in areas of large or complex provision;
- failure to maintain data integrity in the first destination survey.

## QE ISSUES WITH INFORMATION ON QUALITY AND STANDARDS

In terms of developing good practice in this area the underlying principle is to ensure that the right information gets to the right people at the right time in the right format. One way of facilitating this of course is to empower users to access information on demand. It is also important to maintain the distinction between data, statistics and information. Further, it is important to distinguish between description and inference. The following points may be useful in identifying the key priorities for individual institutions:

- Ensure there are clear arrangements with designated responsibilities for checking the accuracy, internal consistency, currency and adherence to house style of public information on the Web.

- Ensure that information is put on the Web in a manner that is fully accessible (this is particularly important in terms of MS Excel spreadsheets which are preferred by HEFCE for student feedback data).
- Ensure that information put on the Web is appropriately integrated with other pages on internal and external Web sites in such a way as to enable the reader to access appropriate contextual or additional information. For example, it would be useful for a programme review report to have a hyperlink to any QAA subject review or recent PSB report.
- Ensure that information put on the Web is presented in an effective and professional style to show the importance of the information to the institution.
- Consider where possible the option of translating key content into languages other than English or failing that, providing an e-mail address where requests for translated material can be sent. Translation will be particularly relevant for programmes with high overseas participation such as computing and business. Although there are some online translation programmes these are variable in quality. Institutions may wish to advise users on the use of these systems.
- Ensure that there are university policies on the function, format and content of institutional responses to external examiners' summary statements.

---

### Reflecting on information on quality and standards in higher education

What type of information do you think the following external stakeholders are most interested in?:

- young applicants for undergraduate programmes;
- parents of young applicants for undergraduate programmes;
- overseas applicants for postgraduate programmes;
- employers.

How many working days would it take you to acquire the following information in your institution for a specified programme? For the institution overall? (All for the most recently completed academic year.):

- student qualifications on entry;
- HESA return on basic demographics;
- student progression and completion data;
- first destination survey data.

Under what circumstances do you think an external examiner would err on the side of submitting a summary statement for public consumption which gave 1) a slightly more positive impression than would be objectively warranted; 2) a slightly more negative impression than would be objectively warranted?

What is the process in your institution for writing and editing the responses to the external examiner's summary? In what ways, if any, has this affected the relationship with the external examiner?

# 5 | Managing quality enhancement (QE)

## WHAT IS QE?

Several attempts have been made to define QE.

'…taking deliberate steps to improve the quality of the learning opportunities made available to students'. Peter Milton (2002) QAA, quoted in 'Quality': the Universities UK quality enhancement report.

'Quality enhancement (QE) in higher education is a deliberate process of change that leads to improvement… QE is an inclusive concept and a collective enterprise. It involves everyone who teaches, supports and guides students and the managers and administrators of HE institutions. It includes significant strategic initiatives and the many small things that people do to try to make things better'. Learning and Teaching Support Network (LTSN).

Quality enhancement 'is fundamentally about trying to make things better'. Jackson (2002).

In higher education at least QE has traditionally been seen as the acceptable face of the quality revolution. In the comprehensive subject review round it was a chance for departments to highlight what they were doing to develop staff, promote innovation and share good practice. The overall relatively poor scores across many disciplines under the quality management and enhancement (QME) aspect under that methodology masked much important work in QE.

'Enhancement' in principle can mean anything from updating the module reading list, through improving laboratory protocols, to staff training in sign language, to the introduction of peer assessment right up to scrapping the entire provision and franchising it all out with a revamped curriculum through a private agency. Some of these changes happen routinely on a daily basis and are almost self-evidently improvements in the programme (such as updating reading lists); others are complex, long-term projects with significant resource implications and involving several teams but with no guarantee of success. If we read the texts that are produced by practitioners in the period 2001–02 when the frame of reference for QA was in crisis we can see that the fundamental narrative is one of rescuing the damsel of enhancement from the dragons of external inspection and internal managerialism.

In 2002 the Universities UK group (UUK) published a report in collaboration with HEFCE and SCOP giving an overview of QA in the UK which highlighted the range of agencies involved in QE and perceptions of these groups across the sector. The report also sought to determine the main priorities for QE as perceived by a range of tutors, practitioners and academic managers. Although the formal definition of QE used by the group is one given by the QAA in fact the range of agencies involved in QE is narrower than that offered by Jackson (2002). The key agencies identified by UUK were:

- The Quality Assurance Agency for Higher Education (QAA);
- Higher Education Staff Development Agency (HESDA);
- The Institute for Learning and Teaching (ILT);
- Learning and Teaching Support Network (LTSN);
- Staff and Educational Development Association (SEDA);
- Joint Information Systems Committee (JISC);
- Society for Research into Higher Education (SRHE).

The UUK report took the view that the roles and relationships amongst these agencies is perceived as complex by the sector and may need to be clarified or rationalized. It claims that 'there is now a complex and fragmented system for quality enhancement, with few practitioners having a clear view of the terrain' (UUK, 2002: para 1.5). The 2003 White Paper subsequently built on this report to propose a Teaching Quality 'Academy' to be established by 2004 to promote best practice in teaching. How the academy will integrate the many strengths of ILT, LTSN and HESDA, which it brings together, remains to be seen.

In the 1990s much of the agenda around enhancement, development and innovation was largely around the *protection* of quality, student engagement and achievement (sometimes through various forms of resource-based learning) in the context of a declining unit of resource. According to the UUK report however the focus is now seen by academic staff as primarily one of addressing the challenges of a diverse student participation in higher education. Specifically, when UUK asked focus groups to identify priorities for QE nine key areas emerged:

- enhancing quality in the context of widening participation;
- developing pedagogy and curricula to increase student retention;
- enhancing quality in the context of lifelong and work-based learning;
- supporting the development of e-learning;
- developing diversity of delivery practices;
- having a more coherent approach to staff development;
- supporting student participation in course design;
- raising the profile of learning and teaching generally;
- promoting innovation.

The UUK report provides a useful overview of the politics and recent history of QE in the UK. However, the identification of a QE agenda is difficult to assess in the absence of more detailed information on relative priorities in relation to different contexts, the relationship between contexts, and the kinds of judgements practitioners were making and expressing in relation to what kind of questions.

Jackson's Enhancement Function Typology

Jackson (2002) has suggested that there are four types of agencies in the UK which address and promote QE in one way or another. There are the agencies who play a 'strategic' role which affect policy and funding initiatives for enhancement such as DFES, HFCE, UUK and SCOP; regulatory organizations such as QAA, TTA/OFSTED, HEIs themselves and Investors in People; developmental agencies operating through brokerage action research and network building include LTSN, ILT, HESDA, SEDA, JISC, ALT and e-University; bodies which support research for enhancement such as the ESRC, SRHE and university-based research units and departments. Jackson's model of enhancement is perhaps more useful than that used by UUK as it relates organization to enhancement function.

There is debate too about the relationship between QA and QE in higher education. QA is principally seen of course as a regulatory arrangement trading on the accountability of universities to funding councils or governments. By contrast QE is typically a broader-based enterprise often drawing on support networks within professional and academic communities. Thus while the former is seen as inspectorial and remedial the latter as seen as collaborative and developmental. For this reason there is ongoing debate for example as to whether or not one unit within a given university or one agency across a university sector can manage both processes.

The shift by the QAA away from comprehensive subject review and towards institutional audit has been presented as a decisive shift towards QE. However, as can be seen from Chapter 3 (on institutional audit) this does not mean that the QAA only inspects QE initiatives. Although institutional audit includes explicit provision for evaluation of the range of effectiveness of QE activities, enhancement of provision is seen as an outcome from the audit methodology, rather than an input to the process. The focus on the reliability and credibility of a university's information about itself in particular is very clearly an audit in the strict sense of the term. Similarly, outcomes differentiated in terms of 'no confidence', 'limited confidence' or 'broad confidence', do not use language calculated to enhance. Overall the claim that significant enhancement of UK higher education will emerge unproblematically from audits of the quality assurance arrangements in universities seems overstated at best.

---

Should units or agencies responsible for QA also be responsible for QE?

The issue over ownership of assurance and enhancement is not limited to the UK. The Australian Universities Quality Agency argues that it is right that it should manage both for much the same reasons that academics can effectively teach and assess their own students. Do you find this a convincing analogy?

AUQA: http://www.auqa.edu.au

---

## REGULATORY AND TRANSPARENCY DIVIDENDS OF QA FOR ENHANCEMENT

There are arguably two specific ways in which QA and QE support each other. First is what we might call the *regulatory dividend* of QA for QE, in the sense that attention to the extent to which aims are being achieved (and the accountability that goes with ensuring that any gaps between aims and achievement are progressively minimized or erased) means that there will be a context and motivation for improvement. For example, consider a situation where a journalism programme has set itself the aim of ensuring that all students have the opportunity to do a marketing placement during their course but it turns out over the year that there are insufficient marketing placements available. The department would be expected to invest resources or provide incentives for marketing companies to increase the number of placement opportunities available. The increase in the number of placements available would be seen as being an enhancement to the provision (in the sense of an improvement minimizing the gap between aim and achievement).

However, quite different in nature is the second kind of contribution of QA to QE. This is where the demands of QA almost force a better understanding of the essential nature of some aspect of the provision thus ensuring that that aspect is dealt with more effectively and coherently. We might term this the *transparency dividend* for QE of QA. In this example if we looked at the idea of applied business communication skills for journalists as a key subject related skill we might while redrafting a programme specification need to be very specific about what 'applied business communication skills' might mean for journalists. If we define this as applying journalistic skills to non-news business contexts then we would have identified the right kind of placements for our students, and would hope to be able to make objective, transparent judgements on shared criteria for why one placement is likely to be more useful than some other for students registered for this programme. The improvement here is the better understanding of the skills set we are seeking to promote in our students.

Both the regulatory and transparency dividend lay the foundations for more extended QE initiatives that may be inspired or motivated by factors other than QA. It is interesting to compare these two types of dividend. In some ways within the existing provision the transparency must precede the regulatory review (how do we know if we have achieved our goal if we are not clear about the goal or the means?). However, often in practice it is precisely the other way round: the regulatory dividend is what triggers the need to explore what is needed more precisely. More generally it is probably also the case that while the regulatory dividend is more easily and more rapidly cashed in, it is the transparency dividend which has the greater longer term value as it provides a deeper more strategic understanding than the operational focus of the regulatory dividend.

---

## REFLECTIVE PRACTICE POINT

Can you think of an example from your own experience where QA monitoring has yielded a 'regulatory dividend'? Was it 'cashed in' in terms of QE?

Can you think of an example from your own experience where QA monitoring has yielded a 'transparency dividend'? Was it 'cashed in' in terms of QE?

Were there differences in terms of the immediate impact, long-term integration or effectiveness of the QE?

---

Thus while the distinction analytically between QA and QE is reasonably clear it is the case that they are closely related in overall quality management. If a process is operating poorly then it needs to be stabilized and reformed before it can be enhanced. Equally, if to maintain academic standards with atypical learners or modes of study, an innovative approach to student learning is required, then enhancement will have been served. Traditionally however, universities have treated innovation in recruitment, delivery or assessment as a threat to academic standards rather than as a means of protecting them. It is appropriate that where a university lacks experience in certain areas such as franchised, distance, electronic or work-based provision, risks have to be managed more carefully than might otherwise be the case.

Some of the later sections of the Code of Practice, as we have noted earlier, have attempted to build the foundations for QE into the QA-focused precepts and their associated guidance points. There are now routine references to having policies in place for staff development, monitoring and review of activities and systems for learning from students' complaints for the areas in question.

While minor changes and initiatives may emerge from monitoring procedures or from review of complaints, significant enhancement can require considerable planning. Genuine, integrated and sustainable enhancement does not happen by accident or incrementally.

---

## REFLECTIVE PRACTITIONER POINT

Which external agencies do you find most useful in helping your own reflections for developing practice and enhancing provision? Are institutional managers supportive, antagonistic or indifferent to the idea of departments working with these agencies?

What are the advantages and disadvantages of merging any or all of the national agencies responsible for QE? How does this affect you?

Which of the external agencies charged with QE has the most credibility with the people you work most closely with? Which provides the greatest support for input of your ideas?

---

## MANAGING COMPLEX ENHANCEMENTS TO QUALITY

Gordon (2002) has suggested that one of the difficulties with external quality review, certainly in the form of quasi-inspectorial visits of the comprehensive subject review round, is that it leads in many cases to the promotion of tactics over strategy in developing quality systems. In particular, argues Gordon, there needs to be clearer leadership and ownership in HEIs in relation to QE strategies. It is certainly the case that many institutions in the 1990s set up teaching innovation funds which sought to promote and resource pedagogical innovation and enhancement. While these local schemes produced several excellent developments which have in some cases gone on to achieve national recognition, in most cases these schemes have not led to significant cultural change. In terms of an integrated total quality approach to enhancement in some respects these initiatives have been limited in their effectiveness, particularly in terms of securing *sustainable* enhancements through embedding the innovations in the mainstream operations of academic departments. There have been many reasons for this, often including unique local factors. However, general issues have included: narrow focus on learning as opposed to broader student experience issues; overemphasis of ICT-led innovation; lack of robust underlying core mechanisms with which to innovate; premature launch and promotion of innovations with students and academic constituencies; resentment from other areas of perceived funding diversion; lack of effective dissemination across institutions; lack of support for the development of project management skills; lack of support from senior managers; lack of follow-on funding; misarticulation with central university support services; failure to secure 'buy-in' from alliances across the institution and a general under-involvement of students at the design stage. Interestingly it could be argued that more recent top–down or central approaches to cultural change for enhancement, including the establishment of educational and learning development units, have been more successful in effecting cultural change due to the lessons learned from these earlier small scale innovation projects. All of this has occurred in a context where most academics have lost whatever enthusiasm they had for QE because of the associations of the concept of quality generally with managerialism, bureaucracy and stress.

## A FRAMEWORK FOR DEVELOPING ORGANIZATIONAL CULTURES FOR ENHANCEMENT

It can be argued that effective planning for enhancement that goes beyond simple amendments to existing local practice needs particular key elements to be taken into account. For example, developing a new system for supporting student induction across a department, introducing work placements into a large programme, incorporating student group assessments or a new scheme for managing student complaints will require collaborative planning over an extended time period and involve dealing with very different types of system elements simultaneously. In order to achieve sustainable enhancements in these and related areas which will be supported by different stakeholders it is important that these different elements supporting change are addressed. There are different ways of approaching this but one framework for 'viewing' change might involve consideration of the 'foundational' (QA derived), cognitive, emotional, interpersonal, and organizational elements. In addition there may be political, financial, technological and external factors that may be more or less crucial for individual enhancement projects, but the ones listed here are likely to be essential to any worthwhile enhancement initiative.

## Key elements of QE in academic contexts

*Foundational (QA derived)*

Key elements:

- effective and stable core systems which have been subjected to different kinds of inputs and are agreed to be effective, and which have sufficient tolerances to cope with innovation;
- clarity and transparency regarding the aims of the relevant area of provision;
- robust monitoring and review data (including complaints data) which enables the effectiveness of the systems to be confirmed and which will allow meaningful comparison between any proposed innovation or development and previous practice;
- a clear model of the relationship between the processes in question and the processes which feed in to it, the processes which it in turn serves, plus any parallel systems which receive input or provide input into similar systems;
- the right kind of staff expertise to build on the above and manage the other elements.

*Cognitive*

Key elements:

- an idea for change and development which is innovative and recognized as such;
- the capacity to express the idea clearly and cogently across a range of contexts, formats and audiences.

*Emotional*

Key elements:

- those leading the change feel passionate and committed about the change and feel comfortable in expressing that passion to others;
- those involved collaboratively in enacting or supporting the innovation feel positive about the enhancement plan;
- everyone involved in the development is able to express concerns, anxieties and doubts about the goals of the plan, or progress towards it.

*Interpersonal*

Key elements:
- a sense of team identity and common purpose amongst those responsible for the enhancement;
- effective, open and inclusive working relationships with significant players in adjacent structural units or projects.

*Organizational*

Key elements:
- a clear link to or location in the organizational structure of the institution;
- a project structure with clearly identified goals, milestones, activities, resource specification and schedules;
- a champion amongst the senior key decision makers of the institution.

If these are the elements required for effective management of enhancement then the question arises as to the ways in which the conditions for such enhancement practices can be built into the organizational culture. In order to maximize the likelihood that effective ideas for enhancement will emerge and be successful it is essential to develop an 'enhancement friendly' organizational culture. Some of the principles shown in the following box will not be relevant in all academic environments and not all will be due equal priority for development at a given point in time. However, the majority of these considerations will be relevant in some form to most institutions at some point.

## Developing an organizational culture for QE in academic contexts

*Foundational (QA derived)*

Action required:

- promoting robust QA as a basis for enhancement;
- ensuring an open and inclusive approach to monitoring, review and complaint management that focuses on feedback as a resource for learning rather than persecution;

- using integrated planning systems which encourage an awareness of the difficulties and priorities of originating and receiving and units;
- having a fundamental and well-resourced commitment to staff development and promoting the institution as a learning organization;
- showing a commitment to supporting innovation, in ways which are not conditional on immediate and complete success of all aspects, allied to an awareness of the unique learning opportunities afforded by innovation projects.

### Cognitive

Action required:

- providing space for outline ideas to be exchanged and developed outside of the funding flurries;
- providing support for ideas for development to be shared widely for discussion and comment before the design and implementation phases.

### Emotional

Action required:

- encouraging potential developers to consider and gauge the responses of other players before taking ideas to the proposal stage.

### Interpersonal

Action required:

- encouraging and valuing cross-function project teams as part of appraisal and reward systems;
- providing staff development support for project related communication;
- having mentoring by more experienced staff of less experienced colleagues.

### Organizational

Action required:

- ensuring effective leadership from senior managers for development and innovation;
- arranging staff development in project management (including mini- and micro-project management).

It is tempting to consider enhancement as a highly bounded management problem where solutions of a fundamental kind are impossible. Most definitions of QE, while sufficiently broad to avoid narrow conceptualizations of what QE might be, in practice do not support consideration of basic issues. Both the Milton and LTSN definitions are sufficiently broad to include resource issues, but in practice neither of these definitions has stimulated debate on the relationship between quality and level of resource. Despite newfangled ideas about complexity theory, leadership alignment, fitness for purpose and quality through empowerment, it remains that the simplest way of improving the quality of provision is to fund it properly. Adequate funding for provision is not a sufficient condition for enhancement but it is a necessary one. As important as scheduling and aligning of available resources with QA outcomes is, the real problem to solve is getting the resources to the problem in the first place. In an operating environment where there are many learning resources of exceptional quality, and a surfeit of highly qualified and potentially extraordinarily committed staff, the relationship between investment and enhanced student experience is an intimate one.

## REFLECTIVE PRACTICE POINTS

To what extent do you feel that an appeal to improving the resourcing of provision is a symptom of higher education not knowing how to effect substantive change?

## QUALITY AT THE EDGE OF CHAOS

Recently there has been extensive discussion on whether or not higher education actually knows how to implement enhancement. Newton (2002) argues that many models of enhancement which assume that universities operate within a context of stable structures and clear policies are missing the point that university strategic development in many areas is a 'messy business'.

An interesting conceptual analysis of the nature of QE in the context of large complex organizations with multiple cultural layers is offered by Tovey (2002). He argues that universities, like most complex organizations, are neither structured nor function in such a way that we can predict the outcomes of interventions in a simple linear manner. For example, if tutors introduce a new set of rules for managing submission of assessments, students will alter their behaviour to adapt to the new regime. More subtly, tutorials aimed at clarifying assessment criteria change the meaning of the criteria and so on. Equally, argues Tovey, universities are not completely unregulated – responses to change are not *random*. Accordingly, and drawing heavily but critically on complexity theory, Tovey suggests that universities can helpfully be thought of as operating between stability and instability developing at the 'edge of chaos' in a condition of organizational turbulence and disequilibrium. For Tovey, this is not a condition to be feared, indeed recognition of this state can be empowering:

> The implication is that systems operate best 'at the edge of chaos'. At the edge of chaos, change can occur easily and spontaneously. It is like a good party; lively, lots of flowing conversations, and fun. A party in stasis would be safe, but probably boring and stilted; one in chaos might be thrillingly anarchic, or perhaps offensive or dangerous. In chaos, a system could self-organise into a higher level of complexity, with novel forms of relationship emerging, or it could disintegrate. (Tovey, 2002: 18)

Tovey argues that in this context the practical implications for QE are that university practitioners need to accept that they are not in full control; they must explore the powers of simple rather than complex rules and structures for change and should recognize that actions in specific spheres are also acts about those spheres (as when an act of teaching is also an act about the context for teaching). Like Newton, Tovey questions fundamentally the very idea of managed QE initiatives which are based on the assumptions that interventions need only have clear goals, organized implementation and collective commitment to make the intended impact.

Tovey's analysis is an interesting angle on enhancement in the context of complex organizational cultures, especially given that universities pride themselves on collegiate, peer-based arrangements which lend themselves to extreme 'connectedness' but limited 'directiveness'. However, as with the application of complexity theory to business settings, the true value or otherwise of this approach for higher education will depend upon the successful implementation of projects guided by the theory which are not interpretable in terms of other simple and familiar formulations. The jury is out on the value of complexity theory and will not return until it is able to show some degree of additionality to existing practices.

---

### Reflecting on QE

What are the three major resourcing issues in your department? If resources were made available overnight to address these issues would your department be a world-class unit? If not, why not?

To what extent do you find it easy to cost proposed innovation – either your own or others' – in your institution? Is this important to you?

Consider your working environment in terms of the aspects that most directly affect students:

What aspects of this working environment do you consider to be stable? What aspects of this working environment do you consider to be unstable? What aspects of this working environment do you consider to be on the 'edge of chaos'?

How comfortable do you feel in each of these 'zones'?

If you were part of a team seeking to effect significant step changes in academic quality, which aspect of supporting enhancement would you find most comfortable: foundational (QA derived), cognitive, emotional, interpersonal, organizational?

What is the relationship, if any, between the four kinds of contributions to the enhancement environment identified by Jackson (2002) and the nature of QE within your university? Are the four functions reproduced or are there different structures and dynamics at work?

To what extent do you feel Institutional Audit achieves its aims in relation to enhancement? Does it do so more effectively than the old comprehensive Subject Review system? More than Academic Review?

The Academic Review methodology is sometimes regarded as inspectorial since it largely focuses on assessments of the provision against external standards rather than against the provider's own aims. To the extent this is true, what are the implications for quality enhancement benefits of such reviews?

# Part 2
# Managing quality in the context of the QAA Code of Practice

# 6 The Code of Practice

The Code of Practice for the Assurance of Academic Quality and Standards in Higher Education, normally referred to as 'the Code of Practice', or simply 'the Code' is a set of guidelines for ensuring good quality of education in all aspects of provision. Although sometimes referred to as the *Codes* of Practice there is in fact only one Code of Practice comprising 10 sections. The Code is central to the overall quality framework promoted by the QAA in several ways. Administratively, it links the FHEQ, subject benchmark statements (SBSs) and institutional audit arrangements. Politically, it reflects the authority of the agency to lay down an agenda for QA, but acknowledges the autonomy of institutions to address that agenda according to their own mission and local circumstances. The Code of Practice is also notably broad in scope. It deals with issues ranging from 'External examining' (section 4) to 'Collaborative provision' (section 2), and the entire student experience from 'Recruitment and admissions' (section 10) to 'Careers education, information and guidance' (section 8) – for an overview of the Code's sections see Table 6.1 at the end of this chapter. Like the FHEQ, the Code was established in response to the Dearing and Garrick reports into higher education.

The Code is seen by the QAA as an evolving and expanding set of guidelines which 'identify a comprehensive series of system-wide expectations covering matters relating to the management of academic quality and standards in higher education. In so doing, it will provide an authoritative reference point for institutions as they consciously, actively and systematically assure the academic quality and standards of their programmes, awards and qualifications' (QAA *Code of Practice for the Assurance of Academic Quality and Standards in Higher Education*, para 2).

Each section of the Code is made up of an introduction followed by precepts and points of guidance. Some sections also have appendices covering relationships between the main content and external contexts. The precepts identify the key areas which the QAA expects universities to be addressing when delivering programmes, while points of guidance are suggestions on what institutions might wish to consider doing in order to address the precepts. Generally speaking the precepts are written broadly whereas the points of guidance are more focused. It is assumed that institutions will certainly address the precepts but they may not necessarily do so in the manner implied by the guidance. When the early sections of the Code were written there was an assumption that the precepts were requirements which would be monitored by the QAA as part of the subject review/academic review arrangements. However, with the shift of emphasis away from QA to QE, implied by the new arrangement for institutional audit, the assumption is that there is much more flexibility around the precepts with institutions required to consider the recommendations implied by the precepts. The truth lies somewhere in between. The precepts are more than just advisory but less than regulatory. The guidance notes however further reflect the tension between the need to amplify and suggest how the precepts might be addressed on the one hand, and the concern of the QAA not to be seen to be directing what are autonomous HEIs on the other.

## STRUCTURE OF THE CODE'S SECTIONS

To illustrate the idea of the precept and guidance structure we can consider an example from section 6: 'Assessment of students'. Precept 12 states: 'Institutions should ensure that appropriate feedback is provided to students on assessed work in a way that promotes learning and facilitates improvement.' The accompanying guidance states:

> In meeting the needs of students for feedback on their progress and attainment, institutions will need to consider:
>
> - the timeliness of feedback;
> - specifying the nature and extent of feedback that students can expect in relation to particular types and units of assessment, and whether this is to be accompanied by the return of assessed work;
> - the effective use of comments on returned work, including relating feedback to assessment criteria, in order to help students identify areas for improvement as well as commending them for evident achievement;
> - the role of oral feedback, either on a group or individual basis as a means of supplementing written feedback when feedback may not be appropriate. (Code of Practice, S6: precept 12)

Note that the Code does not specify any particular schedule for the return of work to students (eg students should receive feedback no later than four weeks after submitting the work) but rather that institutions should consider 'the timeliness of feedback'. Similarly, institutions are required to consider 'specifying the nature and extent of feedback that students can expect in relation to particular types and units of assessment, and whether this is to be accompanied by the return of assessed work'. In other words the QAA itself does not specify the nature and extent of feedback that students can expect, but it expects institutions to make such specifications and to stick to them. In short, the sections of the Code do not set standards, but lay out the kinds of things a responsible and quality focused HEI should be setting standards for.

It could be argued that the Code does not even go as far as that. An institution could, in theory, give extensive consideration to setting standards for the return of student work and decide in the end to set no standard at all due to the particular circumstances of that institution. It is difficult to see why any institution should wish to do this but technically the Code merely requires that these issues be considered. A more contentious example of this is in section 2 of the Code, covering collaborative provision in the context of franchise programmes delivered through partner organizations (POs). Here there is a precept stating that 'the certificate or transcript should record the name of the Partner Organisation'. However, several universities do not record the PO on certificates as they feel the standards for programmes on all sites are the same.

It is further assumed that institutions will have systems in place for ensuring that whatever they specify as the arrangements and standards, they also have systems for auditing that what they say should happen actually does happen, happens effectively and to an appropriate standard. A further expectation is that institutions will actively monitor the arrangements they put in place to address the precepts and will seek to improve their systems over time. In this way the precepts serve to frame the agenda for QA (do you do what you say you do?) and QE (do you to seek to improve what you do?).

## REFLECTIVE PRACTICE POINT

In your institution how would you describe the current level of awareness of the existence of the Code of Practice, its content and its function?

The Code also provides guidance on what kind of information universities should publish in the public domain for potential students, employers and other stakeholders in relation to the areas covered by the different sections of the Code. In the area of assessment for example, the Code states that universities should 'consider' publishing information on the aim and schedule of assessments; the accreditation of prior learning; the marking criteria; how final awards are calculated on the basis of the assessments; grading conventions; rights of appeal against assessment decisions and publication of results and opportunities for reassessment. This focus on publication of procedures, rights and regulations demonstrates how the Code is designed to encourage universities to actively decide on quality policies and publish those policies widely rather than allow potentially inconsistent custom and practice to emerge by default leading to confusion and a lack of transparency. While other sections of the Code, such as section 10 'Recruitment and admissions', also have an explicit focus on the information which should be published regarding procedures and policies, the arrangements for institutional audit (2002) building on the recommendations of the Cooke report (HEFCE 02/15), establish much wider responsibilities for universities in this area, as we shall see in Chapter 15.

The status of the guidance notes contained in the sections of the Code of Practice is important to establish since the QAA does not want to, or be seen to, direct universities on how to run their programmes. However, the guidance notes are intended to cover key areas of the management of the quality of academic programmes. The expectation is that universities will be able to demonstrate that they have at least considered the issues raised by the sections of the Code and considered the implied arrangements for supporting quality which they contain. While the *guidance* elements are intended to indicate how precepts might be implemented and the QAA emphasize that these are 'not intended to be either prescriptive or exhaustive', the QAA expects that, one year after publication of each section, all institutions will be able to demonstrate that they are adhering in some way to the *precepts*. The phrasing throughout the QAA documentation balances the directive element through insisting that institutions will be expected to adhere to precepts, with the reinforcement of the idea of institutional autonomy by ensuring the precepts focus on what there should be clear policies about, rather than stating what those policies should be.

Both FECs and HEIs will want to note that the Handbook for Academic Review explicitly draws reviewers' attention to those sections of the Code that deal with quality and standards: programme approval monitoring and review; assessment of students; external examining and collaborative provision. This reflects the slightly more 'inspectorial' approach of Academic Review compared to Institutional Audit and may in part account for the relatively high number of 'failing' departments (4.8 per cent) under this methodology compared to the old Subject Review Scheme (0.8 per cent) (Times Higher, 14 February 2003)

## REFLECTIVE PRACTICE POINT

How is your institution reflecting the recommendations of the Code of Practice in approval and review? In annual monitoring? In developing policies in specific areas such as the assessment of students?

**Table 6.1** Overview of the Code of Practice by section

| Section | Became Effective | No of Precepts | Special Appendices |
|---|---|---|---|
| Section 1: Postgraduate research programmes | Jan 1999 | 25 | |
| Section 2: Collaborative provision | July 1999 | 38 | |
| Section 3: Students with disabilities | Oct 1999 | 24 | |
| Section 4: External examining | Jan 2000 | 16 | A note on the respective roles of examiners and academic reviewers |
| Section 5: Academic appeals and student complaints | Mar 2000 | 14 | Independent external review of students' complaints |
| Section 6: Assessment of students | May 2000 | 18 | Type of information for institutions to include in published documentation |
| Section 7: Programme approval, monitoring and review | May 2000 | 9 | Programme design, aligning internal reviews with external reviews |
| Section 8: Career education, information and guidance | Jan 2001 | 14 | |
| Section 9: Placement learning | July 2001 | 8 | |
| Section 10: Recruitment and admissions | 28 Sept 2001 | 9 | UCAS guidance on confidentiality |

# 7 Collaborative provision

## TYPES OF COLLABORATIVE PROVISION

Collaborative provision is where one institution, in this case a UK HEI with degree awarding powers, approves the delivery of one of its courses at another institution under its name. Where the programme runs at the UK HEI this is usually referred to as a franchise, where the HEI does not offer the programme the arrangement is usually referred to as 'accreditation'. Collaborative provision falls into two different categories: franchise to overseas institutions and franchise to UK institutions such as further education colleges (FECs). Although these represent two very different types of challenges, the underlying goals in relation to quality remain the same: the need to ensure that the standards of the awarding institution (AI) are not compromised and that the overall student learning experience on the franchise is properly managed at the partner organization (PO). However, the means by which these goals are achieved and the difficulties that beset both types of arrangements are very different and the management of quality and standards in each case is correspondingly dissimilar. In this chapter we shall consider some of the ways in which the QAA Code section 2 on collaborative provision seeks to provide a QA framework for such arrangements. This section of the Code is outlined in Table 7.1 at the end of this chapter.

The majority of franchises are normally part-franchises, with only year 1 or years 1 and 2 of an undergraduate programme being approved for delivery at a PO. This raises the important issue of managing the transition for students from the franchise provision to the host provision. Although this is one of the most important elements of successful franchise management, the Code does not devote a great deal of attention to it.

In some cases part-franchises are the third and final year of a UK programme offered through an overseas PO to students who have already completed a two-year qualification such as a higher national diploma or equivalent. These are often seen as problematic in QA terms since the academic expertise necessary to deliver level 3 (level H) is not always available to the PO (see below). The academic input and support for honours dissertations in particular is seen as an area where quality can be compromised. The demand for such arrangements is high however since POs wish to build on their own two- or three-year level 1 or equivalent programmes but lack the awarding powers for degrees, while individual students cannot afford the cost of studying in the UK. The fact that the year 3 programme builds on an award which was not explicitly designed as a preparation for the honours level of a UK degree means that in some specialist areas of the curriculum students will struggle with the challenging material.

The QAA's Code section 2 'Collaborative provision' (1999), is based on an earlier document produced by the Higher Education Quality Council (HEQC) in 1996. The Code's section 2 was one of the earliest to be published by the QAA and is the most detailed with 38 precepts. The section covers work in preparing for a franchise and post-franchise work. It also covers areas which are not normally associated with QA issues but which are in fact often quite crucial such as the selection of agents and the responsibilities of a UK institution to another institution when it abandons a franchise.

---

### Articulation and franchise

Section 2 of the Code covers franchise arrangements. However, a franchise is just one kind of inter-institutional 'feeder' system for facilitating overseas students' access to UK higher education. These feeder arrangements come in two distinct forms.

In *articulation* agreements, a UK HEI agrees to recognize the academic credits or equivalent accumulated by a defined set of students on a specific named award or set of awards. Successful completion of the PO programme will secure direct entry on to year 2 or year 3 of a specific programme at the UK HEI. In this arrangement the programme taught at the PO is validated by that PO; the UK HEI has no direct role or responsibility in QA and would not have any direct input into the programme's delivery or assessment.

By contrast in *franchises* the programme delivered at the PO is a validated programme of the AI. As a consequence therefore the responsibility for QA, as far as the QAA is concerned, lies with the UK HEI. There is a general sense in which any damage done to the reputation of one HEI in terms of a failure of maintenance of standards is done to the whole UK higher education sector. It is clear then that whatever the business benefits and risks of either, the QA responsibilities of the AI are very much more serious under a franchise arrangement than under any articulation arrangement.

As stated in section 2 of the Code, the main principle underlying arrangements for collaborative provision should be that 'collaborative arrangements, wherever and however organised, should widen learning opportunities without prejudice either to the standard of the award or qualification or the quality of what is offered to the student' (para 7). This assumes of course that the AI itself runs a version of the programme. This is usually (but not always) the case. Where there is no version of the programme running at the AI, it is of course more difficult to assess whether the standards of the franchise are appropriate.

Ironically, the code recognizes that in genuinely *collaborative* provision (ie with two degree awarding institutions operating in tandem to provide a dual validated award) the provision of the Code probably will not be relevant. The reason for this is that the assumption of the Code in this section is that there is a degree awarding UK HEI (the AI) franchising an award to another institution (PO), which does not have UK degree awarding powers (or in some cases no degree awarding powers at all). The underlying spirit of the code in this section is that there is nothing collaborative in the management of the quality of the provision at all, the UK HEI is the lead partner and the franchisee needs to follow that lead partner's QA agenda. This reflects a concern that the commercial instincts of the overseas institution will result in practices which compromise the good name of the AI. As we shall see however, in practice many of the threats to quality which arise under this heading are attributable to the indifference of UK HEIs to the arrangements carried out by departments and the lack of monitoring systems to identify problems early enough.

## REFLECTIVE PRACTICE POINT

What are the non-commercial benefits for UK universities of becoming involved in overseas articulation or franchise arrangements?

If you have been involved in introducing, developing or monitoring a form of overseas collaborative provision what struck you as the most exciting aspects of the proposed or ongoing provision? What struck you as the most difficult issues to manage in QA terms?

## BACKGROUND TO COLLABORATIVE PROVISION

What is the 'mischief' which section 2 of the Code seeks to address? What are the perceived risks to quality? With the gradual reduction in the value of the unit of resource provided to HEIs by HEFCE it has become increasingly important for universities to secure full-cost overseas students to come to the UK. Universities have realized that relying upon the 'retail market' by targeting individual students through recruitment fairs and magazine advertising is unreliable and expensive. In order to manage the 'supply chain' more effectively and to provide a more predictable stream of overseas students, almost every UK HEI has sought to establish links with overseas institutions as a feeder for UK degrees. In parallel with this need for extra fee-paying students, the overseas demand for higher education in general, and for UK higher education in particular, stimulated either by buoyant economies, government policy, or both, has led to a steady stream of requests from potential overseas POs to acquire collaborative agreements. Many of these requests come from small specialist institutions which are partly privately financed, often with a strong sense of customer satisfaction but limited experience in the maintenance of academic standards and their management of the kind developed in the UK. Occasionally, entire awards or the final year of an award is delivered in collaboration with POs. However, the most complicated agreements, and in many ways the most interesting, are part-franchises serving as feeder arrangements.

The precepts cover a wide range of areas that would all be covered within one institution for their traditional campus-based provision. However, the franchise might deal with these different components in different ways and the Code seeks to ensure that there are clear agreements and policies in place to manage these processes. A further effect of this section of the Code is that it effectively confirms the end of serial franchising with or without the authority of the awarding HEI – (see para 9).

It is clear that institutions do not always have a full grasp of the arrangements taking place under their name. A scoping exercise carried out by the QAA in 2001 indicated that institutions in the UK were not able to provide accurate information on whether or not they had any overseas partners in China:

> A number of other UK institutions had responded to the survey claiming to have no collaborative arrangements with Chinese partners. However, it quickly became clear during the visit to China that some of these institutions did, in fact, have established partnership links with Chinese universities. This failure to disclose the existence of established collaborative arrangements caused some confusion during the visit to China, and had the potential to cause embarrassment for the institutions concerned as well as for the QAA. It would be advisable for UK institutions to ensure that this disappointing aspect of the present exercise is not repeated in future surveys of collaborative links with overseas countries. ('UK Collaborative links with China', report of a scoping exercise, 2001)

It seems likely that institutions simply did not know centrally what kind of overseas partnerships were being carried out in their name rather than there having been any deliberate attempt to conceal their activities.

In order to appreciate the significance of the Code in this area it is useful to consider some of the areas where overseas franchises threaten to compromise academic standards. QAA reviews of overseas provision frequently find that while the AI has clear procedures and guidelines for delivery, assessment, staff development and reciprocal visits that these are not always adhered to by the PO. This clearly suggests that monitoring procedures need to be improved. A key consideration here is that monitoring is much more expensive for overseas provision than it is for mainstream or domestically franchised provision. Additionally, since monitoring overseas provision is more complex and requires a greater level of skills and experience, institutions do not always have a large group of specialists to advise on the management of such franchises.

## HOW AND WHY FRANCHISES GO WRONG

### Overseas audit reports

Unique to QAA reports, publication of reports on overseas audits occur with key issues being unresolved. Unlike subject review reports the response of the university to the report is published alongside the final report from the QAA. This occasionally leads to confusing messages to students. On some occasions the unresolved issue is a matter of judgement which leaves the report looking rather untidy as an investigation into standards. However, sometimes the commentary disputes matters of *fact* which in principle could have been resolved one way or another with further enquiry and consideration of evidence.

For universities keen to enter into critical discussion about the most effective way of managing quality and protecting academic standards, such exchanges provide interesting insight into the areas of debate between central auditing and local providers. However, to the rest of the world, such unresolved disputes present a confusing and unseemly image of UK higher education and give the impression of unfinished business.

QAA reports of overseas provision by UK institutions indicate a range of issues which in the view of the auditors need to be addressed. These can be summarized under the following headings – programme design, monitoring and review; staff development; external examining; teaching and learning; and organizational arrangements – and serve as a useful context for consideration of the precepts themselves.

## Programme design, monitoring and review

Changes to franchised provision are sometimes implemented without going through the appropriate revalidation arrangements. This can occur because student demand or staffing changes mean that some modules or parts of the syllabi need to altered quickly and POs, particularly in the private sector, allow their desire to meet customer needs override what appears to them to be the lumbering bureaucracy of the AI.

Many franchises have developed from links established by enthusiastic individuals within a department. As a result the involvement of the institution and the institutional QA procedures are characterized by low awareness and engagement.

Information from departmental monitoring reports about the franchised provision does not always get to institutional level at the AI. This can occur because at each successively higher level there is aggregation in the QA reports. Another problem occurs because reports of the external examiners appointed by the AI are sometimes not shared with staff delivering the programme overseas at the PO.

Individual departmental 'link persons' rather than course leaders for the on-campus provision sometimes take responsibility for reviewing the quality of provision at the PO. The result of this is that there is very limited comparability of standards and this can lead to a lack of ownership for QA actions.

## Staff development

Occasionally there are only infrequent visits by AI staff to the franchise provider. Sometimes this is because the numbers scheduled to enrol on the programme are lower than anticipated and there are limited resources to support the visits.

Where visits from the AI to the PO do occur they sometimes lack focus. This can be because in reality the primary function of many visits to PO by AI staff is to explore the possibility of developing *new* business with the partner rather than to monitor the existing provision. Additionally, since visits overseas are expensive, time spent at any one institution can be brief. Since academic staff can rarely be spared from their responsibilities at the employing institution, the scheduling of the visits inevitably reflects pragmatic considerations rather than, say, key points in the assessment cycle of the collaborative programme.

In some cases there is exploitation of AI staff at the PO. An effective arrangement to support overseas franchise is for an experienced full-time member of staff from the AI to the PO to help support the delivery of the curriculum and the maintenance of standards. However, it is important that the PO does not abuse this:

In one case, the [QAA] audit team found that a first-year franchise was being conducted by an individual seconded from the UK institution, whose responsibilities ranged from admissions and assessment to staff appointments and the monitoring of teaching quality, with what appeared to be very limited requirements for reporting back to the UK. In this case, the commitment of the individual had clearly made a substantial contribution to the success of the franchise, but there was little evidence that the partnership had been underpinned by robust quality assurance mechanisms. (QAA Malaysia overview report)

## External examining

In some franchises there has been concern that external examiners have not been able to be involved in assessing whether standards in the franchise element are comparable to those of the host HEI delivery. Many AIs require external examiners to visit the PO at least once during the term of office. While some external examiners see this as an important part of their duties in confirming the equivalence of standards, and no doubt a welcome opportunity for some expenses-paid travel, others are unwilling or unable to make the commitment to visit the PO and rely instead on reviewing a sample of scripts.

## Teaching and learning

Occasionally a lack of support for subject specific English teaching is noted in audits on overseas franchises. The majority of overseas franchises are taught in English. However, students often struggle to learn in a language that is not their native tongue. It is widely recognized that while lectures and formal tuition and student presentations will normally be delivered in English, tutorial, academic support, technical instruction and feedback on assessment will often be given in the local language. In some areas, such as health and safety briefings, it is essential of course that all students understand what is required of them. The key threshold is that all assessments must be set in English and answered in English. Some universities offer extensive English language support for students when they arrive in the UK, focusing on English for academic purposes (EAP).

Particular issues have been noted with provision where the delivery of curriculum is in languages other than English. Where a programme of study is franchised in its entirety and there is no period of study in the UK, it will, in order to meet local consumer demand, often be delivered in the local language. However, as the course materials and their delivery is taken closer to the customer, it is correspondingly taken further away from the AI. It is essential therefore that UK HEIs have robust systems in place to monitor delivery in languages other the English. The first issue is that all assessments will have to be translated into the local language and a sample of student work will always have to be translated into English for the AI to monitor standards. This translation work is of course time consuming and expensive. It is good practice though rarely pursued for the quality of the translation to be assessed to ensure that the intention of the setter of the assessment question is fully captured. One standard way of doing this is to have a second translator independently translate the first translator's translation back into English. More generally, difficulties arise when translation delays add further confusion and pressure on to an already tight assessment administration schedule.

Further problems arise when monitoring reports or other indicators such as student achievement suggest that there are difficulties with the delivery of the programme in some way. It can be difficult for the AI to review documents such as student handbooks if they are not in English. In this sense translation difficulties can impede not just the QA arrangements for design and implementation, but also impede review and reform if the implementation is imperfect.

Finally, programmes delivered under franchise agreements in languages other than English mean that two crucial systems widely recognized for providing good quality support for franchises – secondments by AI staff to the PO and Web-based support by AI staff – are not fully available and as such leave the delivery at the PO even more cut off than it would otherwise be.

In some overseas franchises there have been difficulties in supporting honours level project work. Where the third level (level H in the FHEQ) or Masters level work is franchised overseas, there is often particular risk to quality in relation to any dissertation, project, thesis or equivalent which has to be completed by the student. While many dissertations are successfully completed each year on overseas franchises, often applying the UK curriculum in imaginative ways to local circumstances, there are a number of specific areas where HEIs should pay particular attention to monitoring the student experience and academic standards:

- Academic staff at the PO may lack experience in dissertation work.
- There may be lack of learning resources, including specialist journals, at the PO.
- There may be limited opportunities for supervision sessions at the PO.
- The prior academic experience of the students, on, say, a local national diploma or equivalent, may not have provided students with the requisite methodological and practical techniques required for an extended project.

Of course all of these issues must be explored fully at any validation or review event, but inevitably systems put in place to address these issues are often resource hungry and can be difficult to maintain.

## *Organizational arrangements*

Particular difficulties have been identified where the organizational arrangements for the franchise involve additional subsidiaries or parent organizations of the principal PO. For example, in the review of a collaborative partnership between one UK university and a private sector educational provider the QA loop involved not only the company which entered into the collaborative agreement but also its quasi-autonomous delivery centre in a different country where the programme was actually taught, *and* its parent company. This led to lack of clarity as to who was responsible for what aspect of planning and monitoring the student experience.

Similarly subfranchising of a technology programme to an established university overseas led to a further subfranchising to a small specialist college. There are two principal and probably ultimately insurmountable problems with these arrangements. First, the difficulties of the AI communicating effectively with the subfranchisee, and secondly the impossibility of delegating to the PO the kind of responsibilities for the protection of standards embedded in the Code. When high turnover of staff is added to these complex hierarchical arrangements there can be significant concern about the risk to standards. Such subfranchises are quality disasters waiting to happen and institutions would be well advised to steer clear of them.

## REFLECTIVE PRACTICE POINT

To what extent are the solutions to the problems raised by the QAA in relation to overseas collaborative provision obvious? To what extent are the solutions easy to implement? Are they likely to have significant resource implications?

## IMPLEMENTING THE PRECEPTS FOR COLLABORATIVE PROVISION

### Responsibility for, and equivalence of, academic standards

*1. The Awarding Institution is responsible for the academic standards of all awards granted in its name.*

*2. The academic standards of all awards made under a collaborative arrangement must be both equivalent to those of comparable awards for programmes delivered by an Awarding Institution itself and be compatible with any relevant benchmark information recognised within the UK.*

These precepts lay down the general principles for the rest of the section. Precept 1 is effectively a 'strict liability' clause – in other words everything that happens on the programme in quality terms is the responsibility of the AI, whether the AI knows about what goes on or not. This ensures that UK HEIs cannot wash their hands of a QA disaster by saying that the PO should have acted more effectively.

Precept 2 contains a requirement regarding benchmark compatibility. While not a major issue it needs to be recognized that benchmark statements have been written primarily for UK-based universities on campus provision. For example, section 3.1.2

of the communication, media, film and cultural studies benchmark states that amongst the things graduates of programmes in these fields will demonstrate knowledge and understanding of is the following: 'an awareness of the economic forces which frame the media, cultural and creative industries, and the role of such industries in specific areas of contemporary political and cultural life'.

Clearly this means something very different if we are referring to the development of the media in the West as opposed to, say, South East Asia. The AI needs to decide on the extent to which the curriculum being franchised has to adapt to local histories and cultures. On the one hand the programme needs to be relevant to students in their local circumstances, on the other hand in the context of a part-franchise there needs to be adequate preparation for the final part of the programme at the AI. In some areas, such as computing or physics, there is little need for extensive review of how the franchised programme meets the benchmark statements. However, in grey areas, such as media, business and marketing, a strategy has to be carefully worked out.

Comparability of student achievement under both programmes must take into account the entry level of the students on to the programme. In some cases the capability of entrants will be higher (as would be the case in relation to numeracy levels in some South East Asian franchises) and in some cases lower (as with literacy levels in English in some business or humanities programmes).

## Policies, procedures and information

Precepts 3–6 set out the requirement for a formal procedure for establishing a collaboration (rather than informal local departmental arrangements), an inter-institutional commitment (and not just a unarticulated understanding), a central register of collaboration (and not just an awareness) and PSB notification in advance (and not retrospectively). This lays out a basic threshold for ensuring that new collaborative projects are carefully designed as *central institutional* developments rather than simply being informal, local initiatives. This is to ensure AI commitment and that there is a clear understanding on the part of the PO that they are dealing with the UK HEI as a whole and not with one section of it. The requirement for a register reinforces the need for institutions to know centrally what is being done in their name, and by implication, that they take responsibility for managing the collaboration at an appropriately senior level.

*Precept 7: The Awarding Institution's policies and procedures should ensure that the financial aspects of the arrangement satisfy any statutory and funding body requirements; activities must be costed and accounted for accurately and fully. There should be adequate safeguards against financial temptations to compromise academic standards.*

Precept 7 contains two quite separate and fundamental exhortations. First that statutory requirements are met and secondly that there are safeguards to prevent the desire for profit to override the interest of quality. The former relates primarily to the Funding Council's rule that HEFCE funds should not be used to subsidize overseas education. For that reason the financial accounts associated with overseas provision have in principle at least to be kept separate from those relating to domestic provision. In practice of course this is almost completely unachievable. Staff costs in particular cannot be easily allocated to overseas activity.

Although several mechanisms can be put in place to ensure that standards are maintained despite the costs involved (such as service level agreements, library agreements, computer agreements and so on) the best defence against the temptation to compromise academic standards is to ensure that there is a viable business plan in place at the outset. In that context, it is the temptation to pursue palpably unprofitable projects that has to be resisted. Clearly, while an institution may wish to pursue some franchises for strategic reasons (as loss leaders in new markets for example) it has to reassure itself that the department delivering the programme will have access to sufficient resources throughout the period of the collaboration. This is particularly true where early institutional enthusiasm for an overseas links wanes as the economy of the PO dips or continues to dip and the prospects of further more lucrative joint ventures become progressively more remote.

A further important issue in protecting quality and standards for overseas collaborations is to ensure that the overseas franchise element (often loss making) is subsidized by the revenue from the provision at the AI. This is partly because the fees charged to students in their home country are less than those levied when those students arrive in the UK for the latter parts of the programme; and partly because the UK HEI would get only 20–40 per cent of that franchise tuition fee element. Although the AI would not be responsible for teaching costs for the franchised component, it would incur significant costs for validation, travel, staff secondment, external examining costs and so on. Institutions expecting the franchise element to be self-financing sometimes find themselves having to cut costs and compromise quality. The HEFCE rules on finance of course encourage this separation since the equivalent provision at the UK AI is normally funded from HEFCE revenue. In brief then, Precept 7 relates to important financial considerations which institutions must take into account when planning franchise provision, but while these considerations are necessary ones they are by no means sufficient since they relate principally to transparency and delivery rather than business viability.

## REFLECTIVE PRACTICE POINT

Does your institution currently have any overseas or FEC-based collaborative arrangements which have not been approved above the departmental level? Or above the faculty or school level? How important is such approval in your view?

## Selecting a PO

*Precept 8: An Awarding Institution should be able to explain the rationale for its choice of Partner Organisations.*

*Precept 9: An Awarding Institution should satisfy itself about the good standing and financial stability of a prospective Partner Organisation. The mission and objectives of a Partner Organisation should be compatible with those of the Awarding Institution.*

*Precept 10: The legal status of the prospective Partner Organisation and its capacity to contract with the Awarding Institution should be examined, together with its ability to provide the infrastructure and the learning resources necessary to ensure that the required quality and standard of the planned provision will be achieved.*

*Precept 11: Where a prospective Partner Organisation is known to have a current, or has had a previous, relationship with another UK Awarding Institution, enquiries should be made of that Awarding Institution as to the standing and effectiveness of the proposed Partner Organisation.*

*Precept 12: Where an Awarding Institution has withdrawn from an arrangement with a Partner Organisation it should, to the extent permitted by law and the contract(s) entered into with such Partner Organisation, and in the event that enquiries are made from another UK Awarding Institution proposing to enter into a collaborative arrangement with the same Partner Organisation, make a frank disclosure to that UK Awarding Institution of any concerns which led to its withdrawal.*

Precepts 8–12 relate to the selection and assessment of potential POs. Few HEIs identify potential POs by strategically assessing their own needs and the different kinds of collaborations which might be beneficial and then actively seeking a partner. Instead most collaborations emerge from individual academic contacts, sometimes through research collaborations, or through a third-party brokerage arrangement. Several overseas POs are private colleges or the income generating arm of an established university or college, and as such are primarily motivated by commercial considerations. In these cases it is difficult to assess the extent to which their 'mission and objectives are compatible with those of the Awarding Institution' (precept 9).

Precept 10 combines two very different considerations: the legal authority to contract and the resources available to support the provision. The assessment of the legal and financial standing of the PO will often involve a 'due diligence' report commissioned from organizations such as the British Council and a review of any accounts made publicly available. In some cases key financial data will need to be requested from the PO though this can lead to misunderstandings. Of course there is no reason why POs should not ask for similar information from the AI, even if in most cases it may look like merely a face-saving *quid pro quo*. Nevertheless, given that 50 per cent of UK HEIs in 2001–02 were technically in deficit, it may be that such enquiries are more than just cosmetic.

### REFLECTIVE PRACTICE POINT

What is the history of the development of partnerships with overseas institutions? Are they selected strategically or on the basis of individual researcher or management contact? If institutions have robust systems for assessing the suitability of any proposed links, does the origin of the link matter?

In relation to the resources of the PO, difficulties can arise if the PO states that the acquisition of specialist resources and additional staffing is contingent on successful franchise validation of the proposed programme. In such circumstances clear agreements in writing need to be in place long before the validation and time needs to be set aside following validation to confirm that the appropriate resources have in fact been put in place. All of this is not far removed from the kind of process which might take place in a wholly UK-delivered programme. The real difficulties arise when a PO indicates that purchase of specialist equipment or reading resources is contingent not only on successful validation of the programme *but on sufficient students being recruited*. This leads to the risk that the programme will recruit enough students to run but not enough students to finance a level of resourcing consistent with high academic standards. Clearly, a threshold level of resourcing to protect the student experience is necessary and cannot be subject to the number of enrolments achieved since the experience of the students who are on the course, even if few in number, needs to be protected. (It is interesting to compare this precept with the more demanding expectations on this score of the QAA guidelines for distance learning – see Chapter 16.)

However, in order to ensure that the student experience and academic standards are comparable to those at the AI, a higher threshold may need to be put in place. In terms of audit and QA monitoring generally, there is always some latitude for new provision to develop, but this latitude must not be abused. This issue reflects the broader tension in QA in collaborative provision between, on the one hand, establishing the level of resourcing required to ensure that the learning outcomes of the programme are to be achieved, and on the other, ensuring that academic quality and the learning experience is comparable to that of provision at the AI (often a more challenging standard).

Precepts 11 and 12 seek to ensure that there is an accumulation of experience across the UK higher education sector of organizations which have not been able to maintain standards for whatever reason. Of course it might well be that the AI and PO were not suited to each other, which is possible given the advice on incompatible missions and objectives. It might well be of course that POs also develop an awareness of those AIs who fail to provide a sufficient degree of support for collaborative programmes. The Code is silent on poaching POs or dealing with more than one PO locally.

Precepts 13 and 14 relate to written agreements. Perhaps the most interesting aspect of this part of the section is that there should be a need to recommend this at all. One would not expect to find in, say, a code on overseas trade for the private sector a recommendation that 'prior to entering into a new long-term business agreement with unfamiliar companies operating in different jurisdictions, in a different currency and with a lack of any statutory protection, it may be wise to consider putting the agreement in writing'. But the advice is needed because many UK HEIs for several years had no clear policies for formalizing overseas franchises.

Although there can be absolutely no exceptions to establishing written agreements for overseas collaboration there are several points worth noting here. First of all, although it was until recently assumed that the agreement would be in English and that the agreement would be covered by English law, this is now increasingly challenged by POs who feel this gives the AI unnecessary legal advantages. The 'solution' is for two versions to be produced, one in each language, with each having equal weight. UK HEIs need to accept that there is always the possibility of any small, new, private sector PO being unable to meet its financial liabilities under the contract and that should that be the case the prospects of recovery on the strength of the contract are remote.

The precepts encourage UK universities to share information with other HEIs about agreements with previous or prospective POs. This is commendable and all HEIs should adhere to this precept. However, this does not address the other and equally important issue of disclosure amongst UK HEIs as AIs about *current* agreements. It is important that universities know what agreements are in place at the PO they intend to collaborate with, not just for obvious business reasons but to ensure that students are not ushered on to the top-up programmes that are most commercially beneficial to the PO rather than beneficial to the students' interests.

## REFLECTIVE PRACTICE POINT

When entering into an overseas collaborative agreement does your institution routinely contact other UK HEIs about any previous or current link with the potential PO?

When entering into an overseas collaborative agreement does your institution find itself being checked up on by the potential partner? What would be the response from your institution if a request for business sensitive information was requested?

Precepts 15, 16 and 17 address the issue of agents. Agents operate mainly in China and South East Asia dealing with both individual students and with institutions. An agent is likely to have several agreements with different institutions, simultaneously.

Brokering franchise and articulation agreements through agents is fraught with difficulty and agents should probably be used for making initial introductions only. Mediation by agents between the AI and the PO (or network of POs) is not consistent with the responsibility of the AI to fully assess the suitability of any potential partners. Agents are also sometimes used to serve as admissions officers in overseas areas on behalf of UK universities. Agents take a percentage of the fee charged by the university and also seek to levy a charge from the student for introducing them to the UK HEI. Further charges will be payable to the agent for visa application support (where relevant) and for securing an application form for the applicant (even when these are freely available from the university Web site's homepage). The most common complaint about some agents is that they make offers to students with insufficient English language skills. Most universities will ask for a IELTS score of around 5.5–6.5 or a TOEFL score of around 600 where still used. The danger of bogus scores and certificates bought through various means should not be underestimated.

Precepts 18–23 cover standards, programme quality and awards. Clearly, the expectations and recommendations contained in these precepts are in addition to the precepts articulated in other sections of the Code, as collaborative provision has to operate within the same general framework as other non-collaborative provision.

Overall the precepts emphasize the need for clear accountability (ie the accountability rests with the AI), formal documented operational procedures, specific responsibilities of AI and PO, comparability of standards, and the management of admissions.

There is detailed guidance for these precepts. The thrust of the guidance here is that a AI should seek evidence that the PO has already got 'an understanding of the current practices and expectations of UK higher education, for example in connection with external examining, assessment arrangements and quality assurance requirements'. While this is clearly important in the sense that the PO needs to appreciate the underlying principles and rationale for these systems, AIs need to accept that they need to work in partnership with their POs to ensure that there is a developmental process of progressive incorporation of UK practices.

The guidance encourages HEIs to ensure that 'there is adequate monitoring, including regular visits by staff from the Awarding Institution, to verify the accessibility and appropriateness of learning facilities and other support services'. As noted above, this is an area where good intentions are frequently not honoured. Visits to overseas partner institutions are expensive and difficult to arrange. The visit may not occur at the time best suited to the development or monitoring of the franchised provision. One area of good practice is to ensure that administrative staff from the AI visit the PO at an early stage to review systems in the PO and to ensure that there is clear understanding of requirements generally, but particularly regarding assessment arrangements and associated systems and procedures. Face-to-face meetings will also help establish good rapport over the longer term. Awareness amongst administrative staff also ensures that the provision is not overlooked when new systems or support staffing arrangements are being developed.

Precept 22 requires the AI to review the proficiency of staff engaged in the programme. There are several issues here. First of all, academic CVs from some overseas institutions will not always be in the same format or follow the conventions of UK CVs. They are likely to be shorter and may not have significant research publications or scholarly achievements. These CVs need to be read in the appropriate context noting the expectations and norms of the relevant country. It may be the case that fuller biographical details are required to flesh out the details of the CVs, which are likely to be translations of originals produced for the purpose of the collaborative project. There are of course many sensitivities here too. The idea that the AI 'consider undertaking its own evaluation of the proficiency of the academic staff involved in a programme and provide development opportunities for such staff' as recommended by the guidance is liable to cause great offence in many countries if not handled carefully.

One of the key problems in this area is that the staff whose CVs were submitted at validation may not turn out to be the individuals actually teaching on the programme. This may be due to several reasons including, in smaller, commercially-orientated outfits, the high turnover in staff. It is not unusual in many countries especially in North Africa, South East Asia and South America for full-time university lecturers from the state sector to complement their salary by teaching in the evening for private universities and colleges. There can be a high turnover in such institutions as lecturers drift in and out of contract. In such cases it is not the calibre of contributing staff which is the issue, it is the lack of *continuity* of staffing that presents a risk to quality.

Where the precepts address accreditation of prior (experiential) learning (AP(E)L) and related issues there is scope for tighter regulation by the AI of PO management of entry on to the programme. Since the AI should not delegate any admissions policy issue to the PO and maintain close review of the operations of admissions, it is advisable for the AI to be directly involved in any AP(E)L or related matters. Certainly in the first two or three years of operation individual AP(E)L cases should be managed by the AI directly.

Precepts 24 and 25 cover assessment requirements with a particular focus on ensuring that the PO understands and adheres to the assessment systems and standards of the AI, a focus that culminates in a common examination board. The guidance here is rather patronizing and assumes that POs (including FECs) have little or no comprehension of the rigours of assessment. The suggestion that the AI should seek 'regular attendance, pre-arranged *or unannounced*, at assessment events organised by the Partner Organisation by an appropriate member of the Awarding Institution's staff, or an external examiner, *to monitor the conduct of assessment;*' seems calculated to antagonize even the most progressive and accommodating FEC. Similarly, in the guidance to precept 24 the recommendation that AIs should seek to understand the examination and assessment philosophy of the PO 'in order that any differences in approach which might compromise the exercise of the Awarding Institution's responsibility for academic standards can be identified and addressed', the possibility that AIs might learn some good practice from their POs seems to have been overlooked. While it is of course the case that some overseas institutions (and perhaps some FECs) might consider that one of the benefits of entering into a collaborative arrangement is precisely that they can benefit from exposure to mature QA in assessment systems, the emphasis in this section is clearly one of policing and intervention, forcing the PO to mend its ways to enable it to achieve the no doubt impeccable standards of the AI.

---

## FRANCHISING IN LANGUAGES OTHER THAN ENGLISH

Included in these precepts is the guidance to consider the difficulties caused by delivery in a language other than English. All of this can be finessed by simply avoiding the delivery of programmes in a language other than English. However, if the desire to pursue this path is deaf to the entreaties of reason, then there are specific policies regarding translation that can be implemented. All of these have resource implications:

- Ensure that the AI takes responsibility for translating all of the assessments.
- Ensure that assessments are translated back into English by a separate translator working independently of the first.
- Ensure that the PO takes responsibility for carrying out all translations of student work.
- Ensure that a sample of student scripts is made available for translation by an independent translator by the AI for QA purposes (including audio or video records of student presentations).
- Ensure that where possible, translators are used who are also reasonably competent in the subject matter.
- Ensure that additional time is built into the assessment schedule to enable full QA systems to be applied to translated materials.

For these and other reasons collaborative provision in languages other than English is to be avoided unless there are extraordinarily strong reasons to the contrary.

Precepts 26–31 cover the responsibilities of external examiners and their deployment in the context of collaborative provision. However, as the Code makes clear, these precepts need to be read in conjunction with section 4 of the Code on external examiners. Here the precepts cover the need for the external examining processes to apply as fully to the collaborative provision as to the main provision, for there to be specific procedures in place to manage these arrangements and that the PO fully accepts and understands these. Specific guidance on overseas collaboration relates to the external examiners' understanding of UK higher education, and the potential need for additional external examiners given the collaborative activity.

Precepts 32 and 33 cover the issuing of certificates and transcripts and encourages AIs to take particular care to avoid the irregular distribution of documentation. Precept 33 states that the certificate should name the PO and declare that English was not the language of instruction if this was the case. The precept goes on to state, perhaps rather tamely, that where such details are recorded on the transcript only, that the existence of the transcript should be stated on the certificate. Precept 33 is controversial, with many institutions unhappy with the perceived interference to award qualifications. There are clearly commercial considerations here (students and the PO would both rather have a 'standard' certificate, not one which implies that the programme was in some way inferior to the main award). However, the argument in terms of QA is that if a university has in fact met the aim of ensuring that collaborative provision is comparable to the main provision in terms of standards, then there is no need to qualify the certificate in any way.

## The award certificate issue

In some cases the location of the award is not stated on the certificate of the award. Although both the HEQC's Code of Practice for Overseas Collaborative Provision, 2nd Edition (1996) and the QAA Code's section 2 on collaborative provision clearly state that the location of study should be stated on the award, this is not always adhered to. There is concern on the part of the QAA that successful students will present their certificate and give the impression that they attended the home institution directly. Institutions who chose not to state the location of study on awards argue that if the quality and standards of the PO programme are intended to be the same as those on the home campus, then there is no reason why certificates should make reference to the location of study.

This is an interesting example of institutions refusing to adhere to the precepts but arguing that they have considered the issue raised by the precept carefully (rather than failing to follow the precept because of failure to appreciate the issue).

Interestingly the guidance talks not just about standards and level but also the 'nature' of the award, a term which is not defined elsewhere in the Code. Specifically the guidance states that 'an Awarding Institution should consider the need for confidence that the award certificate will not mislead students, current or prospective employers or other authorities about the nature, standard and level of the award'. It is difficult to see how students could be misled but clearly there is a danger that despite well-founded claims that standards and learning opportunities are comparable to the main provision, it would be misleading for a student to claim they had followed the programme at the AI rather than at a PO.

A similar debate has been ongoing in the higher education sector in relation to distance learning programmes, with institutions resisting suggestions that certificates issued should state that the award was achieved through distance learning. It should be noted that the guidelines on distance learning do not suggest that certificates should be qualified in this way.

Precepts 35–38 cover the kinds of information that should be made available to applicants and seeks to emphasize that the programme should not be misrepresented. All of the headings to be addressed are unproblematic in themselves though the practice of giving students detailed information in 'course handbooks' or equivalent may not be standard practice in some institutions, so the real issue is to make sure students understand that the handbook is a definitive statement of what is expected of them through, for example, declaring what the schedule of assessments is. The specific recommendations for overseas provisions cover the language of instruction and assessment, professional recognition and the costs of study.

It is of course very difficult to monitor all of the information circulated by POs and their agents about the provision. But there should be systems in place whereby the number of people authorized to produce material is defined and controlled. Clearly, in competitive commercial environments agents and POs are motivated to present their programmes in the most attractive ways possible but generally speaking they will not want to antagonize the AI. Establishing open lines of communication on marketing is essential to ensure that as much monitoring that can be done is done. Many AIs find themselves delegating all of the publicity for programmes since the design and production costs locally are much lower than UK costs plus shipping. The advent of the Internet has in theory made it more possible to monitor what is being said by the PO or its agents about the provision by requiring all materials to be available on the Web.

In practice the most likely form of misleading information in relation to franchises is the implication that a programme has significant teaching input by academics from the AI, when in fact there is a number of visiting guest sessions. However, the most dangerous type of misleading statement is not misrepresenting a franchise as something more, but rather misrepresenting as a franchise something which is rather less. In particular, where an articulation arrangement has been established between a PO programme and an AI top-up year, it is not unusual for overseas POs to present the arrangement as one where the AI 'approves' the programme and, in some unspecified sense, underwrites and guarantees the quality of the programme. More generally there is the problem of a PO which possesses a franchise, or even less, in relation to one programme or part of a programme, and implies that the AI in some unspecified sense approves a much wider portfolio of programmes than is actually the case.

A further complication is that marketing material and publicity, even for programmes that are delivered in English, is that such materials are typically produced in the local language(s). Not only does this cause extra difficulties in monitoring material distributed about the programme, it raises crucial questions about the need for an agreed name for the programme, the form the collaboration, or even the name of the AI in the local language(s).

## QA ISSUES WITH COLLABORATIVE PROVISION

Managing overseas franchised provision is difficult. It presents a whole range of additional risks to quality in addition to those which all programmes face. The areas identified above which have emerged as particular difficulties in QAA audits of collaborative provision highlight the main threats to quality in such programmes:

- failure to ensure that the programme leader takes responsibility for managing the monitoring of the overseas franchise;
- failure of the AI to monitor difficulties in the collaborative provision at an appropriate level;
- failure to follow an agreed plan of staff visits;
- failure to subject PO scripts to the same scrutiny as AI scripts within the external examining process;
- failure to provide adequate provision for English Language support;
- failure to manage translation issues where delivery is not in English;
- failure to ensure that students receive the appropriate learning opportunities in relation to honours dissertation work at the PO;
- failure to maintain basic controls over quality in subfranchise arrangements.

## QE ISSUES WITH COLLABORATIVE PROVISION

Developing the quality of provision in collaborative franchises will be very much dependent on the discipline, the local culture, the history of collaboration and the other joint activities in which the two institutions are involved. However, in terms of the key areas where good practice can help prevent the kinds of difficulties identified earlier from QAA reports some of the following features are likely to be priorities for institutions developing successful long-term franchise arrangements:

- ensuring adequate reciprocal staff secondments by PO and AI prior to start of programme;
- having a clear business plan which lays out all costs and revenue for both the franchise and revenue components;
- building support staff secondments into the business plan;
- ensuring that a copy of the external examiner's report is sent to the PO;
- ensuring that a 'site' programme leader is appointed at the PO through whom all academic contact is routed;
- establishing extensive Web-based support for franchise students including the opportunities to contribute to discussion groups with UK students;
- having a thorough review of operational matters after the first year of delivery.

---

## Reflecting on collaborative provision

How does your institution balance the commercial and quality considerations in the establishment of an overseas franchise?

How effectively would you say your institution manages the admissions arrangements for overseas franchises?

In what ways is the monitoring of assessment similar and different for franchises to overseas partner institutions and UK further education partner institutions?

What are the implications for annual monitoring of franchise, accreditation and articulation arrangements?

In what ways if any can and should an AI get involved in the staff development process for staff at the PO? What are the implications of your answer for quality enhancement for the programme?

To what extent is it feasible and desirable to amend curricula under a franchise agreement to reflect the local context of the culture of an overseas PO? (You may wish to refer back to Chapter 2).

In what ways does your institution ensure that it has information relevant to the Cooke report (HEFCE 02/15) 'Information on Quality and Standards in Higher Education' in relation to franchise provision? Are both your institution as AI and your PO using the same categories or the same criteria for data capture?

What is your institution's policy and system on monitoring and responding to complaints from students on franchised programmes? Are the arrangements as robust or effective as systems for your own students? What are the implications for QA and QE?

**Table 7.1** Code of Practice for collaborative provision: key issues, risks and good practice

| Precept | Key Issues | Risks | Good Practice/Risk Management |
|---|---|---|---|
| **Responsibility for, and equivalence of, academic standards** | | | |
| 1: The Awarding Institution (AI) is responsible for the academic standards of all awards granted in its name | 'Strict liability' rule – even if, eg an overseas college or FEC has its own protocol for running franchises | Lack of clarity in Partner Organization (PO) agreement | Acquire examples of agreements from other programmes or institutions |
| 2: The academic standards of all awards made under a collaborative arrangement must be both equivalent to those of comparable awards for programmes delivered by an AI and be compatible with any relevant benchmark information recognized within the UK itself | 'Comparability' is more than just a threshold level of quality<br><br>Benchmark content may need application to local circumstances | Applying curriculum to local circumstances may not prepare students for 'top-up element' | Regular review of the relative achievement levels at the PO and AI<br><br>Comparisons of the PO and AI originating students in the final year of any top-up arrangement |
| **Policies, procedures and information** | | | |
| 3: Collaborative arrangements should be negotiated, agreed and managed in accordance with formally stated policies and procedures of the AI | *ad hoc* discussions are fine but no *ad hoc* agreements | The PO has its *own* formally stated policies of good practice for the management of such awards which conflict with the AI<br><br>Extension of existing provision becomes a new activity | Establish central register at institutional level not just of current approved franchises but of developing links |
| 4: The AI's policies on collaborative arrangements should include a requirement that the commitment and support of both the AI's and the PO's central authorities must underpin any arrangement | Collaboration cannot be departmental, it has to be owned by both institutions centrally | | |

**Table 7.1** continued

| Precept | Key Issues | Risks | Good Practice/Risk Management |
|---|---|---|---|
| 5: An up-to-date, authoritative and easily accessible register of all approved collaborative arrangements should be maintained within the AI | Institutions should know, and be able to answer simple questions from the QAA | | A register of approved collaborative awards should be kept separate from the database on proposed collaborations or defunct collaborations |
| 6: The AI should inform any professional or statutory body (PSB) which has approved or recognized a programme which is the subject of a possible or actual collaborative arrangement of its proposals and of any final agreements which involve the programme | | PSB requirements can change over time. Collaborative provision (CP) as validated may no longer be acceptable. Can the changes be made in time? | Ensure early notification to PSB of collaborative plans |
| 7: The AI's policies and procedures should ensure that the financial aspects of the arrangement satisfy any statutory and funding body requirements; activities must be costed and accounted for accurately and fully. There should be adequate safeguards against financial temptations to compromise academic standards | | Inadequate business plans for CP, ring fencing of franchise element revenue | Develop a full business plan for collaboration well in advance. HEIs should develop a template |
| **Selecting a partner organization** | | | |
| 8: An AI should be able to explain the rationale for its choice of POs | | Opportunism rather than strategic alliances. Failure to monitor overall portfolio | Carry out strategic review of overseas collaboration with specification of key features followed by proactive exploration of potential partners |
| 9: An AI should satisfy itself about the good standing and financial stability of a prospective PO. The mission and objectives of a PO should be compatible with those of the AI | | Failure to assess viability and standing of POs or spin-offs which will actually deliver the programme | Enter into low risk non-franchise or non-teaching collaboration to acquire better knowledge of the PO culture and standards |

**Table 7.1** continued

| Precept | Key Issues | Risks | Good Practice Risk/Management |
|---|---|---|---|
| 10: The legal status of the prospective PO and its capacity to contact with the AI should be examined, together with its ability to provide the infrastructure and the learning resources necessary to ensure that the required quality and standard of the planned provision will be achieved | | PO provision of resources being contingent on a certain level of recruitment to programme | Seek information from other partners and ex-students on experience with PO |
| 11: Where a prospective PO is known to have a current, or has had previous, relationship with another UK AI, enquiries should be made of that AI as to the standing and effectiveness of the proposed PO | | Incomplete disclosure by UK HEI | In addition to formal statement from HEI, arrange informal discussions. Essential to get views of those directly involved in working relationship 'off record' |
| 12: Where an AI has withdrawn from an arrangement with a PO it should, to the extent permitted by law and the contract(s) entered into with such PO, and in the event that enquiries are made from another UK AI proposing to enter into a collaborative arrangement with the same PO, make a frank disclosure to that UK AI of any concerns which led to its withdrawal | | Incomplete enquiries by the AI | Provide opportunities for off-the-record briefings |
| **Written agreements** | | | |
| 13: There should be written and legally binding agreements or contracts setting out the rights and obligations of the parties and signed by the heads of the AI and the PO. The written agreements or contracts should at least cover: | | The legal status of any written agreement in different jurisdictions | Establish exit strategy contingency based on zero recovery of committed funds |
| i) the aspects of the arrangement concerned with the relationship of the AI with the PO, and | | | Assess through business plan scenario of complete contractual collapse with no remedy |
| ii) the aspects of the arrangement relating to individual programmes | | | |

**Table 7.1** continued

| Precept | Key Issues | Risks | Good Practice/Risk Management |
|---------|-----------|-------|------------------------------|
| 14: The agreements should include termination and arbitration provisions and financial arrangements and should describe the respective responsibilities of the contracting parties for academic standards and quality. They should include provisions to enable the AI to suspend or withdraw from the agreement if the PO fails to fulfil its obligations. The residual obligations to students on termination of the agreement should also be covered in the agreement or contract. Unreasonable confidentiality provisions which would preclude the AI from sharing with other AIs any concerns which led to its withdrawal from the agreement should be avoided | | Unilateral withdrawal by the PO | Encourage the PO to see longer term development opportunities which will provide motivation for long term partnership |
| **Selecting an agent** | | | |
| 15 : An AI using agents to broker or facilitate collaborative arrangements must be satisfied that an agent's interests do not conflict with those of either the AI or the students recruited to join the programmes provided under the collaborative arrangement | | The agent's commercial interests conflict with students' interest | Use agents only exceptionally |
| 16: The legal status of the agent, its financial standing and reputation within the local educational community, should be investigated fully by the AI | | The agent is unlicensed | Require credentials to be presented at an early stage |

**Table 7.1** continued

| Precept | Key Issues | Risks | Good Practice/Risk Management |
|---|---|---|---|
| **Agreements with agents** | | | |
| 17: There should be written and legally binding agreements or contracts with any agents involved with collaborative arrangements. Agreements should define the role, responsibilities and delegated powers of the agent in each arrangement. The agreements should include monitoring, arbitration and termination provisions and financial arrangements and specify the legal jurisdiction under which any disputes would be resolved | | | |
| **Assuring academic standards and the quality of programmes and awards** | | | |
| 18: The AI will be accountable for the quality and standard of all programmes and awards offered or made in its name which are provided under the collaborative arrangements | | Damage to reputation of the AI in relation to programmes which it does not in fact validate but is perceived to be in some sense associated with | Subscribe to monitoring agency in relevant country. NB: digital archiving services do not normally store advertising copy |
| 19: Procedures and decisions concerning all programmes, whether for accreditation, validation, articulation of franchising, must be based on specific criteria which are systematic and open to scrutiny | | Procedures exist but they do not drive the decisions | Procedures must identify responsibilities and time scale for action, to be agreed at point of validation |
| 20: The respective responsibilities of the AI and the PO for quality assurance and control should be clear, explicit and documented | | | AIs to sign off responsibilities to the PO only when the officer responsible has also been identified |
| | | | Establish reciprocal monitoring/shadowing/support teams to ensure key tasks are done on time |
| | | | Web page with weekly updated task list and schedule can monitor and motivate progress on both sides |

**Table 7.1** continued

| Precept | Key Issues | Risks | Good Practice/Risk Management |
|---|---|---|---|
| 21: The AI should be able to demonstrate that the quality of the programmes provided through the partnership is appropriate to meet the aims and objectives of those programmes and comparable to the quality of any similar programmes provided by the AI itself | | Quality of programmes may be appropriate and comparable but the learning experience is significantly poorer | Where appropriate video recording of lectures and common Internet-based bulletin boards can help PO students access AI lecturers<br><br>Borrowing rights and IT access rights should be supported from the AI library |
| 22: The AI should ensure that effective measures exist to review the proficiency of staff engaged with collaborative programmes | | Staff turnover, insensitive handling of CV review, insufficient detail | HEI should provide person specification for teaching posts, laying out core skills. This needs to be negotiated with the PO |
| 23: The AI must determine the admission requirements and acceptable entry qualifications for students joining a programme provided under the collaborative agreement. It should monitor the application of the requirements, paying due regard to the expectations set out by any professional and statutory bodies where appropriate. Particular care needs to be taken with any arrangements for the Accreditation of Prior (Experiential) Learning (AP(E)L) that may be in place. The AI should review information on student progression | | Insufficient experience in local qualifications and relevance of prior learning to make robust judgements<br><br>Over-accreditation of prior learning by the PO | Where AP(E)L is likely to be a major issue joint processing of applications needs can help provide staff development for the PO. Final approval of all AP(E)L applications should normally be retained by the AI and not delegated |
| **Assessment requirements** | | | |
| 24 : The examination and assessment requirements for programmes provided under a collaborative arrangement must be devised so as to ensure that the academic standards of the awards are equivalent to those of the same or comparable programmes delivered by the AI and, as such, reflect any national benchmarks | | Where the same assessments are used at the PO as are used at the AI and developed by the AI staff, danger that the PO students will be disadvantaged through remoteness from discussions and debates on a hidden or preferred curricular agenda at the AI | The AI must always manage design of assessments<br><br>Actively invite proposals for assessment questions from the PO. Provide feedback on why any questions are not suitable. The PO should provide examples of any case studies used to inform assessment details<br><br>Past papers or sample papers should be produced for the PO at an early stage especially in early years |

**Table 7.1** continued

| Precept | Key Issues | Risks | Good Practice/Risk Management |
|---|---|---|---|
| For franchised programmes the examination and other assessment requirements should be the same as those required by the AI when it delivers the same or comparable programmes itself. If variations are essential these must only be made with the prior approval of the AI which must be able to demonstrate that academic standards will not be compromised as a result | | Assessments are diluted by the PO | The AI must produce all assessment items including questions (or equivalent) and any supporting material |
| | | Additional and inappropriate support and guidance given by PO staff to students with assessments | PO to clearly state and submit assessment procedures to the AI in advance of operation |
| | | | Establish and agree clear protocols for managing assessment. This must go beyond simple invigilation and cover revision teaching, collaborative work, plagiarism and feedback |
| For programmes delivered under an accreditation or validation arrangement the examination and assessment requirements should be equivalent to, and as effective as, those employed by the AI when it delivers the same or comparable programmes itself | | Limited experience at the PO of managing invigilation or coursework submission | AI to offer staff development opportunities to the PO, including shadowing during 'examination season' at the AI |
| 25: The AI should ensure that the PO understands and follows the AI's requirements for the conduct of assessments | | The information gets to the PO but not to the right person within the PO | Establish good lines of communication with key administrators and academics |
| | | | Make it easy for PO staff to ask questions without going through PO managers anonymously if necessary (possibly through Web-based forms) |
| **External examining** | | | |
| 26: External examining procedures for programmes offered by a PO should be the same as, or demonstrably equivalent to, those used by the AI for its own internal programmes. The procedures should be clearly specified and documented, and rigorously and consistently applied | | External too remote from early inputs to assessment board to influence overall grades and marking standards | Ideally external examiner should visit the PO to meet staff, advise on procedures and reinforce importance of role |
| | | External examining system slowing down assessment process generally, or being rushed through administrative schedules | Can serve as 'honest broker' for the PO with the AI to clarify ambiguities or concerns of the PO |

**Table 7.1**  continued

| Precept | Key Issues | Risks | Good Practice/Risk Management |
|---|---|---|---|
| 27: The AI should have specific policies and procedures on the recruitment and selection of external examiners for programmes provided under a collaborative arrangement. These should reflect the AI's normal approach to the recruitment and selection of external examiners and be clear, explicit and communicated to the PO | | External examiner appointed with no experience of CP | Provide introduction in general induction for *all* external examiners on CP, even those not involved, as this will enable them to act in this role in the future |
| 28: The AI must retain responsibility for the appointment and functions of external examiners | | | AIs, as well as underscoring the importance of the external examiner's role, to emphasize how working closely with the external examiner will be beneficial in developing knowledge of UK higher education and UK systems |
| 29: The role of external examiners in ensuring that the AI can fulfil its responsibility for the academic standards of the awards made in its name must be clearly defined and communicated to the PO and to the individual external examiners | | | The AI and the PO to exchange at an early date organizational diagrams and procedural charts (in translation if necessary) |
| 30: The respective obligations and responsibilities of the PO, the AI and the external examiners, should be appropriately and clearly communicated by the AI | | | In addition to formal documents on briefing the package for external examiners should include: |
| 31: External examiners must receive briefing material and guidance from the AI sufficient for them to fulfil their role effectively. They should be expected to participate in induction or training events provided by either the AI or the PO | | | – information on local academic culture; <br> – full list of key contacts at the PO; <br> – contact name of experienced external examiner on other collaborative provision programme within the HEI |

**Table 7.1** continued

| Precept | Key Issues | Risks | Good Practice/Risk Management |
|---|---|---|---|
| **Certificates and transcripts** | | | |
| 32: The issuing of award certificates and transcripts should remain under the control of the AI | | Lack of security for certificates or transcripts | Have high profile local award ceremonies |
| 33: Subject to any overriding statutory or legal requirements or constraints in any relevant jurisdiction, the certificate or transcript should record the name of the PO and the language of instruction where this was not English. If the language of assessment was not the same as that used for the instruction this should also be clearly recorded on the certificate or transcript. Where the information is recorded on the transcript only, the certificate must refer to the existence of the transcript | | | Consider not running programmes where the language of instruction is not English

If necessary put a Web address on the certificate or transcript so that employers and others can read in more detail a balanced overview of the programme, emphasizing the comparability of standards even though taught in a different language |
| 34: The words and terms used on the certificate should be consistent both with those used by the AI on the certificates for the same or comparable programmes it provides, and with any relevant qualifications or awards frameworks | | | A local language translation of the award will be required for local employers |
| **Information for students** | | | |
| 35: Information given by the PO, or an agent, to prospective students and to those registered on a programme, about the nature of the programme, the academic standards to be met and the quality of the provision which is offered should be approved by the AI; define clearly the nature of the collaborative arrangement and outline the respective responsibilities of the parties | | Difficulty of monitoring all information sent to students | The AI to set up a Web page which provides definitive information on the programme. Information should be in the local language to enable parents and other sponsors to assess the suitability of the programme |

**Table 7.1** continued

| Precept | Key Issues | Risks | Good Practice/Risk Management |
|---|---|---|---|
| 36: The information should be comparable with that given by the AI to its own potential and registered internal students. The information should be monitored regularly and updated as appropriate | | | |
| 37: The information should include directions to students about the appropriate channels for particular concerns, complaints and appeals | | Some cultures will not see appeals and complaints as appropriate for students. In some cases requirement to put a complaint in writing will be difficult to implement. The PO will not promote the information, or if it does, staff at the PO will be offended | The AI to negotiate with the PO systems for appropriate implementation of complaints and appeals systems and these should be reviewed by an independent party |
| | | There is a risk that AIs will use bureaucratic procedures to minimize student complaints | Make provision for students to achieve a rapid informal local solution without recourse to even minimal bureaucracy |
| **Publicity and marketing** | | | |
| 38: Effective control over the accuracy of all public information, publicity and promotional activity relating to the programmes and awards for which it has responsibility should be retained by the AI, and particularly so where the information is published on its behalf. The AI should satisfy itself through active means that this control is exercised consistently and fairly and that the public cannot be misled about the collaborative arrangement or about the nature and standing of the programmes and awards provided under the arrangement | | Materials published in local language | |
| | | Institutional listings and advertising are more difficult to monitor than programme-specific promotional material | |

# 8 Students with disabilities

'The object of the Code is to assist institutions in ensuring that students with disabilities have access to a learning experience comparable to that of their peers.'

(QAA Code of Practice, S3)

## THE CODE AND THE SPECIAL EDUCATIONAL NEEDS AND DISABILITY ACT 2001 (SENDA)

The Special Educational Needs and Disability Act 2001 (SENDA) amended Part 3 of the Disability Discrimination Act 1995 (DDA) to remove the exemption of education and introduced a new section, Part 4 (Education). This creates new legal rights for students with disabilities. The Act makes it unlawful for relevant institutions to treat a disabled person 'less favourably' than a non-disabled person for reasons related to his or her disability (without 'justification') and requires institutions to make 'reasonable adjustments' to ensure that a disabled student is not placed at a 'substantial disadvantage'. The DDA 1995 originally only covered universities to the extent that they were providers of goods, facilities and other services. The implications of this new legislation are wide reaching and the ramifications still to be fully evaluated. The Disability Rights Commission (DRC) has published a 'Code of Practice for providers of post 16 education and related services' which provides useful guidance on the Act and its implementation.

It should be noted that the Act focuses on the actual experience of individual students not the intentions, policies or practices of the institution as such. It should not need stating that compliance with the Act requires more than enthusiastic adherence to the QAA precepts. Adherence to the precepts in conjunction with other initiatives may be used as part of a defence for HEIs in the event of action being taken against them under the Act but there should be no confusion about their relative status. Indeed it might even be the case that because the QAA Code does not go as far as the Act in many ways, adherence to its precepts might give academic departments a false sense of security. More generally, the existence of the Act legitimately informs and raises the expectations of students with disabilities and therefore frames all interactions between the student and the institution including those related to the quality of academic provision. Therefore, not only can the Code not be read without full consideration of SENDA at every turn, but achieving quality in this area can only be in the sense of successfully operating within the Act. There can in no meaningful or useful sense be high quality unlawful provision.

> If a claim under the Act is made against a responsible body based on anything done by an employee, it is a defence that the responsible body took such steps as were reasonably practicable to prevent such acts. (S58 5) Examples of such steps could be developing policies on disability matters and communicating these to employees and ensuring all staff are aware that it is unlawful to discriminate against disabled people. (DRC Code of Practice, S8.6)

It is likely that actions which serve to address the QAA Code serve to address the Act. Nevertheless, it has to be emphasized that compliance with the law requires more than adherence to the precepts.

---

The introduction of responsibilities for HEIs under the Act is phased over a three-year period, to enable institutions to comply.

- The main new sections of the Act came into effect on 1 September 2002. These sections make it unlawful to discriminate against disabled people or students by treating them less favourably than others. In addition, they require responsible bodies to provide certain types of reasonable adjustments to provision where disabled students or other disabled people might otherwise be substantially disadvantaged.
- The duty on responsible bodies to make adjustments involving the provision of auxiliary aids and services is effective as of 1 September 2003.
- The duty on responsible bodies to make adjustments to physical features of premises where these put disabled people or students at a substantial disadvantage comes into effect on 1 September 2005.

---

## COMPARING THE CODE'S PRECEPTS AND THE ACT

One of the most obvious ways in which the assumptions of the QAA Code's section on students with disabilities and the 2001 SENDA legislation diverge is in the definition of who is a disabled student. Even though the Code takes no particular definition it does not go as far as the Act which states that anyone who has been disabled in the past – even if now fully fit – still classifies as disabled. Anyone successfully managing the symptoms of their disability or impairment is also still covered by the Act. Note that it does not follow from this that institutions need to treat students who once experienced impairment as though they still experience that impairment but technically such students are covered by the Act and this needs to be kept in mind in terms of disclosure for example.

---

### Links to other legislation and responsibilities

Not only must the Code be read in conjunction with the SENDA legislation, but the SENDA legislation needs to be read in conjunction with a whole matrix of legislation. Not all of this legislation relates to academic matters but almost all relates to a student's broader relationship to a university. The DRC Code of Practice states that:

> The DDA (1995) as amended by SENDA 2001 has to be considered in the context of other pieces of legislation affecting the rights of disabled people and the responsibilities of public bodies towards those rights:

- the Data Protection Act 1998 (10.2)–(10.3);
- the Health and Safety at Work Act 1974 and related regulations (10.4)–(10.5);
- the Fire Precautions Act 1971 and related regulations (10.6);
- the Occupiers' Liability Act 1957 and the Occupiers' Liability (Scotland) Act 1960 (10.7)–(10.8);
- the Defective Premises Act 1972 (10.9);
- building regulations, planning permission and other property issues (10.10);
- the Human Rights Act 1998 (10.11);
- the Race Relations Act 1976 and the Race Relations (Amendment) Act 2000 (10.12)–(10.15);
- the Sex Discrimination Act 1975 (10.16)–(10.17);
- the Welsh Language Act 1993 (10.18);
- common law duties (10.19)–(10.20);
- statutory responsibilities of other bodies (10.21)–(10.23).

---

Much of this legislation is convergent in terms of what it implies HEIs must do, but in some cases the provisions of the Act are at first glance at odds with the actions implied by other acts. In particular the sections in the SENDA regarding disclosure (where disclosure to any employee is treated as disclosure to the institution) can be seen as being in conflict with the Data Protection Act (which makes it unlawful in some circumstances to disclose sensitive personal information without permission). Many of these conflicting responsibilities need to be tested in court to see how the balance of responsibilities should be managed. The DRC Code of Practice states that 'should a student request confidentiality under the Disability Discrimination Act, information may not, from that point, be passed on for the purposes of making reasonable adjustments' (p 64). It does not follow from this that reasonable adjustments cannot continue to be made, simply that the confidential information cannot be disclosed to others in order to bring them about.

---

### DISABILITY PROFILE OF UK HIGHER EDUCATION

Over 30,000 students with a disability started programmes of study in 2000–01 UK HEIs, representing over 4 per cent of all new students. Of those students with a disability, approximately 34 per cent were dyslexic; 3 per cent blind or partially sighted; 7 per cent deaf or hearing impaired; 5 per cent were wheelchair users or had mobility problems; 4 per cent had mental health difficulties; 27 per cent had an unseen disability; 6 per cent had multiple disabilities and 13 per cent had some other disability. These numbers probably underestimate the total number of students who consider themselves to have a disability, the number with a disability and the number covered by the Act.

The number of students with disabilities and declaring is equivalent to a large university student population.

(Source for statistics: HESA Table 11 2000–01 Student Data: First year domiciled HE students by level of study, mode of study, gender and disability 2000/01)

---

## IMPLEMENTING THE PRECEPTS

### *General principles*

*Precept 1: Institutions should ensure that in all their policies procedures and activities including strategic planning and resource allocation consideration is given to the means of enabling disabled students' participation in all aspects of the academic and social life of the institution.*

The aim of this precept reinforces the message that catering for disabled students is not and should not be seen as something additional which has to be done to amend or qualify 'proper' standard provision. Providing effective learning opportunities for students with disabilities is not something that is external to and separate from providing effective learning opportunities *per se*. Ensuring that learning opportunities meet the needs of all students might require additional thought given the history of provision in universities but that is a different matter. The guidance here emphasizes the need for views from those with a disability, and from disability specialists, to be incorporated into the mainstream decision-making process.

The guidance states that institutions will need to ensure that 'senior managers and other key staff have an adequate understanding of the legal framework concerning disabled people'. While this is true of course it should not be overlooked that it is essential that all staff working with students have an awareness of their responsibilities under the SENDA 2001 legislation. Quite apart from the general advantage of all staff being aware of the legal framework, there is the specific issue that under the SENDA legislation a university is deemed to know about a student's disability *even if the student has only told one member of staff informally about that disability*. All employees and not just academics, or those whose job description involves regular contact with students as students, need to be given clear advice on their responsibilities under the Act. SENDA and the other related legislation are complex and in some ways counterintuitive pieces of legislation thus the training and support involved in ensuring that senior managers, 'key staff' or anyone else have 'an adequate understanding' should not be underestimated.

Precepts 2 and 3 cover the physical environment focusing on the need for access to locations of study and to resources for study. Broadly speaking, the design, construction and commission of new buildings, facilities including car parking and related site activities in HEIs now routinely incorporate the needs of disabled students. However, the subsequent *site management* of premises, particularly in relation to building repairs, utilities management and security developments are not usually so effective. Additionally, while building layout and movement within physical spaces is of particular importance to students with mobility problems, the management of buildings, including the refitting of new laboratories and upgrading of seminar rooms, do not always give full consideration to students, or users generally, with sensory disabilities. While induction loops are always incorporated into new lecture theatres and Braille information is embedded in walls near doors, consideration is not always given, for example, to facilities for signers or the aural environment at entrances of buildings. The Code makes useful attempts to highlight these issues. While the guidance focuses on the design of buildings and their layout, a key issue here is staff development for lectures in terms of more inclusive use of their teaching environment including, for example, the use of lighting and slide projections.

## Information for applicants, students and staff

*Precept 4: The institution's publicity programme details and general information should be accessible to people with disabilities and describe the opportunities for disabled students to participate.*

The challenge here is to ensure that the broad information on what is possible is balanced by consideration of individual applicants' needs. It is of course important not to overstate what is possible generally when a service or form of support may only be available at certain times of the year or at certain locations. It is particularly important where universities have multiple campuses that a service available at only one site is not presented as or implied to be available more generally. Where students need to travel from one site to another for specialist services this needs to be clearly stated.

## GOOD PRACTICE POINT

An example of good practice here is to operate, possibly through the university's Students' Union, a focus group of students with disabilities to assess the clarity and accuracy of information in the university prospectus.

### The selection and admission of students

*Precept 5: In selecting students institutions should ensure equitable consideration of all applicants.*

*Precept 6: Disabled applicants' support needs should be identified and assessed in an effective and timely way, taking into account the applicant's views.*

There are at least two general areas for consideration here. First, the need to make sure that the programme does not indirectly exclude students, and second that the applicant's disability does not compromise the effectiveness with which he or she is able to present his or her suitability for a programme.

The DRC Code of Practice offers interesting advice on the likely lawfulness of certain situations. The example is offered of a university which requires selected applicants to attend an interview and discusses the case of where 'one applicant has a speech difficulty which gets worse when he is nervous. This means he needs more time to express himself. The university refuses to allow him any extra time at interview. This is likely to be unlawful' (DRC Code of Practice, example 3.9b). This seems quite straightforward but this kind of case perhaps illustrates the difference between having procedures in place and the application of those procedures, and more generally the actual experience of individuals. It is likely that most institutions will now have in place a policy whereby the special needs of disabled applicants to have extra time for any selection activity is recognized and implemented. It is further the case that any admissions officer receiving, say, a letter from an applicant stating 'I have a speech difficulty which gets worse when I get nervous. This means I will need more time to express myself' would almost certainly get a reply indicating that this request will be accommodated. However, the experience of the applicant might remain unsatisfactory. It is the case that many applicants, disabled or not, find that interviews are shorter than they would like to present themselves effectively. A further difficulty arises if, say, the request is made at the interview itself. It might be construed as a 'reasonable' adjustment to give an extra 10 minutes on the spot, because 10 minutes is not an unreasonable time to take out of one's day. But is an extra 10 minutes for one candidate unreasonably preferential in the context of a competitive admissions interview? Setting selection procedures, which in their standard unadapted form might discriminate against disabled applicants is not likely to be unlawful providing reasonable adjustments are made. But assessing what adjustment is reasonable is not objective, and different parties may have different views. While it is ultimately a judge who will decide definitively what a reasonable adjustment might be, and may consider what a layperson might consider to be reasonable, in the practical delivery of university admissions procedures 'reasonable adjustments' are very much a matter of subjective judgement.

## REFLECTIVE PRACTICE POINT

What training has your institution offered admissions tutors regarding SENDA and admissions procedures? Have administrators who organize open days been advised on who to pass information on to about an applicant's disability?

A further difficult area for which there are no easy solutions is the situation where an applicant with a disability claims that his or her performance in an examination (such as GCE A-levels or AS-levels) understates his or her ability because the impact of the disability had not been fully recognized, or that it was particularly incapacitating at a key period. Medical documentation may not always be available to substantiate this kind of claim but it is important that, where an applicant is indicating that it is an important consideration, effort is put into considering the case and that effort is part of a clear protocol.

Many applicants processed through UCAS are offered a place (or not) on the basis of a standard application form alone. It is important therefore that arrangements are in place to ensure that assessment of students' learning support needs can be made at any time and not just during interviews. One of the notes of guidance states that institutions should 'where appropriate, (offer) disabled applicants the opportunity to demonstrate their ability to use alternative ways for meeting programme requirements'. This needs to be distinguished from an admissions test which will discrimi-nate against disabled applicants. It is important that where any such opportunities for demonstrating capability are offered their purpose is well-defined, clearly communicated to applicants and used only for the purposes stated. So, for example, if a journalism course had a literacy test for dyslexic applicants only this would be unlawful. But if there was a separate arrangement whereby dyslexic students could demonstrate they could use a spell checker and grammar checker on a word process-ing package then this is likely to be acceptable. However, if disabled applicants *perceived* the word processing activity as a test then obvious difficulties might arise. It would not be unlawful to reject a student who had not been able to show that he or she could meet the needs of the course in some other way. In some senses the guid-ance is now too conservative since it assumes that it is good practice to allow students to show what they are capable of, when in fact it is unlawful to exclude students without so doing.

Students are able to state on the UCAS form whether they feel they need special facilities, support or accommodation, or extra time to complete a course. However, they are not compelled to do so, though clearly is as mentioned several times in the Act and the DRC Code of Practice, such non-disclosure makes it easier for institu-tions to argue that they were not being unreasonable in failing to make adjustments.

SENDA makes it clear that applicants with disabilities must not be treated less favourably on account of their disability either in relation to the arrangements an institution makes for determining admissions to the institution or enrolments to courses; or in the terms on which it offers to admit or enrol them by refusing or delib-erately omitting to accept an application for admission or enrolment. This makes it unlawful to set special assessments for disabled applicants, enroll disabled appli-cants on special conditions not specified for able applicants or to pre-process or screen applications from disabled applicants.

## Enrolment registration and induction of students

*Precept 7: The arrangements for enrolment registration and induction of new entrants should accommodate the needs of disabled students.*

Increasingly, new students are taken on a local fieldtrip or equivalent to promote induction, help foster a cohort identity and to help students meet each other and staff. It is important that students with disabilities, especially if recruited through clearing, are not excluded from this important kind of activity. More generally the needs of students with disabilities need to be anticipated in advance of induction in order that full participation in academic, social and support activities can be achieved.

## Learning and teaching, including provision for research and other postgraduate students

*Precept 8: Programme specifications should include no unnecessary barriers to access by disabled people.*

*Precept 9: Academic support services and guidance should be accessible and appropriate to the needs of disabled students.*

*Precept 10: The delivery of programmes should take into account the needs of disabled people or, where appropriate, be adapted to accommodate their individual requirements.*

*Precept 11: Institutions should ensure that, wherever possible, disabled students have access to academic and vocational placements including field trips and study abroad.*

*Precept 12: Disabled research students should receive the support and guidance necessary to secure equal access to research programmes.*

The guidance here suggests that 'programme specifications and descriptions give sufficient information to enable students with disabilities and staff to make informed decisions about the ability to complete the programme'. Clearly the more detailed programme specifications are, the more useful their contribution to applicants' understanding of the programme. However, this approach must not amount to a situation where an inflexible statement of what the programme involves prevents the exploration of alternative means by which students with disabilities can achieve the programme outcomes. Although the SENDA legislation makes provision for the protection of academic standards to be used as justification by an HEI to not admit a student on to a programme, this argument cannot be used unreasonably. The precept is correct in stating that there should be no unnecessary barriers but that extends to parts of the programme that are not essential to maintain academic standards.

The DRC Code of Practice makes it clear that the threat to academic standards is not a defence to be used lightly or as a catchall and states: 'The academic standards reason should not be used spuriously. Where elements are not central or core to a course, they are unlikely to provide a reason to justify discrimination based on academic standards' (DRC Code of Practice, S4.27). So the fact that a programme specification states that a particular skill or activity is part of the programme does not in itself mean that a student with a disability could, within the terms of the Act, be justifiably excluded from it. The test is likely to be whether substitution of that part of the programme, or an alternative form of delivery or skill development could be used to achieve the specified programme outcomes. If this is possible without compromising academic standards then this cannot be justified and may be unlawful.

SKILL (the National Bureau for Students with Disabilities) has argued that:

> ...academic standards cannot be cited as an all-embracing reason never to look at, and adjust, the accessibility of course content and structure. Academic staff will need to give proper thought to what the essential skills, knowledge and aptitudes required by the course really are, and what elements of a course are incidental or unimportant. Practices that really just represent tradition or convention do not count as academic standards.

## REFLECTIVE PRACTICE POINT

The DRC Code of Practice indicates that the protection of academic standards defence cannot be applied to non-core aspects of a programme. However, some academics might argue that the standards of, say, an optional module are just as important to the overall academic standards as the elements of a compulsory module. What if a student with a mobility impairment wants to enrol on a module which in its standard form has a practical outdoor exercise which is considered core to the module? Perhaps different conceptions of 'core' are being used here, but the issue does highlight the complexity of implementing the Act.

In the light of the DRC Code of Practice what would you consider to be the core elements of your programme (or a programme you are familiar with)? Are all these core elements essential for the maintenance of academic standards? Are there any non-core elements which are important either directly or indirectly to the maintenance of academic standards?

Precept 11 addresses the issues around support for placements by disabled students, and should of course be read in conjunction with the Code's section on work placements. Where a university arranges for a third party to provide education, training or other related services for students on its behalf then, to the extent that this training or education remains the responsibility of the responsible body, it is covered by the Act. However, in the case of work placements, broadly speaking, the training and education experience is not provided by the HEI, it has merely arranged for the experience to occur. Providing the placement location is not under any commercial contract to the university then the university is not, within the terms of the Act, liable for any treatment received by the student on the placement (DRC Code of Practice, S3.5).

It should be noted however that the DRC Code of Practice assumes significant 'distance' between the placement host and the HEI. It may be the case that where HEIs have arranged for some staff at regular placement providers to become 'associate tutors' or 'co-supervisors' etc and crucially are involved in the university's assessment of , say, the student's placement report, the law might construe the responsibilities of the university differently. This might be limited though to ensuring that any advice of assessment was consistent with good and lawful practice in relation to assessing the work of students with a disability, and not more broadly in relation to, say, restrictions on mobility in the office environment. This is another area where academic practice is more complex and diverse than the legislation assumes.

## Examination assessment and progression

*Precept 13: Assessment and examination policies practices and procedures should provide disabled students with the same opportunity as their peers to demonstrate the achievement of learning outcomes.*

*Precept 14: Where studying is interrupted as a direct result of a disability-related cause this should not unjustifiably impede a student's subsequent academic progress.*

Ensuring that students with disabilities are not unfairly disadvantaged in assessments now involves much more than simply allowing additional time to complete unseen examinations. As assessments have become more complex, so too have the challenges involved in either making adjustments to enable students with disabilities to participate fairly, or making alternative and comparable arrangements for students to demonstrate their achievement.

The guidance encourages universities to develop flexible systems of assessment which nevertheless protect academic standards. Amongst the adjustments recommended is 'flexibility in the balance between assessed course work and examinations'. However, some professional or statutory bodies (PSBs) require examinations to ensure that students' work is their own and departments will not have much discretion in this area. Of course the PSBs cannot operate unlawfully either so departments need to square QAA guidance, institutional policies and PSB requirements all within the context of SENDA.

While the guidance points to ways of supporting students in relation to assessments, there is no guidance on *how* this should be done in such a way as to maintain academic standards. However, consideration of what learning outcomes need to be evaluated can lead to review of the assessment system in a department. For example, if a student with dyslexia can be assessed through a practical exercise rather than through an unseen examination, then why can everyone not be similarly assessed? There is certainly a ritualistic element to unseen examinations which still lies deep in the academic mentality. There are broader views from external stakeholders that only examinations *really* test the students and that they are indispensable in the context of plagiarism. Some academics have also justified unseen examinations on the grounds that being able to write accurately and cogently under pressure, using only one's own remembered knowledge, is a skill which is relevant to many circumstances in the world of work and elsewhere. This argument would be more compelling if universities made any attempt to train students in these skills or if such a skill set appeared anywhere in a programme specification.

One of the functions that assessment serves is to test student achievement, and since student achievement is at the core of the management of standards, it is essential that that function is preserved in any alternative arrangements that are organized for students with a disability. However, good practice in this area is built on a recognition that assessments serve many other functions than just evaluating achievement *and that these other functions should also be preserved in the alternative arrangements*. First of all we need to note that almost all assessments, even those which contribute towards formal grades, serve a formative function. That is to say assessment (if designed sensibly) serves an educational function – in the preparation for the assessment, in the carrying out of the assessment and in the feedback received subsequently. Ideally, alternative assessments should capture some of this formative function.

It should also be noted that in a carefully designed curriculum there should be a carefully designed assessment strategy which may involve progressively more detailed or challenging assessments through a course or module. If this is the case then it is important that alternative arrangements for assessments occurring early in the sequence do not unfairly disadvantage students in relation to this preparatory function for subsequent assessments (if a student with a disability would be taking the same assessments as other students later).

Although few assessments are designed to foster greater group cohesion, it is a beneficial side effect of group work and group assessments that important social links are formed, especially in the early periods of a course or module. Ideally, alternative assessments for disabled students should either try to reproduce this social function or alternative opportunities should be offered to ensure that students with disabilities are not excluded from social groupings. Alternative assessments should also be organized in such a way that they not only assess fairly the level of achievement obtained by the student, but that they offer scope for a similar level of feedback from the tutor. For example, if an analysis of a conceptually rich case study was replaced by a multiple choice test, while the basic summative function might be served, the formative function would have been diminished due to the limited feedback that would be possible. Finally, one of the side effects of assessment is that it creates an end product which can serve to show to employers and others what the student is capable of. Alternative assessments should ensure that a student's portfolio of assessed products does not diminish prospects for further study or employment. Overall, while the main function of alternative assessment arrangements for students with disabilities is to ensure that they are able to show their achievements in comparable ways, it is important that where possible the other functions and consequences of assessment are recognized and that students with disabilities are not denied the benefits of these.

**REFLECTIVE PRACTICE POINT**

To what extent does your institution's guidance on alternative assessments for students with disabilities incorporate recognition of the formative function of assessment?

In your experience what is disabled students' perception of assessment management by your institution?

Are there assessments in programmes with which you are familiar which do not obviously lend themselves to alternatives that would retain both summative and formative features?

## Staff development

*Precept 15: Induction and other relevant training programmes for all staff should include disability awareness/equality and training in specific services and support.*

All institutions should now have opportunities for staff development in this area. The difficulty is that such staff development programmes are usually not compulsory so there can be no assumption about what an individual member of staff will know. Some staff may feel that they have had training in the area in the past three or four years and therefore do not need to prioritize any further similar staff development. Of course, as we have seen, SENDA changes everything and many old assumptions about the institution's relationship to disabled students need to be revised. This is an area where staff development has to be supplemented by accessible, relevant, up-to-date and practical advice. Many universities now have intranet sites which provide online guidance on dealing with individual disabilities and the options that are available. The best of these are designed in such a way that they can be accessed by students and staff in order that, where appropriate, final decisions on any alternative arrangements can be made in full consultation with the students themselves. There are also many excellent Web sites that cover the provisions of the Act and suggestions for best practice, such as SKILL at www.skill.org.uk.

One issue that has to be carefully addressed is getting the balance right between individual students' needs on the one hand and consistency across students on the other. Similarly, while there are advantages in empowering individual courses and departments to establish appropriate methods for assessing the learning outcomes of individual programmes, there is also a need to ensure that disabled students in one department are not treated less favourably than students in another, *or are seen to be* treated less favourably. Precept 18 rightly emphasizes the need to address individual needs of each student with a disability and that must be the initial point of departure.

## Access to general facilities and support

*Precept 16: Students with disabilities should have access to the full range of support services that are available to their non-disabled peers.*

This precept emphasizes that students with disabilities should be able to benefit from non-academic as well as academic services. These services need to be accessible and the service provided should be relevant to disabled students' needs. This needs to be carefully considered when central services are being restructured, relocated or restaffed.

The duty on responsible bodies to make adjustments involving the provision of auxiliary aids and services becomes law on 1 September 2003. This means that it will be unlawful for any HEI to treat students with disabilities less favourably in relation to services which support the educational function.

## Additional specialist support

*Precept 17: Institutions should ensure that there are sufficient designated members of staff with appropriate skills and experience to provide specialist advice and support to disabled applicants and students, and to the staff who work with them.*

While each academic department should have its own disability coordinator it is good practice to have at school, faculty or campus level a number of academic staff who have expertise in relation to common disabilities and how these are likely to interact with the student learning experience. This experience can be invaluable in course design, library or study centre development or the introduction of new technology. While academics in such roles can raise issues and make suggestions for improvements or reforms, it is essential that for major initiatives specialist external professional advisers are consulted.

*Precept 18: Institutions should identify and seek to meet the particular needs of individual disabled students.*

*Precept 19: Internal communications systems should ensure that appropriate staff receive information about the particular needs of disabled students in a clear and timely way.*

*Precept 20: Institutions should have a clearly defined policy on the confidentiality and disclosure of information relating to a person's disabilities that is communicated to applicants, students and staff.*

Precepts 18–20 seek to ensure that the specific needs of individual students with disabilities are addressed by institutions. Not only are the needs of students with different disabilities vastly different, the needs of students with the same label are different also. This can be in terms of the severity or nature of the disability, the presence of multiple disabilities, the extent of effective medication in controlling symptoms and the interaction of any disability with other social circumstances (including ethnic identity, sexual orientation, religious beliefs, gender, financial circumstances and personal relationships).

However, there is a need to respect privacy and confidentiality even if, in the view of a tutor, administrator or counsellor non-disclosure is not in the best academic or other interests of the student. The Data Protection Act explicitly prohibits disclosure to a third party of 'sensitive personal information', which would include information about disability, its management and its likely effect on the individual's capacity to study.

## Complaints

*Precept 21: Institutions should ensure that information about all complaints and appeals policies and procedures is available in accessible formats and communicated to students.*

*Precept 22: Institutions should have in place policies and procedures to deal with complaints arising directly or indirectly from a student's disability.*

Clearly students with disabilities have as much right to prompt and just consideration of their complaints as any other student. However, given the potentially sensitive nature of the information that might be at issue and for that matter the legal framework for the relationship between a HEI and its students with a disability, it is necessary that particular attention is given to the effective and appropriate handling of complaints by students particularly where these relate to their disability. Not only will the substantive issues in any case be likely to be sensitive given the student's status, but the means of communicating and of conducting any inquiry or review must recognize any particular needs a student might have. The guidance emphasizes that information about complaints procedures should be accessible and that there should be specific procedures in place for dealing with complaints that are related to the student's status as a disabled person.

## Monitoring and evaluation

*Precept 23: Institutional information systems should monitor the applications, admissions, academic progress and nature of impairment of disabled students.*

*Precept 24: Institutions should operate systems to monitor the effectiveness of provision for students with disabilities, evaluate progress and identify opportunities for enhancement.*

These final precepts and their associated guidance emphasize the need for clear planning systems around disability issues in such a way that progress can be monitored. Good practice here is to compare institutional performance with similar institutions and with national data. This can be done both through comparisons of publicly available information or through working with other institutions to share aggregate data on a confidential basis. This can be further supported through sharing of good practice and establishing regular inter-institutional visits to review new developments, perhaps also forming part of a staff development series for academic, support and administrative staff.

With the advent of SENDA, institutions will find themselves required to plan more strategically to support students with disabilities. Institutions for example have 'anticipatory duties' under the Act, which means that they must put measures in place prior to any specific student requiring them. There is also the schedule of adjustments which means that there is a duty on responsible bodies to make adjustments by 1 September 2005 to physical features of premises where these put disabled people or students at a substantial disadvantage.

## QA ISSUES WITH STUDENTS WITH DISABILITIES

It is understandable that SENDA legislation offers institutions the defence of maintenance of academic standards to justify not making adjustments for students with disabilities. However, this gives the impression that students with disabilities and their education is in some way intrinsically inimical to academic standards. QA and the maintenance of academic standards are though in many ways reinforced through thorough consideration of students with disabilities and their special needs. Forcing departments to be clear about what is core and what is custom and practice, and about which functions of certain assessments are indispensible, encourages a focus on what actually matters in a course of education and what is just so much pedagogical window dressing. The key risks to quality in this area might be said to be:

- failure to assess early enough the implications of a student's disability for full participation in a course of study;
- failure of a member of staff to pass on information about a disability to someone able to address the issue;
- failure to distinguish between students with different disabilities, or within categories of disability when making 'reasonable adjustments';
- failure to clarify responsibilities for decision making in relation to implementation of policy;
- failure to specify the authority of departmental or other staff working directly with students with disabilities on a day-to-day basis to make urgent adjustments to standard practice.

## QE ISSUES WITH STUDENTS WITH DISABILITIES

There are a number of ways in which provision can be enhanced in this area, but these will vary depending on the progress already made by institutions to provide fully accessible and inclusive provision. The major principles for enabling enhancement in this area could be described as follows:

- Ensure full involvement of students with disabilities and representative groups in the design and planning of all significant new arrangements.
- Establish differentiated staff development for all staff reflecting their particular needs in different roles. This is an area where although there are basic threshold awareness issues, such as disclosure, generic staff development sessions are unlikely to be helpful.
- Have policies that explicitly focus on ensuring that alternative arrangements for students in teaching, learning or assessment meet not just the immediate aims of the relevant activity but the contribution of those activities to the overall learning, teaching and assessment strategies.

### Reflecting on quality of provision for students with disabilities

Do you consider yourself to have a disability? Does the QAA Code assume that the reader does not have a disability and that the category of persons being discussed are outside the readership? Does this chapter?

The QAA Code of Practice and the DRC Code say little about the role of staff with disabilities and the contribution they might be able to make to enhancing practice in their own institutions. Why do you think that is?

How does your institution solicit feedback from students with disabilities about their experience? How is action taken, or not taken, on the basis of this feedback monitored?

What would you consider to be your main staff development points after having read this chapter? Are they the same as before reading the chapter?

Comments in this chapter should not be relied upon as legal opinion or advice. Institutions, employees and students must seek independent legal advice in addressing issues relating to SENDA or related legislation on proceedings.

# 9 External examining systems

'External examining provides one of the principal means for the maintenance of nationally comparable standards within autonomous higher education institutions.'

(QAA Code, S2)

## EXTERNAL EXAMINERS, QUALITY AND POLITICS

The idea of academics from one university visiting, as individuals, the academics of another university at their invitation and then commenting on their standards is a distinctively British arrangement almost unknown throughout the rest of the academic world. Although external examiners are notoriously poorly paid for the work they do, the external examining system is designed to uphold standards across the sector, both in the sense of monitoring the consistency with which a university implements its own standards but also more generally in the sense of maintaining (largely undefined) sector-wide standards.

The role of the external examiner has attracted much discussion since the Dearing and Garrick reports. Dearing, famously, recommended a new cadre of dedicated externals nominated by institutions who would do little else but externally examine. This proposal was a well meaning if utterly misconceived attempt to deal with the discrepancy between the importance of the routine external peer scrutiny which external examiners bring and the limited resources they had to devote to it.

However, the external examining system has been subject to extensive criticism over the years with accusations of cronyism, off-the-record reassurances by departments that problems would be fixed and rubber-stamping. Conversely, conscientious external examiners are dismayed when concerns about standards have been raised but overruled or submerged in institutional bureaucracy. The external examining system has been under pressure since the 1990s with the increased volume of students and increasing bureaucracy and formulaic nature of modular schemes. Many subject review visits in 1995–2001 identified serious weakness in some areas of provision which had been completely missed or ignored by successive external examiners. There is increasing pressure to provide more structured professional training for external examiners possibly through the new Teaching Quality Academy. Additionally, the institutional audit methodology requires external examiners' reports to be published more widely by institutions, which will give the examiners' reviews more credibility. Ultimately, any reforms of the external examining system will place greater demands on external examiners, which they are already reluctant to absorb.

In 1994 the Higher Education Quality Council declared the aim of the external examining system as 'to ensure that degrees awarded in similar subjects are comparable in standard in different institutions of higher education in the UK' and to 'ensure that the assessment system operated by an institution is fair and is fairly operated in the classification of students'.

Indeed there has already been a proposal for a 'college of accredited external examiners' overseen by the QAA. Inevitably, universities have seen this arrangement as a potential threat to their institutional autonomy to set, maintain and monitor their own standards. Vice-chancellors do not want an Ofsted for universities. The shift from the subject review methodology to the lighter touch audit approach was based on the assumption that the external examining system would be beefed up.

---

How many committees or groups receive copies of external examiner reports in your institutions? What kind of response do each of these groups make? Are all of these responses fed back to the external examiner?

---

## IMPLEMENTING THE PRECEPTS

*Precept 1: An institution should require its external examiners, in their expert judgement, to report on:*
i)   *whether the standards set are appropriate for its awards, or award elements, by reference to published national subject benchmarks, the national qualifications frameworks, institutional programme specifications and other relevant information;*
ii)  *the standards of student performance in those programmes or parts of programmes which they have been appointed to examine, and on the comparability of the standards with those of similar programmes or parts of programmes in other UK higher education institutions;*
iii) *the extent to which its processes for assessment, examination, and the determination of awards are sound and have been fairly conducted.*

The content of the precept is uncontentious, but the key word is 'require' in the first sentence. Some universities still follow the practice of inviting external examiners to comment on whatever they feel is worth commenting on. Other universities have almost moved entirely to what is effectively a multiple choice arrangement, with external examiners asked to respond to items such as 'the arrangements for moderation were poor/good/very good/excellent' and so on. This has arisen because a small minority of external examiners submit perfunctory (if glowing) reports which will not do in today's audit intense environment. If a university does *not* explicitly request external examiners to comment on certain issues then they are unlikely to, or at least there will be no consistent practice. This in turn means that when a university is asked how it reassures itself that, say, arrangements for internal moderation are effective, whatever else it is able to say it will not be able to say that the external examiners have said that they are. An interesting situation arises when the university provides external examiners with a multiple choice questionnaire or pro forma for completion which contain specific questions or sections for completion and then the external examiner submits *a narrative report not covering all the identified areas.* Technically a university should request that the external examiner does complete the standard report but few do, such is the relief in some cases to get any sort of report at all. In extreme cases external examiners can be relieved of their responsibilities due to a failure to submit reports, this is more common than it was even five years ago but still rare.

The invitation to external examiners to comment on the comparability of standards with institutions elsewhere predates the QAA Code. Yet external examiners, even experienced ones, have in truth limited evidence to draw on to make claims about standards in other institutions, especially in the sense of concurrent standards (though this changed for a time with the advent of comprehensive subject review).

Precepts 2 and 3 cover the roles of external examiners – specifically that their role should be documented and that they should endorse pass lists.

*Precept 2: Institutions should state clearly the various roles, powers and responsibilities assigned to their external examiners.*

*Precept 3: Prior to the publication of mark lists, pass lists or similar documents, institutions should require external examiners to endorse the outcomes of the assessment(s) they have been appointed to scrutinise.*

The guidance notes invite institutions to consider whether there should be institution-wide job descriptions for external examiners or whether each programme should have its own. This is indeed an important issue and which should probably be resolved through a generic template defining minimal threshold standards that each programme is able to amend within the context of institutional approval. A further complication arises where there are two-tier board systems where the rights of the subject-based external examiner are different from those of the programme- or award-based external examiner.

In relation to precept 3, institutions need to decide the conditions under which externals have been insufficiently involved in the process to sign off a set of results. This is particularly important for resit or January boards where external examiners may not be present but may have been involved in confirming some of the marks. There is a possible danger here: say an institution mindful of the importance of the role of external examiners, and the need for consistency in the monitoring of academic standards, creates a policy stating that an external examiner must be present at any assessment board considering finalists. Then the institution finds that external examiners cannot attend September or January boards where one or two finalists are being considered. It then has the dilemma of deferring the decision to award a degree or ignoring its own regulations.

In the guidance it is stated that institutions should consider whether external examiners 'should have the power to adjust marks or decisions for individuals or students collectively, and on what basis of (sampled) assessed work.' The idea that external examiners should alter the marks of any individual student's work is rapidly losing ground especially if they have not seen the work of the entire cohort. Since some cohorts may contain over 100 students this is not always possible. Exceptionally, where the external examiner has seen all of the cohort (or possibly all the scripts in a class or in adjacent classes) he or she may wish to recommend changes to individual scripts. The most common case however, is when a candidate, is, or looks like, falling on a borderline, and the internal markers ask the external examiner to consider whether there are reasonable grounds for raising the mark. Institutions need to be clear about whether they wish to permit external examiners to recommend a change of mark alongside consideration of requests from the department to look at individual scripts with a view to changing marks.

In the preamble to these precepts the Code states that 'Institutions employ external examiners in a range of roles. Besides the primary role in the assurance of the academic standards of their programmes and awards, institutions may ask external examiners to undertake additional roles. Any such additional roles should not conflict with or compromise the primary role.' These additional roles might include serving on a validation panel for a related programme (especially in specialist subjects with limited practitioners nationally) or as an examiner for a doctoral candidate. If managed appropriately there is no reason why such roles should conflict with the external examiner role. A much more grey area is research collaboration between the external examiner and a member or members of the department. There are no hard and fast rules here but clearly institutions will wish to ensure that external examiners are able to retain sufficient detachment from a department to exercise their judgement independently. There is always the danger that an external examiner who identifies too much with the department will be reluctant to make too much of minor blemishes with the result that inappropriate or ineffective practices become entrenched in the provision. While the number of such instances is probably low, it has to be conceded that given the low level of remuneration external examining attracts, academics take on such a role through a genuine sense of responsibility (and a little kudos). However, given that external examining is seen as the 'the principal means for the maintenance of nationally comparable standards', the independence of the role is allowed to be compromised in a way that would not happen in other professions.

*Precept 4: Institutions should define explicit policies and regulations governing the nomination and appointment of external examiners, and premature termination of their contract.*

*Precept 5: Institutions should ensure that their external examiners are competent to undertake the responsibilities defined in their contract.*

*Precept 6: Institutional procedures should ensure that potential conflict(s) of interest are identified and resolved prior to appointment of external examiners.*

One issue here is that conflicts of interest may arise *during the course* of the tenure. External examiners may through regular visits to an institution develop alliances for bids to research bodies. These need to be managed carefully and may in some circumstances require a termination of the external examining arrangement. The precepts assume the main danger is an external examiner who may be too close to the provision or its tutors to 'blow the whistle' if things go wrong. However, there is also the possibility of an external examiner who is, for whatever reason, unduly antagonistic to the provision. This is rare but does occur. Sometimes this can arise when external examiners from one side of the old binary divide serve as external examiners to institutions on the other, a problem that can cut both ways. Alternatively, there is the problem of the external examiner who identifies with the discipline more than the role of assuring standards to the extent that reports overstate the dire consequences that will befall the provision if, say, two, or possibly, three new lecturers / computer laboratories / studios are not approved immediately.

## REFLECTIVE PRACTICE POINT

In your view should external examiners have any kinds of links with their examining universities apart from their external examining role? If so what kind of links would be acceptable and which would not?

*Precept 7: Institutions should ensure that potential external examiners are provided with sufficient information to enable them to identify whether they can carry out their responsibilities effectively.*

Generally the expectations on external examiners are the same all over the UK. A central issue is that external examiners should not take on too much (two concurrent examinerships usually being considered the maximum that anyone should undertake). Specific features which need to be made clear to prospective external examiners include: the number of students on the programme and the number of assessed items involved; the number of other external examiners for the provision who will share the load; the existence of any franchises of the programme to FECs or overseas POs; and the university's policy on external examiners' attendance at any resit boards outside the normal summer period.

## Preparation of external examiners

*Precept 8: An institution should provide for the proper preparation of its external examiners to ensure that they understand and can fulfil their responsibilities. This should include a written briefing, for all of its examiners, on the institution's policies for assessment and external examining in general, together with appropriate specific course documentation.*

Ideally of course the external examiner should attend a briefing event and meet key staff involved in assessment at the department. Examples of the previous year's coursework could be displayed and discussed (especially if non-traditional in format), issues relating to the previous year's assessment raised, and any developments or anticipated developments in the curriculum or its delivery or assessment could also be covered.

*Precept 9: At least one external examiner should be appointed for all educational programmes or parts of programmes that contribute to an award of an institution.*

The guidance goes on to encourage institutions to consider whether external examiners 'are to be involved in scrutinizing work required solely for progression to subsequent stages of a programme leading to an award', in other words in relation to an undergraduate honours programme for year 1 or stage 1 assessments. Most post-1992 institutions would have external examiners for all courses and modules whether those components contribute to the final award or not. Clearly the introduction of the FHEQ, and the greater clarity of level C and associated awards, means in principle that the criteria for end of year 1 performance and the actual achievement of students in that context is more closely related to the overall academic standards of a programme than has been the case in the past. It follows perhaps that external examiners should be more involved in monitoring this level. The anomaly arises because year 1 is both a milestone on the path to an honours degree and also technically a substantive endpoint in its own right.

**REFLECTIVE PRACTICE POINT**

To what extent is there scope for a national training scheme for external examiners to be delivered locally by universities who hire them? Would this be 'the thin end of the wedge' in terms of a national college of examiners or would it raise standards amongst external examiners? Or both?

One issue raised by the guidance is 'how examiners will be deployed to assess the overall standards and coherence of combined studies and multidisciplinary programmes'. Most institutions do have an overall examiner for combined studies programmes, however, his or her role is principally to ensure that there is parity of treatment across all subject combinations at combined studies examination boards. There might be an opportunity for him or her to receive and review external reports from constituent subjects but these reports do not usually give separate consideration to combined studies students when they are taught alongside single honours groups. Certainly there is rarely an expectation for external examiners to scrutinize the degree of *coherence* in combined honours programmes. Indeed it might be said that there is not expected to be coherence in such programmes, which are after all combined honours not coherent honours. Such integration as might be possible or desirable occurs in the student's head, not the curricula. The monitoring of interdisciplinary programmes especially at postgraduate level does provide more scope for the external examiner to query and review whether flexibility and coherence are being effectively balanced.

An opportunity for good practice where institutions are particularly concerned about departmental performance against internal or external benchmarks might be to provide external examiners with the relevant university or HESA and HEFCE performance indicator data, for both the programme and the subject nationally, on such points as progression and degree classification.

*Precept 10: Institutions should discuss with their external examiners the evidence the examiner deems necessary to discharge his/her responsibilities.*

The guidance for this precept raises the issue of whether external examiners should be entitled to hold vivas with students. Most universities ensure that their regulations retain the provision for such vivas but they are increasingly seen as inappropriate and unmanageable. Since students are not trained to perform in vivas the ordeal can give little or no meaningful information for an external examiner. Additionally the practicalities of ensuring all students are in principle available for vivas are often insurmountable. In the end few universities would want to have discussions with individual external examiners on this matter – the university policy might just be that they simply do not happen.

Additional good practice here would be to ensure that on appointment an external examiner was provided with the previous three years' external examiner reports and the previous three years' course reports. This will be particularly important in identifying recurrent issues that appear not to have been addressed. More positively this will give the external examiner a stronger feel for the ongoing discussions in the department on curriculum development, assessment strategies and student views. External examiners should also be advised that they have a responsibility to comment on the department's responses to their predecessor's reports.

*Precept 11: In respect of collaborative provision, external examining procedures for programmes offered by a partner organisation should be the same as, or demonstrably equivalent to, those used by the awarding institution for its own programmes. The procedures should be clearly specified and documented, and rigorously and consistently applied.*

This precept is particularly challenging for overseas franchises where the very tight deadlines for marking, moderating and approving grades are even more difficult to manage. An attempt by an external examiner to get additional information about other scripts, the circumstances of assessment or extenuating circumstances is not always likely to be successful.

Additional good practice here, particularly in the context of overseas franchises but also for FEC work, is to ensure that the external examiner at least once in her or his term of office is able to attend a examination board (or pre-board) in the partner institution, both to confirm the equivalence of procedures and to enable detailed and well-founded comment to be made in the end of tenure summative report.

*Precept 12: Institutions should require external examiners to prepare at agreed times a written report that provides comments and judgements on the assessment process and the standards of student attainment.*

The guidance here does not emphasize some issues that many institutions are already building in to their procedures. For example, external examiners need to be asked to identify issues which by their nature, or by virtue of the degree of threat to quality, require immediate action by the institution or an immediate response from the head of department or programme leader. These 'areas requiring urgent attention' would then be used as the trigger for the report to receive wider discussion.

*Precept 13: Institutions should indicate the required form and coverage of external examiners' reports.*

The guidance for this precept encourages institutions to clarify the issues on which externals will be required to comment. The principal areas are normally student achievement, award standards, assessments, external examiners' access to information, comparability of student achievement and the external examiner's role.

Additionally the external examiner might be asked to comment on the curriculum, resources, the basis for any judgements made, teaching quality and cohort academic strengths and weaknesses. As noted above, institutions need to be clear what their policy is when external examiners, for whatever reason, do not comment on areas on which they have been asked to offer a view.

The areas identified by the guidance appear to omit a small number of important areas. Additional areas which universities might consider inviting external examiner comment on are: effectiveness of university regulations for dealing with plagiarism; the management of extenuating circumstances; the appropriateness of university regulations for determining classification of awards and the conduct of the examination board; and, of course, the effectiveness of the external examiner's report form. Many of these are in fact already incorporated in universities' external examiners' report forms.

Finally, the guidance emphasizes adherence to standards and benchmarks – and rightly so – however, most institutions would strongly want to encourage external examiners to comment explicitly on examples of *good* practice within the provision they have examined, both in terms of the delivery and assessment of programmes and the management of the external examining process. The external examiner's focus on the maintenance of academic standards nevertheless allows him or her to see aspects of intelligent, progressive management of delivery and assessment and as such this is an example of the 'regulatory dividend' from QA to QE (see Chapter 5 on QE).

## REFLECTIVE PRACTICE POINT

If you have been an external examiner in the past did you raise issues in your formal report that you were not able to raise directly with the course team? Were there occasions when you discussed issues of concern with the course team but did not include them in the formal report? Why did this happen?

*Precept 14: Institutions should request that external examiners' reports are formally addressed to the head of the institution, or to specific individuals designated by the head of the institution to exercise responsibility for the handling of these reports. Institutions should ensure that the reports are considered within the institution at a senior level.*

*Precept 15: Full consideration should be given by the institution to comments and recommendations contained within the reports of external examiners, and the outcomes of the consideration, including actions taken, should be formally recorded.*

Precepts 14 and 15 ensure that institutions take seriously their responsibility for acting on external examiners' reports. It also serves to ensure that external examining is seen to be taken seriously. Many institutions still formally require external examiners to submit reports direct to the vice chancellor's office, even if it is widely recognized that the likelihood of the vice chancellor reading any of the reports thus received is remote. Many institutions process external reports through a central QA office which will flag up serious issues to the pro-vice chancellor with responsibility for quality.

The guidance for Precepts 14 and 15 appear to assume that external examiners will only raise issues about the assessment process and the way it is managed by the *department*. However, the real challenge is to ensure that institutional issues of assessment policy and management are dealt with appropriately.

There are at least two types of institutional issues. The first relates to central services – often, of course, library and computing resources. Additionally, however, comments increasingly are related to the procedures for the calculation of the final degree award and the participation of the external examiners in that process. It is essential therefore that there are effective mechanisms in place to ensure that the library, academic computer services (or equivalent), academic registry and other central support services are informed of external examiners' comments and required to respond.

The second institutional issue is where several external examiners express a particular concern independently. For example, several external examiners may express concern about the degree of plagiarism in year 2 courses, indicating perhaps that measures taken to warn and advise students on the matter in year 1 are not effective. Universities need to be proactive on the matter of identifying patterns across different reports. Where collation of reports is devolved to schools or faculties there is the danger of problems common to more than one faculty not being picked up institutionally. Although universities will normally have an academic standards committee of some kind the effective discharge of any responsibility such committees have for reviewing institution-wide issues very much depends on the quality of summative reports they receive from departments, schools or faculties.

Of course, reading external reports is a specialist skill in its own right, with reading between the lines and being sensitive to what is not said being particularly important. It is a truth universally acknowledged that external examiners err on the side of praise and support in the language of their reports. As current or recent practitioners themselves they are only too aware of the increasing pressures and limited resources that impinge on course leaders and tutors. In the climate of intensive subject review few external examiners wanted to write about problems which would provide ammunition for QAA reviewers. This in turn led to a degree of scepticism on the part of reviewers about how much could be taken from the external examiners' reports on matters of detail. External examiners are encouraged to go beyond the recording of the symptoms of a threat to quality, but to further specify the underlying malaise and then make proposals for a remedy too. The difficulty here is misdiagnosis. If scripts do not get to the external examiner on time he or she might recommend bringing forward the coursework deadlines. In this context institutions can decide whether this is the best remedy and, if it is, whether it is feasible or not and whether the knock-on effects on other aspects will be manageable. The problem arises where external examiners offer remedies *without indicating what symptoms the remedies are meant to address*. Thus simply recommending bringing forward deadlines may be read as an attempt to link assessment to learning more directly when in fact it is meant to address an entirely different problem. This highlights the dangers of checklist reports where the ratings of problems is not always clearly linked to the recommendations for development.

*Precept 16: Institutions should ensure that external examiners are, within a reasonable time, provided with a response to their comments and recommendations, including information on any actions taken by the institution.*

Additional good practice here is to send the external examiner a copy of the annual course report, which will of course contain a response to the external examiner's comments from the previous year.

One of the difficulties here is that external examiners do not always clearly express their comments as recommendations for action: 'I noted that X…' or 'I was surprised to see that Y…' or 'Although Z is not yet a cause for concern it is something which the department will have to watch closely' and so on. This underlines the limitations of the narrative report where external examiners' loose language allows them to equivocate about the seriousness of the problem or the urgency involved.

External examiners are rarely asked to justify the claims that they make. Particularly interesting are those external examiners who express concern at the 'low/high number of firsts' or the 'poor/excellent first year progression figures', when these areas are now subject to complex data analyses to determine whether the figures are in fact high or low given that cohort in that subject. The assumption is, and has to be if the system is to work at all, that external examiners have enough experience and expertise to be in a position to make judgements on the basis of their recognition of patterns and relationships.

Additional good practice here would be to encourage external examiners to comment on the programme in relation to HESA and HEFCE statistics on admissions, progression, achievement and first destination. Of course all of this puts an additional burden on the external examiner. Nevertheless, it has to be acknowledged that if external examiners are determined to comment on such matters they need to be encouraged to draw upon objective national data when doing so.

External examiners are asked to comment on the comparability of standards of the provision they are examining with other courses of the same kind with which they are familiar, and yet the size and relevance of this reference base is never made explicit or challenged. To some extent the content of external examiners' reports reflect the disciplinary base in question. External examiners in English literature sometimes produce reports which reflect an attention to the precision of language in assessments and the clarity of exposition in students' handbooks. Examiners in the sciences are much more likely to be interested in the distribution of marks, the standard deviation of grades within modules and the inter-rater reliability between moderators. This can make the integration of reports slightly more difficult. It also means in extreme cases that issues which rely upon recognizing the significance of complex numerical evidence may be slightly more likely to surface in the sciences than in some areas of the humanities and issues which depend upon reading and integrating extensive documentation may be more likely to be spotted in the humanities. Equally of course these issues are more likely to be picked up by course teams themselves.

## REFLECTIVE PRACTICE POINT

In your experience what are the differences in the style of external examiners' reports? How do different external examiners react to different kinds of pro forma for their report? Are there differences between external examiners from the humanities and from the sciences?

## QA ISSUES WITH EXTERNAL EXAMINING SYSTEMS

Section 4 of the Code (on external examiners), when read in conjunction with section 6 on the assessment of students, provides many clear points of guidance for managing external examining. The external examiner is not an aspect of the provision but an aspect of the QA system itself. If the external examiner is not able to make judgements on the academic standards set and achieved, or on the management of the assessment process, then the QA for the programme is severely compromised. The following are common difficulties in external examining which can threaten the confidence in the quality of the provision:

- failure to enable external examiners to make judgements on the quality of academic standards achieved through late or unrepresentative samples;
- failure to encourage external examiners to raise concerns formally;
- failure to require external examiners to comment on all those areas which the institution has determined are essential to the management of quality and standards;
- failure to adhere to any institutional rule regarding external examiners' presence or involvement in final award decisions (such policies can be a hostage to fortune and are best avoided);
- failure of the external examining system to assure the overall academic standards of combined or joint honours awards.

# QE ISSUES WITH EXTERNAL EXAMINING SYSTEMS

There are several ways in which external examiners can enhance the quality of the provision they examine. But how can an institution enhance the quality of the external examining system? Several possibilities are listed below. Not all will be appropriate for all institutions or areas of provision, but all are worth considering:

- Send the external examiner a copy of the annual course report which will of course contain a response to the external examiner's comments.
- Monitor the quality of external examiners' comments. Consider periodically inviting academics at your institution to review anonymously the external reports from other disciplines and write confidential reviews of the effectiveness of the reports. These can be sent under sealed cover to the external examiner in question (ie without anyone at either institution knowing about the report, or the reviewer knowing who the external examiner is).
- Trace whether any important enhancements to provision have come from external examiners' comments.
- Appoint a senior institutional examiner whose role it is to draw out of a wide range of external examiners' reports quality themes, much along the lines of QAA subject reports but bringing together the messages from different subjects at the one institution, rather than messages from different institutions on the one subject.
- Bring together all of your institution's external examiners and your course leaders for training and sharing of experience and practice. While this superficially aids the quality of provision in other institutions, there are several pay-offs for the host university, including greater awareness of QA issues in external examining, staff development for academics interested in becoming external examiners and identification of sector-wide good practice and emerging issues.

## Reflecting on external examining systems

What are the implications, in your view, of the requirement for HEIs to publish a summary of external examiners' reports on each programme for the relationship between external examiners and the teaching staff?

What are the advantages and disadvantages in terms of QA of having external examiners from a university in the same geographical region?

It is often stated that academics new to external examining should be only be appointed to programmes where there is also an experienced external examiner in post. While this is primarily to ensure academic standards, what opportunities does your university provide to help experienced external examiners to share their expertise with newer external examiners or answer their queries?

What are the processes in your institution for linking external examiners' reports to QA? To standards? To QE?

Under what circumstances are vivas likely to be useful? How should they be assessed and quality assured?

Drawing on experience at your institution, both in terms of external examiners for your programmes and of colleagues who are external examiners, to what extent does the Code in this section adequately address the different role of subject or module external examiners and programme external examiners in two-tier systems, such as modular schemes? What are the implications for the publication of the summary external examiner's report?

# 10 Academic appeals and student complaints

## THE NEW CULTURE OF COMPLAINT MANAGEMENT

Section 5 of the Code reflects the broader concern noted by The Nolan Committee on Standards in Public Life and the Dearing and Garrick reports, that public bodies must be more transparent, consistent and fair in the way complaints from service users are handled. In addition, greater awareness of the possibilities of legal redress, fuelled by 'no win no fee' deals, has concentrated the minds of universities to ensure that students have a local solution available as an alternative to pursuing matters through the courts. Additionally, the perceived ineffectiveness of the 'visitor' system used at pre-1992 universities has brought renewed calls for greater externality and independence in the final stages of review and appeal. Proposals for a UK ombudsman, of the kind used to resolve grievances about local authorities, have not met with uniform support from the higher education sector, with universities fearing the 'thin end' of a regulatory 'wedge'. The 2003 White Paper, however, proposed the establishment of an 'independent adjudicator' to take effect from September 2003, acknowledging that legislation would be required to implement the system. Consideration of these issues by the sector, in conjunction with the increased focus on the student voice in institutional audit, has led to the development of a new culture of complaint management, centring on greater systematicity, broader transparency, early resolution and linkage with service and QE.

The increasing formalization, codification and centralization of the systems for managing student appeals and complaints mean that there are inevitably legacy issues around managing the previously local systems, roles, cultures and remedies. While centralization (of policy if not quite of management) of complaints and appeals in principle will improve consistency, transparency and monitoring, there is the danger of losing the supportive and solution-focused pragmatism which probably characterizes much of the work of senior tutors and academic advisors around the sector. There seems little awareness amongst some institutional managers of the irony of entries in student handbooks of the type 'Section 4, Subsection 2b (ii): Informal resolution of minor Type 3 complaints'. If the complaint and appeals procedures are not fully owned and understood by academics and departmental administrators, then ways will be found to circumvent them, with the inevitable short-term benefits and long-term disasters that such arrangements produce.

---

## What is a complaint?

For the purpose of the Code, a 'complaint' is defined as 'any specific concern about the provision of a programme of study or related academic service'.

Since universities do not normally have separate complaints procedures for academic and non-academic matters, this definition may in practice be extended to 'any specific concern about the provision of a programme of study, academic service or related facility or service provided by the university'.

Exclusions would normally cover:

- harassment issues;
- appeal against assessment board decisions;
- Students' Union issues;
- complaints about other students' behaviour;
- public interest disclosure.

## What is an appeal?

'An "appeal" is defined as a request for a review of a decision of an academic body charged with making decisions on student progression, assessment, and awards.'(QAA Code, S4)

---

The definition of complaint in the Code is arguably over-inclusive, since it does not specify the form, context, addressee or content of the 'specific concern'. Obviously, and trivially, no-one would suggest that the code is trying to cover an institution's response to jocular comments overheard in the student bar about a lecturer and his illegible handwriting. However, the status of, say, an e-mail by a student about the continued difficulty of getting library books for an essay is less clear.

The definition of an appeal is less problematic and is assumed to include the notion that the request for a review of a decision is made to the right person at the right time in the right format. Confusingly perhaps, some institutions have systems which are referred to as 'Request for a review of assessment results' which are explicitly designed to allow students to query module registration details, programme alterations, and resit/reassessment schedules following receipt of computer-generated results or transcripts without having to trigger the whole lumbering machinery of the appeals process.

## IMPLEMENTING THE PRECEPTS

The Code covers the **general principles** (formal, reasonable procedures which are transparent and implemented effectively) and states that there should be accurate **information** and sources of advice for students as complainants, that **internal processes** such as the decision about a complaint or appeal should be characterized by objectivity, support for students and opportunities for appeal, that **remedies** should be clear and swiftly implemented and finally that institutions should periodically **review** the effectiveness of their systems in this area.

### *General principles*

*Precept 1: Institutions should have effective procedures for resolving student complaints and academic appeals. Students should have a full opportunity to raise, individually or collectively, matters of proper concern to them without fear of disadvantage and in the knowledge that privacy and confidentiality will be respected.*

*Precept 2: The procedures should be ratified by the governing body or other body with ultimate corporate responsibility and should form a part of the institution's overall framework for quality assurance.*

*Precept 3: Institutions should ensure that their procedures are fair and decisions are reasonable and have regard to any applicable law.*

*Precept 4: Institutions should address student complaints and appeals in a timely manner, using simple and transparent procedures. Informal resolution should be an option at all stages of the complaints procedure which should operate, in the first instance, at the level at which the matter arose.*

One of the key issues to note here is that it is an implicit assumption that individual departments should not be running their own independent and potentially idiosyncratic complaints and appeals processes. The thrust of this part of the section of the Code is that there should be institution-wide procedures approved and underwritten by the ultimate authority of the institution. While there might be some local variation to cover particular circumstances (such as some programmes with strong professional body involvement) essentially all students will have the right to the same due process and standards of decision making, appeal and remedy. The challenge in managing quality in this area is undoubtedly the fact that while for many years institutions have had central policies on such matters, there has been extensive local discretion tolerated on implementation, diverse approaches to remedy and appeal and almost no central monitoring of outcomes or implementation. Once again the Code seeks to encourage institutions to regularize policies and their implementation.

It should be noted that the precepts do not lay down who is responsible for handling student complaints in the context of collaborative provision, but requires that jurisdictional authority is made clear to students. Universities need to be aware that whatever arrangement is put in place, the effective management of student complaints in the context of collaborative provision is particularly complex and challenging. Issues to be considered include whether the normal timeframes for appeals is to apply, whether all terms and definitions are appropriate and unambiguous (eg 'the student's head of department'), the extent to which the student is complaining or appealing under the awarding institutions' rules or those of the PO, and whether in the case of multiple and interrelated grievances the same jurisdiction applies to all grievances. In terms of adhering to the equal opportunities requirements of the Code here, it is important to ensure that panels are fully inclusive and representative of all groups for all hearings and appeals, and not just for those hearing for, say, students from ethnic minority groups or with disabilities.

It is important to ensure that student complaints and appeals procedures are consistent with the Data Protection Act, SENDA and Human Rights legislation, not only in their conception but in their application. Universities will find it worthwhile to review cases to ensure that record-keeping procedures and good practice are being adhered to. Universities will want to pay particular attention to identifying how any *informal* practices underpinning formal arrangements are being developed to manage decision making and reassure itself that it is comfortable with these.

## Information

*Precept 5: Information on complaints and appeals procedures should be published, accurate, complete, clearly presented, readily accessible and issued to students and staff.*

*Precept 6: Sources of impartial help, advice, guidance and support should be advertised widely within the institution.*

## GOOD PRACTICE POINTS

A potential form of good practice here is for the HEI to lay out the sequences of the complaints or appeals procedure *diagrammatically* rather than purely textually. This will help clarify the links between different processes and the way in which contingencies are handled. It will also help students, or the advisors of students, for whom English is not the first language.

Further good practice in the context of collaborative provision is to give the full external address for offices and clarify that terms such as 'The Registrar's Office' or 'Academic Programmes Office' equal the University of X's Registry or APO (as appropriate). Lack of clarification can be a problem where an institution overzealously declares that it has one complaints procedure for all students without reflecting on how guidance on that policy will be read in local contexts.

Further good practice here is to make complaints and appeals information available on university Web pages with hyperlinks to advisory notes. There needs to be clear responsibility assigned to relevant officers to ensure that the information is up to date and consistent.

Although the Code emphasizes, rightly, that students will not be penalized for making complaints in good faith, there should be indications at an early stage in the information provided of the right of the university to take appropriate action in the case of frivolous, malicious, speculative or vexatious complaints.

### Internal processes

*Precept 7: The complaints and appeals procedures should identify the persons or bodies from whom authoritative guidance may be sought on the applicability and operation of the procedures.*

*Precept 8: Those responding to, investigating or adjudicating upon complaints or appeals must, as required by law, do so impartially, and must not act in any matter in which they have a material interest or in which any potential conflict of interest might arise.*

*Precept 9: A complainant or appellant should be entitled to be accompanied at all stages of the complaints or appeals process by a person of his or her choosing.*

*Precept 10: The documentation should indicate what further internal procedures, if any, are open to a student dissatisfied with the response to a complaint or outcome of an appeal.*

In the context of managing the internal process of complaints and appeals, universities should clarify not just whether a student can be accompanied at any hearing or meetings by a representative, but what role this representative can have at meetings, including whether for example he or she is attending in a supportive, representative or advisory capacity. Additionally, HEIs should clarify under what conditions if any they are prepared to enter into correspondence with a representative of the student. Occasionally, difficult issues can arise when the representative is another student, a parent, or a legal representative and universities should not allow themselves to fall into a position where they are making decisions about such situations on the spot.

The guidance on the precepts relating to internal processes highlights that following an initial decision there should be provision for that decision 'to be reviewed by a more senior member of staff should the student remain dissatisfied'. Although universities are reluctant to be seen to be preventing students having their cases heard at an appropriately senior level there is a danger here that if complainants have an *automatic* right of appeal they will simply go through the motions at the lower hearing, undermining its credibility and effectiveness in the process. Where there is effectively an automatic right of appeal, it is not unknown for complainants to assert during the hearing that if they do not get satisfaction they are determined to take the matter further. There is an argument that in order to resolve issues at the lowest possible level of formality, even where there is in effect an automatic right of appeal, complainants should be required to state *why* they are dissatisfied with the lower 'court'. They might helpfully indicate that they variously found the administration of the hearing flawed, that new evidence has come to light, or that the person hearing the complaint or appeal was in some way lacking full independence – supported by any relevant evidence. If complainants simply want to appeal because they got the wrong result at the lower level and remain unhappy, then should such a right of appeal be open to them, they should be encouraged to make a statement to that effect. This at least would ensure that complainants were able to confirm (or otherwise) that the complaints and appeals procedures were correctly applied.

The guidance for these precepts helpfully lays out a range of issues for complaints and appeals procedures to address. A common issue is not addressed however: appellants who seek to have extenuating circumstances for assessment taken into account retrospectively because circumstances meant that they were unable to communicate their situation to the relevant university authorities. Where students have experienced psychological difficulties related to personal circumstances it can be almost impossible to obtain convincing medical evidence either way. The 'gatekeepers' for any departmental-based system are normally very sympathetic to students in these circumstances, not least because they have already been supporting them over a period of time. Universities will want to reassure themselves that such flexible and supportive arrangements, however well meaning, do not lead to the effective abandonment of any notional schedule of deadlines for appeals.

## Remedies

*Precept 11: Institutions should ensure that where a complaint or appeal is upheld, appropriate remedial action is implemented.*

*Precept 12: Institutions should meet reasonable and proportionate incidental expenses necessarily incurred by a successful complainant or appellant.*

The guidance on remedies rightly emphasizes the desirability for all parties of early, informal low level resolution of complaints where possible. However, this strategy requires attention being paid to consistency of outcome both in terms of fairness to all students affected at any given point in time (and not just those who complained) and in terms of setting precedents. Universities will want to advise whoever is empowered to make decisions on the ground of the desirability of taking advice from more senior or more experienced colleagues to ensure that the remedies proposed do not have undesirable wider consequences.

Precept 12's statement that 'Institutions should meet reasonable and proportionate incidental expenses necessarily incurred by a successful complainant or appellant' is interesting. Substantively there are a wide range of views on whether or not such expenses should be paid, how 'reasonable' and 'proportionate' might be defined, who would be responsible for a definitive decision on such matters, and, of course, whether being denied the expenses requested would be grounds for further complaint (and so on). More interestingly perhaps, however, is the fact that the Code should go so far as to take a view on the matter at all. Code-speak here would be 'Institutions should make clear whether or not they will meet any expenses incurred by a successful complainant or appellant'.

## Monitoring, evaluation and review

*Precept 13: Institutions should have in place effective arrangements for the regular monitoring, evaluation and review of complaints and appeals.*

*Precept 14: Institutions should keep their monitoring, evaluation and review arrangements under scrutiny, taking into account current good practice.*

The flow of information into a central complaints register will of course reflect different ideas about what counts as a complaint. While letters and e-mails received directly at this central point are often automatically logged as a complaint, no matter how trivial or vague, the flow of information from local departments or services will reflect local organizational subcultures.

The definition of 'complaint' is slightly loose so it may be that different sections of a university will trigger the record system in different ways as a function of the level of the threshold they are applying. It is important that this is recognized since being able to manage informal expressions of concern without them developing into full blown complaints lies at the heart of any positive approach to dissatisfaction or disappointments. However, it may be the case that some departments or services are loath to refer complaints to a central logging system for fear that it will reflect badly on their activities. Still others hold off reporting complaints until they have put in place some kind of informal response or remedy.

Record-keeping systems that seek to log the 'location' of a complaint need to distinguish between the course of study of the student, the person or office to whom they complain and the service or department which they are complaining about. Examples of complex complaints would include students on modular programmes complaining about their least satisfactory subjects as opposed to the subject they identify with most, parents complaining to a head of department about enrolment queues, or postgraduate students complaining to deans about the lack of car parking spaces. If complaints are simply logged against the department or service which receives complaints then service standards will fall as service and departmental heads refer the complainant to the 'correct' section with a consequential aggravation of the complainant.

The Code rightly emphasizes the need to review practice and complaints management in the light of external reference points including legislation. The inputs into any review will be both quantitative and qualitative. The former need to be handled carefully since the information provided can only be as useful as the quality of data captured and the categories under which it can be entered. In monitoring complaints there is sometimes an assumption that complaints are about issues which are 'located' in central units or academic departments. However, the basic building blocks of students' experiences of learning at an institution do not necessarily map on to the organizational building blocks or systems. This is compounded by the fact that students, while able to articulate the symptoms of their problem ('The library computer didn't let me borrow books so I couldn't hand my essay in on time'), are not necessarily able to deduce the diagnosis ('There is a large pile of library registration forms sitting in Student Records not processed'). However, simply logging this as a complaint against Student Records rather than the library (and having the annual summary of student complaints show it as such), is still not enough if it fails to deliver the most appropriate remedy ('Encourage academic staff in Department X pass on library enrolment forms to Student Records more quickly').

Managing student complaints and appeals is a difficult area since it strikes at the heart of the complex relationship between students, their rights, their university and their university's position in law as an autonomous public body. As such any serious cases are likely to have multiple legal, academic, governance, policy and public relations dimensions. More generally however, a university with clear statements of what it expects of its students, and what students can expect of it, and that takes seriously violations of those expectations in a timely, transparent and fair manner is likely to build up stakeholder confidence as a responsible and effective public body without compromising aspirations to maintain a sense of a supportive and inclusive academic community.

## QA ISSUES WITH STUDENT APPEALS AND COMPLAINTS

Complaints and appeals systems are capable of contribution to QE through identifying where things could be done better. However, as systems in their own right they have areas which can go wrong. It is in relation to both these contexts that the following threats to quality can be identified in these systems:

- failure to ensure that there is consistency in the recording and referral of students complaints;
- failure to implement an improvement rather than blame culture approach to complaints;
- failure to brief students about their rights and the procedures, so that further complaints are bound up with the management of the complaints system itself;
- failure to prevent re-hearings of the same case at progressively more senior levels on the grounds that the complainant is not satisfied with the outcome at the lower level.

## QE ISSUES WITH STUDENT APPEALS AND COMPLAINTS

Complaints systems can contribute to enhancement through:

- ensuring that complaints and appeals are used positively to identify areas of poor service, inaccurate information, inappropriate expectations or system-to-system failures;
- ensuring that unsuccessful complaints are not seen as uninformative and that successful complaints are not seen as indications that systems need to be completely overhauled;
- ensuring that complaints, and the processes for exploring them, do not become personalized or confrontational;
- ensuring that where possible the messages from complaints systems are triangulated with information from other sources such as course feedback questionnaires;
- ensuring that chairs of complaints panels have adequate training, not just to manage the case competently and fairly, but to identify the underlying issues which have given rise to the complaint;
- ensuring that there are systems to identify and interpret patterns of complaints across different academic departments or central services.

## Reflecting on student appeals and complaints

Do you find the definitions of a 'complaint' and an 'appeal' too narrow? Or too broad? Do the definitions correspond to students' views of what a complaint or appeal is?

At your institution can complaints be submitted to a higher level simply because the complainant is not happy with the outcome at the lower level? How does this affect the participants of the lower hearing?

Does your institution have policies in place to prevent repeat complaints on trivial matters by the same individual(s)? How are these managed?

What is your university's policy on group complaints? Are they treated differently? How should they be treated?

How does your institution manage cases where a student is involved in disciplinary proceedings and makes a complaint about a related matter? How should these circumstances be handled?

What strategies or processes are used in academic departments and central services for the informal management of complaints?

In terms of appeals, what procedures are in place for a student to query an administrative error in his or her results? Are these subsumed under appeals?

# 11 The assessment of students

## THE ACHILLES HEEL OF QUALITY

Assessment has long been a lightening rod for local and national debates about the nature of standards in higher education. It also looms large in students' experience of education and has often been the first point for the withdrawal of labour in industrial disputes. Until the advent of subject review little was known outside individual departments about the procedures and practices of assessment. The subject review cycle 1995–2001 identified several areas of assessment, which generally speaking some institutions had not been managing well.

Extracts from the subject overview reports for politics, economics and business studies give something of the flavour of the issues in this area:

> Assessment procedures require further consideration by some politics staff, particularly in relating assessment methods to the learning objectives and providing clear assessment criteria and helpful feedback on student work. However, some providers do not use the full range of marks available. (Politics subject overview report)

> In teaching learning and assessment the grade reflects good teaching and learning which in some instances contrasts with poor assessment practice. (Economics subject overview report)

> …reviewers noted a lack of clear assessment criteria and of matching assignments to learning objectives. Additionally, the reviewers considered that the range of assessment methods was limited, and students could be briefed more effectively about both the requirements of assignment tasks and the computation of grades. In some institutions, marking and internal moderation processes needed to be more rigorous… In more than 40 per cent of institutions, (feedback) was of variable quality, lacking focus and being too brief. There was also evidence that formative feedback was provided too late for it to be of value. (Business studies subject overview report)

It should be noted that these three reports reflect subject reviews carried out at the end of a five- or six-year period of comprehensive discipline-based subject reviews when institutions would have been more, not less, aware of the expectations of reviewers in this area. It is interesting to reflect that assessment was noted as an area of concern in the 1994/95 round of assessments carried out by HEFCE. In business and management studies for example reviewers noted 'considerable variation in the quantity and quality of written feedback given to students' (Business and management studies subject overview report, 1994, para 21).

In some respects it can be argued that bringing information about quality of assessment management across different disciplines and institutions into the public domain was one of the major and most valuable outcomes across the entire comprehensive subject review process. Assessments were occasionally found to be poorly designed both in the sense of complex assessment arrangements not being fully thought through, or in having unclear relationships to the learning outcomes for specified modules or courses, where these relationships were not always consistently applied or were not clear to students.

This lack of planning in design and remoteness from curricular specification led in some cases to limited transparency for the entire assessment process. The privileged position given to subject specialist expertise had led in some cases to subjective judgements which in the absence of moderation were not consistent across markers on the same programmes. The opportunities provided by assessment for developing students' understanding of the curriculum, their skills development and their progress through a programme of study was further undermined by the limited effectiveness of feedback arrangements in some areas of provision. In some cases there was effectively no feedback at all, especially if students themselves did not initiate the process. In some cases feedback was not clearly linked to any explicit or implicit criteria for the piece of work. Where some feedback was provided against criteria, it would rarely clarify what students would have to do to improve in subsequent assessment tasks.

Knight (2002) has argued that there are too many local institutional factors affecting assessment to make nationwide comparisons reliable or meaningful and for that reason internal quality monitoring has to be given priority over external quality monitoring in this context. This position is supported by Larrington and Lindsay (2002) who have demonstrated the lack of credible evidence that can sometimes underpin external reviewers' claims about the overall achievement level of students in one institution.

## REFLECTIVE PRACTICE POINT

It is interesting that the QAA declares external examiners to be 'the primary safeguard of academic standards in UK higher education' when the only substantial independent review of assessment in the UK identified the design, management and standards of assessment to be one of the least well managed areas. The question to be asked is: why did external examiners fail to notice the lack of coherence and consistency in assessment in so many areas of provision in higher education throughout the 1990s?

## IMPLEMENTING THE PRECEPTS

Section 6 of the Code, which covers the assessment of students, must be read (and applied) alongside section 4 on external examiners. The only significant reference to assessment in the *Handbook for Institutional Review* is to the fact that when making their judgements institutional auditors will pay particular attention to the QAA's expectations that 'institutions are making strong and scrupulous use of independent external examiners in summative assessment procedures' (para 16).

In the Code assessment is defined as 'a generic term for a set of processes that measure the outcomes of students' learning' and the distinctions between diagnostic, formative and summative are noted. The Code however deals principally with summative assessment. The pedagogic role of assessment is noted as is the opportunity it provides for tutors to assess their own effectiveness as educators. Because assessment in many ways serves to evaluate the extent to which a student's subject knowledge and skills in a certain area are commensurate with a formal level of academic attainment and award, this section of the Code needs to be read and implemented alongside guidance on SBSs and the FHEQ. There is no meaningful way to assess the effectiveness of assessment, or the arrangements for ensuring its quality, if we do not also review the knowledge and skills under assessment and the qualification under consideration. An assessment scheme that works for a level I award in marketing may not work for a level H award in computing, in ways which go beyond the fact that one will have questions on brands and the other on software.

Precept 1 lays out the general responsibilities of institutions in the area of assessment: that they should have effective procedures for assessment strategies and rigorous assessment practices. Essentially these two components refer to the overall framework for assessment – making sure that assessment is linked to the outcomes, that there is not too much of it and that it should be integrated across a programme of study with minimal gaps or duplication given the curriculum; and that the system for assessing students' efforts should actually work in practice – with no idiosyncrasies, an appropriate degree of moderation, double marking, anonymity and objectivity. Both the grand plan and the nuts and bolts of assessment have to work, and institutions need to able to show that this is the case, that they have thought it through and that they regularly monitor their systems. Clearly, there are many processes involved at both these strategic and operational levels.

### REFLECTIVE PRACTICE POINT

To what extent does your university have institution-wide policies on assessment of students? How is the balance between departmental autonomy to design assessments relevant to the discipline balanced with the need for consistency across different programmes?

The guidance encourages institutions to pay attention to validity, equity and reliability in assessment. Validity is not defined in the Handbook but in measurement theory validity is taken to mean that an assessment device actually does measure what it claims to be measuring. Thus a thermometer should accurately measure temperature, a ruler length and a dissertation, perhaps, the capacity to work independently on a sustained project. Reliability is the extent to which an assessment device is consistent in what it measures. Thus a car trip meter which gives different mileage readings for the same journey is unreliable. An assessment device that is reliable is not necessarily valid of course. Equity is simply an issue of fairness. Assessments in education should not favour one ethnic group, class, sexual orientation or health status over another. Staff should not grade one student's work more favourably than another's on the grounds of favouritism or anything unconnected to academic ability and application. Validity of assessment can be achieved through ensuring that a wide range of specialists is involved in the construction of the assessment materials. Reliability can in principle be assessed through checking whether there are any significant fluctuations amongst successive or parallel cohorts. In some cases, statistical analyses may be required to confirm that the assessment arrangements are genuinely valid, reliable and fair.

A general principle is that a narrow range of types of assessment is unlikely to fairly or effectively measure a broad set of learning outcomes. The classic situation is where innovative learning outcomes declaring that students will throughout the programme acquire all kinds of interpersonal, transferable and employment-related skills are assessed through a moribund and predictable diet of 2,000 word essays and 3-hour examinations. It is not unusual for programme specifications to run ahead of assessment strategies, typically because they are written by different tutors. Assessment schemes are typically designed by module leaders while programme specifications are designed by programme leaders.

## REFLECTIVE PRACTICE POINT

Think about a course development in which you were involved. Which came first – the programme specification or the module learning outcomes? In what ways, if any, did one inform the other? How ideally in your view should the production of these two levels be organized?

One key issue here is the extent to which assessment principles are applied consistently across the institution. Clearly, students in drama will not expect to be assessed in the same way as history students but the underlying principles of assessment strategy and thorough and conscientious application of those principles should be in evidence.

*Precept 3: Institutions should have effective mechanisms to deal with breaches of assessment regulations, and the resolution of appeals against assessment decisions.*

It might be usefully noted here that this precept implies that procedures should be in place for both student cheating and staff malpractice. The guidance section states that institutions should have procedures to deal with concerns raised about the 'unfair operation of assessment procedures'. These could be concerns raised by the student, or possibly another member of academic or support staff. With the advent of the Freedom of Information Act (2000) it will be interesting to see whether, given that students cannot appeal against academic judgements *per se*, they will use the Act to secure information from academic departments which will enable them to form a view as to whether the published assessment procedures have in fact been adhered to. If a department has a policy which states that all work is moderated, what is the response to a student who asks for proof that his or her essay was moderated? At what point does the need to promote confidence in the assessment process give way to the need to prevent over-bureaucratizing and to avoid speculative and frivolous request for remarking?

## Assessment panels and boards

*Precept 4: Institutions should implement effective, clear, and consistent policies in respect of the membership, procedures, powers and accountability of assessment panels and boards of examiners. Where there is more than one such body the relative powers of each should be defined.*

The guidance for this precept effectively encourages institutions to ensure that external examiners attend examination boards; that there is an academic from another department present; that personal interests in students are declared; that there be a quorum; that student work is available; that extenuating circumstances are consistently considered and that proper records of decisions are kept. The 'relative powers' clause is essentially referring to modular schemes where two-tier systems operate, with lower subject-based boards making decisions on module performance and higher programme, scheme or university examination boards making decisions on awards. Institutions should not have difficulties adhering to this precept.

Specifying rules of attendance at examination boards by external examiners is an area fraught with difficulty. In traditional single honours boards with a single summer finals board, the attendance of the external examiner (or one of them) was seen as essential and not difficult to achieve. However, with the advent of modular schemes and hence at least two levels of boards, resit boards, January boards, year 1 boards and stage boards, there are a lot more boards for external examiners to miss. While summer boards process the vast majority of finalists, the existence of other boards, created by greater flexibility in reassessment policies, means that finalists can come up all year round. It seems unlikely that external examiners would want to engage in a 500-mile round trip to nod sagely when candidate 75032 goes through with a mark of 62 per cent and a upper second. Some institutions finesse this difficulty by the use of preprinted forms for external examiners which simply state 'Although I was unable to attend the examination board for BSc (Hons) X, due to reason Y, I was fully briefed on the department's deliberations and recommendations for this candidate.' One of the ironies of recent practices concerning external attendance is that, in parallel with greater expectations for external examiners to attend boards, there is corresponding reduction in the discretion that external examiners can exercise once they finally turn up. Quite rightly, the traditional principle that external examiners could alter the marks of any of a sample of scripts that had been sent to him or her, but not the others that were not sent, has been abandoned. However, subject external examiners are frustrated by two-tier modular schemes where they attend the module board to confirm module marks but have no influence on the final classification which is determined, sometimes mechanistically, by a separate superordinate scheme board. Such a board may cover over 50 subjects but have only two or three external examiners to approve the process, who in turn are no doubt disaffected by their lack of contact with individual students and their work.

## Scheduling and amount of assessment

*Precept 5: Institutions should ensure that the scheduling and amount of assessment are consistent with an effective and appropriate measurement of the achievement by students of the intended learning outcomes and that they effectively support learning.*

Traditional degree programmes often had summative assessments at the end of the course, often using only unseen examinations. There have been concerns that modular schemes however have gone too far in the other direction, with too much weighting on coursework and too much volume of assessment generally. Additionally, modular schemes can lead to the difficulty that students taking as many as five modules simultaneously will find themselves with too many assessments over too short a period of time as a consequence of a lack of coordinated assessment planning between module leaders. These difficulties are compounded in combined and joint honours programmes which straddle more than one department. There is no easy answer to assessment scheduling. Objectively, it is clear that students cannot be assessed before they have learned something to assess, while if all modules finish with the assessment process then there is too much pressure on students at the end of the semester. Subjectively for students, if the assessment is too early they will be frustrated that they are being assessed prematurely, before they have grasped and consolidated learning; if the assessment is too late feedback is unlikely to help future performance. There is a view that with the increasing emphasis on learning outcomes, the need to assess learning outcomes and the need to incorporate knowledge, generic and subject skill in those outcomes, the volume of assessment is always going to be high. There is a perception that any attempt to reduce the volume of assessment would run the risk of that greatest of quality misdemeanours – the unassessed outcome. In order for assessment to facilitate learning there needs to be less assessment, or better, the assessment needs to be integrated into the learning. The problem with assessment can be not so much the assessment process but the assessment activity. Students do skip lectures because of looming deadlines and academics collude in this. Assessment can be built into seminar activities, field trips, group work and presentations, but all of these require careful planning and moderation arrangements.

## GOOD PRACTICE POINT

Some institutions seek to manage assessment loadings for students across combined honours programmes by scheduling assessment weeks differently for different categories of timetable slots. This means that subjects which students are able to combine do not have coursework deadlines in the same week.

### Marking and grading

*Precept 7: Institutions should publish, and implement consistently, clear criteria for the marking and grading of assessments.*

*Precept 8: Institutions should ensure that there are robust mechanisms for marking and for the moderation of marks.*

The Code requires institutions to consider the guidelines for marking, advantages and disadvantages of anonymous marking, sampling and moderation. There are many different kinds of systems with combinations of each of these features which institutions use. However, occasionally these are historical, reflecting local academic preferences, or pragmatic considerations to manage workload rather than extended reflection of the most effective system. An institutional policy on marking and grading does not necessarily mean that a single set of rules will be applied to all programmes in the same way. The institutional policy might simply be that each department will publish its own policy. The advantage of the former in terms of quality is that there is consistency in adherence to a minimum specification across the institution, students constructing programmes from across the institution will not be dealt with differently on the same programme, and most importantly, truly weak practice in poorly managed departments can be eradicated quickly. The disadvantages in terms of quality of a centralized rather than federal policy is that academics will resent the central imposition and implement it grudgingly, if at all, local needs and circumstances will not be accommodated appropriately and the areas which need radical reform will not change.

## REFLECTIVE PRACTICE POINT

Does your institution have a central assessment policy which specifies minimum standards of moderation, sampling or blind double marking or are departments left to specify their own standards? What have been the advantages of the system your institution has adopted? Have there been practical or political problems with the implementation of the policy?

*Precept 9: Institutions should evaluate periodically the maintenance and development of their academic standards.*

- *maintaining and using an archive of sample marked scripts in all subject areas;*
- *analysing trends in results to identify, for example, the relation between student entry qualifications and assessment outcomes; and the evaluation and comparison of the distribution of marks, grades or honours classes.*

The wording of this precept does not perhaps fully convey the thrust of its intention. The guidance notes imply that institutions should periodically review the effectiveness of their assessment processes not simply by inviting external examiners, students or academic staff to comment on trends or patterns, but through the systematic analysis of actual scripts over a period of time. This is a departure from current practice for most institutions. The first issue here is that some assessment activities resist archiving. The second issue is that a systematic review of entry qualifications and assessment outcomes involves more than just a simple correlation of one with the other. Students with lower entry qualifications may also come from low participation neighbourhoods, may have a wider range of personal issues and may be entering different courses compared to those coming in with better entry qualifications. Care must be taken in the analysis of such data. The review of degree classification data is simple enough at the descriptive level but fraught with difficulties when it comes to drawing conclusions such as whether or not there are more, or less, firsts or upper seconds than there should be given some input variable. The statistical technique known as multiple regression analysis (of which there are many varieties) or the non-parametric equivalent loglinear analysis would be among the techniques appropriate to use on data of this kind. Larrington and Lindsay show how involved such analyses can be, and the difficulties that arise when such matters are foregrounded during QA (Larrington and Lindsay, 2002) .

*Precept 12: Institutions should ensure that appropriate feedback is provided to students on assessed work in a way that promotes learning and facilitates improvement.*

As noted earlier, the subject reviews during the period 1995–2001 identified inconsistent and ineffective feedback as one of the areas where quality has not been well managed. The guidance notes effectively recommend that feedback seeks to be timely; that students know what to expect on feedback across different assessments; that there are criterion referenced comments, and that there might be supplementary oral feedback either involving the whole class or with individuals.

One of the difficulties noted here has been the fact that often it is a small number of modules where students have not received feedback that is timely, helpful, supportive or developmental. It is probably the case that where institutions fall down on assessment of quality in general, and in feedback in particular, is neither in the design of sensible strategies nor the broad implementation at departmental level, but rather the failure to deal effectively with departures from the strategy – of which it might be said there are two main varieties. First there is the failure to manage the rogue element where one or two tutors in a manner widely known to colleagues and to which students quickly become resigned, return work with perfunctory comments or fail to provide feedback at all. The second, more forgivable reason (for the individuals if not those responsible for quality), is the part-time member of staff who through lack of effective induction, inexperience, or the sheer volume of marking he or she is expected to get through, fails to provide adequate feedback. This failing is something in which others collude since they recognize the excessive demands and pressures under which such individuals ply their trade. This relates also to Precept 13 which states that 'Institutions should ensure that all staff involved in the assessment of students are competent to undertake their roles and responsibilities' and which must be taken to cover part-time staff and not just full-time permanent academics. It is essential therefore as a matter of good practice that part-time, possibly short-term contract staff be properly inducted and supported in developing their understanding of assessment and the institution's expectations around the management of assessment.

Although the Code here refers to the guidelines on distance learning it does so only in relation to precept 5 which covers rigour, fairness and security – in other words in the sense that distance learners have more opportunity to cheat and need therefore to be watched particularly carefully. Be that as it may, it is unfortunate that distance learning is not highlighted in relation to this precept since in distance learning feedback on assessment is one of the most important teaching channels the tutor has. The management of distance learning should seek to incorporate additional consideration on the way in which feedback will be handled. Not only are the comments particularly important in helping the student to gauge progress and reflect on his or her own developing subject knowledge, they constitute one of the few customized elements of the programme. As such it is crucial even more than in campus-based delivery that feedback is supportive and developmental.

*Precept 14: The languages of assessment and teaching will normally be the same. If, for any reason, this cannot be achieved, institutions must ensure that their academic standards are not consequently put at risk.*

The issue here is that students whose first language is not English, if assessed in their own language, may not be demonstrating the learning outcomes associated with their programme. No UK HEI would wish to promote this even if it had the resources to support the translations of the assessment materials and the subsequent translation of the student scripts. The real issue arises with franchised provision to countries where English is not the first language. There will always be concerns that some of the teaching will not be in English and that although the actual assignment papers may be in English, guidance notes by local tutors may not. Of course this may be more of an issue in business studies than, say, in mathematics since in the former the learning outcomes will almost certainly emphasize not just the knowledge of certain business systems, but also the capacity to communicate clearly in English about those systems and therefore the assessment of skills needs to be in English. Conversely, differential calculus, set theory and probability are the same the world over. More generally, it has to be borne in mind that the possession of a degree from a UK HEI is understandably seen to attest to the bearer's linguistics skills so it is important that where a significant amount of teaching or assessment is not in English, this is clearly stated on the degree certificate.

## GOOD PRACTICE POINT

Where English is not the language of instruction or where there is, for whatever reason, a significant amount of material provided to students about assessment in another language, it is good practice to have the initial translation translated back into English by a different interpreter. This ensures that the original meaning is not lost. This process is resource intensive and yet another reason why many institutions are abandoning programmes where the language of instruction is not English.

*Precept 15: Institutions should ensure that where a programme forms part of the qualifications regime of a professional or statutory body, clear information is available to staff and students about specific assessment requirements that must be met for progression towards the professional qualification.*

This is unlikely to cause institutions much difficulty. Modules or courses are normally aligned with PSB requirements not their constituent assessments. It would be unusual and ill advised to arrange PSB recognition around an examination rubric that stated, 'Candidates for admission to the Chartered Institute of X, should attempt questions 2, 5 and 6, but not questions 1, 8 or 9.' In some cases however the dissertation or project may need to be in a particular area if PSB or other national body membership is to be achieved. In psychology for example some universities will allow students to submit a theoretical or literature review dissertation as part of their final honours work and still get a degree in psychology. However, the degree would not attract recognition by the British Psychological Society. Houghton (2002) has highlighted some of the difficulties involved in ensuring that intended learning outcomes and their assessment can reconcile the sometimes *conflicting* demands of PSBs and SBSs.

*Precept 16: Institutions should have effective mechanisms for the review and development of assessment regulations.*

It is inherent in the management of any system that change should be as far as possible proactive and strategic, a managed process which adds value, minimizes risk, is based on consultation and gets everyone on board. This is particularly important in the area of assessment. The review of assessment regulations is a necessary part of a systematic QA strategy as it will take some time for the implications of SBSs and the FHEQ to be fully incorporated in the delivery of programmes. Assessment is the lynchpin that holds outcomes and awards together and cannot be allowed to drift by indifference or stagnate by neglect.

*Precept 17: Institutions should ensure that assessment decisions are recorded and documented accurately and systematically.*

Ostensibly Precepts 17 and 18 cover the 'recording, documentation and publication of assessment decisions' and seem to be stating the obvious and add no value. Clearly precept 17 on its own has no detractors – recording degree classifications 'accurately' and 'systematically' seems wholly reasonable and exhorting universities to do so seems superfluous. However, as is often the case, it is in the notes of guidance that we see the fuller picture. The guidance states that there should be 'clear statements of the responsibilities of all those involved in computation, checking and recording of assessment decisions'. It is worth remembering that while final degree classifications and resulting awards are the most numerous of the results that have to be processed by administrators, approved by boards and published by registry or departments, it is essential that *all* pass lists, progressions lists, resit lists and individual appeals and reviews for subdegree programmes and foundation degrees as well as full honours programmes are also properly managed. Once this is conceded it can be seen that there are many more opportunities for inconsistency and error. The areas of risk here are:

- insufficient attention paid to candidates processed outside of the normal schedule of assessment boards;
- ambiguity in the balance of responsibilities between academic staff and administrative staff;
- ambiguity in the balance of responsibilities between central administrative staff and local departmental administrative staff;
- any lack of clarity in the nature of the powers delegated to the chair of examination boards and its relation to the notification of examination results.

The injunction to have back-up systems is commendable and is why most academics will hold on to their marks in hard copy or their own spreadsheets until the pass lists are published and the deadline for appeals has expired – the constraints of the Data Protection Act notwithstanding.

## QA ISSUES WITH THE ASSESSMENT OF STUDENTS

Assessment is a key area for QA with small failures often having significant ramifications. Although the institutional, departmental and programme context will all affect the level of risk of different areas, the major areas of risk for the assessment of students might be said to be:

- failure to match assessment activities to learning outcomes within courses or modules;
- failure to derive grades from marking criteria;
- failure to make grading criteria transparent to students;
- failure to manage the scheduling or sheer volume of assessment for students;
- failure to provide feedback to students that is educative;
- inconsistency of assessment practice across a programme (particularly when inconsistencies are widely known and ignored);
- failure to induct or support new or part-time staff;
- failure to review, at an institutional level, the effectiveness of institutional policy on assessment, whether centrally controlled or devolved.

## QE ISSUES WITH THE ASSESSMENT OF STUDENTS

Enhancing the quality of assessment procedures also serves as a risk management strategy which might be effective in minimizing the likelihood of the potential problems identified above. This enhancement is likely to include some or all of the following measures:

- extensive sharing, collaboration and scrutiny of module intended learning outcomes as part of approval and review processes;

- resourcing and empowering academic staff to adopt good practice through for example the production of standard programme assessment briefing sheets and feedback sheets after consultation;
- encouraging students to ask for greater transparency in marking criteria;
- encouraging a culture of openness across the institution where problems and difficulties in relation to managing the bureaucracy, workload and management of assessment can be shared.

---

### Reflecting on the assessment of students

Think back to when you were a student. What information did you receive about the aims and criteria for assessments? Did you receive satisfactory feedback on your work? How much have things changed in your discipline? Are students at your institution over-assessed or under-assessed? What would you feel would be the right level of assessment? What would you say was the general perception of assessment by students at your institution or in your department?

What does the QAA subject overview report say about assessment in your discipline? Does it correspond to your own direct experience of assessment? How would you explain the common finding from subject reviews that inconsistency in feedback to students was a common feature?

To what extent do you feel that students in programmes with which you are familiar select their option modules on the basis of perceptions of the marking reputations of the module or course leader? Do students accept this as a part of academic life or are they frustrated about it? How can inconsistency in assessment practices be addressed? Would you rate it as a major priority for your department or institution?

# 12 Programme approval, monitoring and review

## THE METACODE

Section 7 of the Code, covering programme approval, monitoring and review (AMR), is of particular importance within the Code overall for several reasons. First of all, the section relates to what is in many senses the core of QA in higher education: the standards of programmes of study, which in turn reflect the defining authority of HEIs: namely the right to award degrees. Secondly, the arrangements for AMR need to incorporate systems for ensuring that other sections of the quality framework are being addressed by an HEI, such as the curriculum content (through the benchmark statements), award structures (through the FHEQ) and the management of course delivery (through other sections of the Code). In that sense this section of the Code serves as a metacode, articulating how institutions should ensure that other sections are being addressed. Thirdly, there is the issue of alignment, that is, the extent to which institutional arrangements for internal QA map onto external arrangements. This can be a general issue in the sense that both internal and external processes may seek to reflect the underlying principles of transparency, QE and quality design, but can also be a pragmatic and concrete issue, such as the exhortation by the QAA for annual programme review statements to have a format and focus which anticipates the requirements of a SED for external QAA audit. Alignment serves to reduce duplication of effort, often criticized during the comprehensive subject review cycle, but alignment has the consequence of replicating at institutional level the externally specified quality framework. Thus, although alignment may serve to reduce duplication of effort it can heighten alienation of academic staff from the QA process.

While section 7 of the Code emphasizes quite rightly that AMR systems need to be linked to and integrated with each other, it is important in terms of quality management to recognize that the skills, risks and enhancement issues in each of these components is different. Nevertheless, the existence of an overall strategy for AMR which cross references actions and review points will make mobilizing the skills, minimizing the risks and maximizing the enhancement more straightforward.

Before addressing the precepts and guidance of the AMR section, it is worth reviewing the background issues which indicate considerations which need to be borne in mind when designing AMR systems.

## MANAGING QUALITY IN APPROVAL, MONITORING AND REVIEW (AMR)

All sound course proposals are sound in similar ways, but unsound course proposals are unsound in different ways. Validation and review of programmes of study reflects several different types of decisions and these decisions need to acknowledge the differences in programmes in the context of common standards. Institutions are concerned to ensure that their programmes are of a high standard and that there are adequate resources to support them. The canonical form of a validation is the presentation by a department of a new single honours course drawing on staffing expertise within the course team for delivery. The arrangements for validation will generally reflect a number of key principles, which are explored below.

### Externality

There is an assumption that the course team must draw on sources of expertise and commentary from outside the immediate circle of those developing the provision, and that the validating institution, the awarding body, must incorporate external views on the appropriateness of the validation. Sources of expertise and commentary might be academic peers who run a similar programme elsewhere, contacts in industry or the relevant professional sector and, of course, students. In terms of programme development or review, the benefits of incorporating externality at an early stage can be significant. Academic peers can pass on lessons from mistakes learnt elsewhere. Industry contacts can identify emerging industry practices and concerns to enhance the curriculum and can identify skills needs from the employer's perspective. Students can comment on the overall clarity of the programme and the level of interest that might be shown by potential future applicants.

However, there are also potential issues around incorporating external elements in programme development. For example, there may be a conflict of interest from competing courses leaders in commenting on a new programme which may reduce their own market share. Sharing new programme design with peer academics serves to reveal a new product line in ways which would be unthinkable in the private sector. Even though the vast majority of academics are much more interested in helping peers in other institutions and developing and maintaining their credibility as professionals, there is the risk that intellectual property rights and 'time to market' advantages can be compromised. This issue is particularly acute in relation to distance learning programmes, particularly e-learning provision. The small number of practitioners and the effective eradication of market boundaries means that externality in relation to programme approval must find the right balance between peer review and support on the one hand and commercial sensitivity on the other. The involvement of external academics in the approval process is one of many contradictions in HEIs' attitudes and practices towards access to documentation. If an academic at University X phoned the academic registry at University Y and asked for a full draft of a new programme, with complete CVs and a resource analysis, the information would be refused on the grounds of commercial sensitivity. However, such information, and more, is routinely sent to external panel members for validation. The fact that in the latter case the academic panelist has been invited by the university does not make the documents any less sensitive.

All of which is not to suggest that universities should stop using external academic peers to review programmes or that commercial sensitive information should be handled more cautiously. Rather, it is noted to show up the ways in which the legacy of collegiate principles of inter-institutional academic collaboration sits uneasily alongside the commercial imperative of institutions that are also multi-million pound businesses in an increasingly competitive market.

There is also an issue in relation to the role of industry specialists in the approvals process. No single individual can easily represent experience across an entire industry sector, and views offered on graduate skills deficits, emerging markets and industry trends generally will inevitably draw heavily on the company's own experience. Private sector representatives working as owners or employees in ongoing commercial concerns will be able to offer commentaries on changes in demand for specialist products or services, while representatives from trade or sector bodies tend to be more useful for information on emerging government policy initiatives or legislative changes that are in the pipeline. One would hope, of course, that academics specializing in particular commercial markets would already be passingly familiar with most of the major trends at the sharp end. Nevertheless, for academic programmes which seek to provide graduates with skills relevant to a particular market sector, there is no substitute for an enthusiastic industry representative who can spell out business and employers' needs. Such intelligence enhances the vocational relevance of the curriculum and the overall employability of graduates and as such will make the programme not only more coherent, but more credible with both potential students and potential placement companies.

---

## Externality and market research

Externality has an interesting relationship to market research in the development of new programmes. The approach of some universities is that consultation rather than survey is the more appropriate and realistic method to get information on whether the course will work or not. In some ways it is almost like a multinational consulting the Consumers Association for their view on the suitability of a new chocolate confectionery line rather than listening to children as they eat the actual chocolate. Course development teams rarely ask potential students whether a proposed course would be attractive to them. At best existing students on similar courses are asked their views, which while better than nothing is not the same as asking someone who has got to make a choice.

---

Overall externality is an important part of QA arrangements for the approval of new programmes and the review of existing ones – as long as the different ways in which different external stakeholders relate to the proposed course needs are carefully considered in order to ensure that the most appropriate and useful information is elicited.

In practice the management of externality in approvals by universities can be poor. Documents are typically received by external stakeholders too late to comment on them and the whole exercise can appear rather too much like a box-ticking exercise. External panel members are regularly sent four or five 100–150 page documents to read less than a week before a validation or review event. External panelists have barely enough time to read the documents and make their comments at the validation event itself let alone engage in any meaningful dialogue with the course team. Since the comments are fed into a point in the process where a final decision or approval (or otherwise) is at stake, course teams can find themselves defending their final draft document rather than incorporating the suggestions of external commentators. It need hardly be added that external panelists are paid a pittance (if paid at all) for this consultancy work. It is essential that plenty of time is built into the course development schedule to enable comments from external stakeholders. Of course the reverse problem is also rife – where external stakeholders do not provide comments at all, or provide them too late, and this leaves course teams cynical about the role of external consultation.

## Procedure

Most approval systems are characterized by two properties: an assertion that validation is a process and not an event; and detailed specification of the authority of the validation panel during the validation event.

Ideally, in a mature and quality aware academic institution, the validation event should be little more than a light touch confirmation that key issues have been addressed and that the team has the resources required to deliver a decent programme of study for students. As such it will be just one part of a more extended process of careful design and preparation for the delivery of a programme of study. In practice however, the validation event drives the rest of the process. The date for the validation drives the deadlines for the other processes and given the limited time often made available for consultation by correspondence, the validation serves as the primary forum for discussion and debates on academic quality and programme development. Many institutions now operate a two-stage system. A preliminary or stage 1 validation seeks to check that basic requirements are in place such as known resource needs, a credible programme team and a basic working document for the curriculum and programme specification. The quality and detail of the responses to the conditions of this preliminary validation is one of the primary points of departure for the full or formal stage 2 validation. While the former is often managed at faculty, school or departmental level, the latter will normally be owned at university level with the chairs appointed by deans and institutional quality units respectively.

For practical purposes the idea that the preliminary validation should be a relatively informal local affair, with a more formal panel with significant external representation later, makes sense and it is difficult to envisage how it could be otherwise. However, in some ways it should be the other way around. The preliminary panel is in some ways dealing with more fundamental matters than the stage 2 validation, such as team credibility, resources and realistic market assessments. As such it needs to be more probing and more prepared to say that the proposal is misguided and should not go ahead. However, in practice such preliminary validations panels are populated by the more or less immediate peers of the course team and as such have at least a degree of conflict of interest. In some ways the true health and maturity of an institution is measured not by the rigour and robustness of the discussions and decisions of the formal panel, but by the preparedness of preliminary panels to veto further development of possibly ill-judged unrealistic programme development proposals.

## Documentation

One of the key aspects of the whole exercise of programme approval is the production of appropriate documentation. However, the documentation required and the way it is managed varies considerably from university to university. There are many types of core documents that are normally produced in relation to the approval of a new programme of study. Some institutions will require all of these but not all would necessarily be scrutinized at any full validation 'event'. The most common of these are as follows:

## Definitive course document

This document will lay down the programme structure including programme specification, details of constituent modules, entrance requirements, any academic regulations additional to institution arrangements, assessment regulations and the composition of a course committee or equivalent. The course document will also lay out the resources required by the programme and how these will be met.

## Student handbook

This document serves as the *vade mecum* for students when they join the programme. This will lay out a guide to the programme structure, assessment, modules and so on, but will also indicate support systems, library registration, student societies etc. This is increasingly used as the main documentation for validation panels as it serves to focus attention on the student experience.

## Business plan

Increasingly, course teams are being asked to develop business plans for new programmes to demonstrate the sustainability of the programme given the start-up investment the staffing requires, the number of likely students and, where appropriate, the fee they are likely to be expected to pay. Where universities run two-step procedures this area is likely to be covered in the first step with appropriate written undertakings by head of department, dean or other resource manager to confirm that the necessary resources, human and otherwise, will be available if the programme is validated. Occasionally, a short period is set aside in the main or second-step event to ensure that any queries or concerns regarding resources are properly addressed.

## Development document

Occasionally, course teams are asked to keep and submit 'logs' of the development process to demonstrate the scope and content of discussions with external stakeholders, university registry, professional bodies, students and so on. This is intended to promote and confirm the extent to which the course team has engaged in dialogue with relevant parties and with each other in a reflective manner, and in such a way as to ensure that the course development process itself has served to enhance quality. Such a document might be no more than the minutes of course development team meetings and copies of correspondence with relevant parties, but it can serve to illustrate how the team's thinking has developed over the course of the development process. In some cases, the document can provide answers to panelists as to why one particular course of action has been decided and others abandoned. Unfortunately, where the production of such documents is a requirement it can, by creating another bureaucratic burden for the course team, flood the very space it seeks to create and track. Cynically, it has been noted that the existence of such a file can serve to document, and bring attention to, voices of dissent and minority views in the development of a programme, which in turn can provide the opportunity for mischievous amusement on the part of roguish panelists.

> ## REFLECTIVE PRACTICE POINT
>
> How does your institution monitor the effectiveness of its approval and review systems? Are there criteria for the effective management of the process? To what extent is the process devolved and how does this affect how the systems work in practice?

## THE APPROVAL PROCESS

There are two fundamental tensions often apparent in the approval process. The first is the tension between on the one hand the business imperative (normally driven by heads and deans) to introduce new or revised programmes which will attract more students or at least maintain a department's student numbers, and on the other hand the need to maintain academic standards. The second tension is between the need to recognize that the vast majority of programme developments are carefully thought out and reflect sensible planning by a dedicated course team (and as such need support and the least possible amount of bureaucratic interference), and the fact that a small number of proposals are below a minimum threshold of quality and need to be aborted before they are inflicted on innocent and unsuspecting students. These two tensions are often related but not always in obvious ways. Programmes which enjoy the patronage of deans and pro-vice chancellors rarely find access to new resources problematic, and proposals for programmes which reflect traditional academic traditions rather than transient commercial imperatives are not always the most carefully thought through.

The tension between the rush to market and the need for quality is not unique to higher education, of course. In the private sector all kinds of products and services are withdrawn or hastily revised following an indecently hasty journey from the drawing board to the marketplace. In academia however, it is often the case in some areas that the market demands new courses which some institutions are not yet capable of delivering. Ironically, it can often be the new universities with traditionally closer links to industry and faster decision-making processes which are quicker to identify a new need and seek to meet it, but which lack the capacity to dedicate significant resources to meet that need. Accordingly, in new universities the ideas for products run ahead of the capacity to deliver, while in older universities the recognition of markets lags behind the resources available.

The tension between support and policing is different in character however. While every programme that is presented to first- or second-stage validation will have some feature which needs addressing, the vast majority of proposals do get validated subject to conditions being met at the formal validation. When the experience of academics in their subject area is wedded to tightly formulated specifications for which areas need to be addressed, which in turn reflects the brief for the validation panel, there should be few difficulties. However, a small number of programmes are likely not to meet a threshold level of quality at each hurdle and it is essential when designing effective approval systems that there is no likelihood of such programmes getting approved when they should not be.

## IMPLEMENTING THE PRECEPTS

*Precept 1: Institutions should ensure that their responsibilities for standards and quality are discharged effectively through their procedures for:*

- *the design of programmes;*
- *the approval of programmes;*
- *the monitoring and review of programmes.*

The key point to note in this precept, which is so fundamental that it might be overlooked, is that AMR is central to the institution's management of standards and quality. It is not just that arrangements for AMR need to be effective in general terms (including business terms) but in terms of academic standards and quality. It is worth noting this at the outset since, as we will see in consideration of other precepts, one of the central issues is ensuring that this function is discharged despite pressures pushing in the other direction. Although not explicitly stated here or in the guidance, the underlying expectation is that institutions will develop arrangements for these three areas which ensure that the procedures, practices, expectations and terminology in one of these areas articulates with those from another area.

So, how should institutions ensure that their responsibilities for standards and quality are discharged effectively in this area? The guidance emphasizes the importance of external reference, articulation with institutional mission, planning and existing provision. However, this still leaves unanswered how due account will be taken.

The key players in this area are going to be:

- The *academic board* or *senate* which has the ultimate authority in matters relating to academic standards.
- An *academic standards committee* which takes a direct role in the formulation, monitoring and review of quality issues, occasionally taking a role in confirming the appointment of external examiners or a schedule of new programme propos-

als from faculties. If authority for QA matters is significantly devolved to faculties, there will often be a faculty-based academic standards committee with a similar remit for the faculty or school in question. A university or faculty academic standards committee often has a distinctive role in relation to annual monitoring, by ensuring that faculty- or institution-wide issues are brought together because of common problems or because a broader, often institutional, response is required (in relation to computing systems for example).

- A central *quality unit* or equivalent which implements academic board or senate policy and supports the work of faculties, schools or departments in the context of any devolution of AMR arrangements.

- The *panel* for validation (approval) and review, made up of peers with varying degrees of detachment from the course team and the development, which takes time to scrutinize proposals and then, at some event, reassures itself through discussion, debate and dialogue that the appropriate academic standards will be maintained. Its judgement is then referred to faculty or quality unit as appropriate.

- A *monitoring committee* that receives the annual monitoring reports from course teams or equivalent which ensure that course teams are maintaining academic standards, that threats to academic standards are being addressed, and that due consideration is being taken of annual external examiners' reports, student course evaluations and employers' fora as appropriate. This may be a committee convened purely for the purpose of receiving annual course reports or it may be a faculty or school academic standards committee sitting in 'special session'. In some smaller institutions this would be done on an institution-wide basis by one committee.

Additionally, there needs to be a set of documents that define the policy for AMR. In relation to approval there needs to be at a minimum:

- An overarching statement of the QA arrangements for approval (and review) which will normally lay out the sequence of steps for approval, the responsibilities of key individuals or units, the information required for submission, and the normal timetable for each annual cycle of approval. Additionally, where QA arrangements are decentralized, clear statements should be given as to the reciprocal responsibilities of the central and local units. The overall statement should explain how the other documents should be used.

- A series of templates (preferably available in electronic form) which ensures that information requested is submitted in a standard fashion, consistent across all programmes and limited to relevant areas. If properly designed these templates can reduce paperwork by focusing only on those areas where information is required. Templates may be produced for areas such as programme specifications, module information, franchise arrangements and details of external commercial partners.

- A protocol for the composition, authority and frame of reference for validation and review panels. Particular clarity is required on the role of the chair.
- Any special arrangements for the validation of distance learning, overseas, franchise, jointly accredited or subdegree provision.
- A handbook of guidance for all parties expected to participate in the approval and review process that describes in non-technical language the aims and procedures involved. Particular sections of this may be particularly useful for student representatives, employers or other non-academics.

It is increasingly common to find all of the above documents on university intranets, an arrangement which serves several aims. First of all there is no dispute over which version of a document is current (assuming the Web site is properly maintained), course developers can rapidly get copies of key documents and templates, and through the use of hyperlinks the relation between documents and strategies can be clearly presented.

In relation to external reference points it is essential that submissions for new proposals clearly demonstrate how the proposed programme draws on the relevant benchmark statement. However, it should be noted that benchmark statements are broadly disciplinary-based and therefore not necessarily directly relevant to inter-disciplinary programmes. The benchmark statements apply principally to undergraduate provision and therefore alternative benchmarks are required for subdegree and postgraduate provision. To comply with the FHEQ should not be problematic. All that is required is that a clear statement is made of where the qualification falls and how through the programme specification the relevant descriptors are addressed.

Reference to PSBs in relation to curriculum should be covered by the SBSs, since professional bodies have been heavily involved in their construction. However, care needs to be taken that any PSB requirement regarding delivery is taken into account. Some PSBs still have requirements in areas that validation panels nowadays pay limited attention to such as specific SSRs (staff–student ratios), the number of hours spent in particular learning environments (for example the workplace, the laboratory or the classroom), the qualifications of staff and the entry qualification of students. The appropriate way to manage this is to ensure that the proposal is seen by as wide a range of peers and practitioners as possible.

In terms of documentation, a list of these points can provide an agenda for the validation or review panel and for the yearly monitoring report. For the validation and review arrangements the chair of the panel might be required to sign off a statement that these areas have been addressed to the satisfaction of the panel. In terms of monitoring, it can be useful to encourage course leaders to address these areas in the context of recent or anticipated developments in the PSB requirements and what the course team is doing to ensure that the appropriate curricular or delivery arrangements are being amended as required.

Ensuring that the programme is compatible with the university's mission or goals is an interesting area. It is difficult to think of programme proposals for any institution that were not *compatible* with an institution's mission, even if they do not address directly the distinctive areas of its mission. While some institutions emphasize widening participation as a pivotal part of their strategy and mission, that does not mean that they will not validate specialist masters programmes or taught doctorates, or that they would not put on programmes which would primarily attract highly qualified applicants on a national or international basis. Equally, universities with explicitly research-led missions still often provide access programmes and courses designed to attract local students. Finally, while universities with a business and vocational orientation would probably think twice about putting on medieval studies, there is no reason why they should not, and should not do so successfully. It is difficult to see what value this guidance adds to the section, especially if we set aside cynical interpretations about policing mission drift.

Ensuring that there is appropriate strategic, academic and resource planning requires two types of information to be in place: 1) the context of the overall strategy for academic development and associated resource allocation system; and 2) an analysis of how the particular proposal or review is located within that context. Further, it is not enough that a university has an academic strategy: that strategy has to be seen to be widely owned and make an active contribution to course development, monitoring and review. In terms of resources, the key issue is that the institution needs to have a system whereby the resource needs of new or revised proposals can be identified, and resource managers can make decisions on whether the resources can be released for that purpose, in the context of other competing priorities. There also needs to be a system in place whereby the extent to which promised resources have in fact been released following validation can be incorporated into annual monitoring arrangements. More generally, at an institutional level there needs to be a clear strategy that clarifies how resources are allocated to departments, how departments know what resources they are likely to receive well in advance of the academic year and how continuity of provision is maintained in the eventuality of shortfall in departmental recruitment.

It is widely recognized that institutions have limited resources but there is an expectation that institutions should have systems for managing those resources effectively and in accordance with their academic strategy. It is not the business of quality auditors to assess the resourcing levels of individual institutions, but there is a need to demonstrate that there are procedures for ensuring that new developments are not approved without adequate resources and that course teams are aware of those procedures and how to engage with them.

The guidance to institutions to take into account existing provision within the institution can be taken to relate to three separate areas. First of all there is the obvious area of duplication. Depending on the configuration of departments, schools or faculties there is a danger that similar or overlapping programmes will be offered in different parts of the institution. This is particularly likely where there is significant devolution of validation authority with a concomitant reduction in central academic planning. Occasionally, programmes are revised through local 'minor change' arrangements which leads to drift in the character of the programme while leaving the programme specification untouched. Curriculum areas where duplication is likely are access programmes, IT programmes (especially business information systems programmes), media, social policy/sociology and psychology/counselling/health studies. This needs to be managed through an annual planning cycle that requires expressions of intent by all relevant parties. The second aspect of this area of guidance relates to expansions and developments within modular schemes and there are several issues here, including the possible subject combinations, the progression arrangements in the context of prerequisites and co-requisites and duplication with existing provision at the modular level. Finally, in the context of review, an issue will be whether there are proposals for abandoning certain modules or courses as they no longer meet the needs of the students on the programme. If other courses have adopted such modules, there is a need for consultation about the proposed decommissioning with all affected departments.

## REFLECTIVE PRACTICE POINT

What is the general view of academic staff in your institution about the bureaucracy that surrounds approval and monitoring? Is it considered too heavy or appropriate? What about the paperwork around review? Is that felt to be unnecessarily detailed or appropriate? If opinions are that the processes are too bureaucratic, how does this affect attitudes towards QA in general?

## *Authority*

*Precept 2: Institutions should ensure that the overriding responsibility of the academic authority (eg senate or academic board) to set, maintain and assure standards is respected and that any delegation of power by the academic authority to approve or review programmes is properly defined and exercised.*

With the growth in student numbers and the programmes they pursue, it has become increasingly necessary for university sovereign bodies to delegate authority within their institution. The increasing scrutiny on how institutions manage the quality of their programmes has meant that proposals going through on the nod after a perfunctory discussion at academic board is not good enough. As QA matters have been taken more seriously it became clear that for any real evaluation of proposals to be done significant devolution would be required. In larger institutions much QA work has been devolved to school or faculty level. Devolution to departments within schools or faculties is rare and devolution is not always total.

Although there may be a requirement for a summative report to be submitted to a central academic standards committee, the monitoring element of programmes is almost always devolved locally. Review is also typically devolved and it is now common for the initial approval to be devolved also. Although institutions will vary in their practice, authority to approve new overseas franchises and distance learning programmes is typically not devolved (though the authority to monitor and review normally is). Some institutions have engaged in a rolling programme of review with different functions gradually devolved to faculties. In some cases the devolution happens faster in some areas than others, leaving a not always satisfactory hybrid arrangement in place, which becomes particularly problematic with interfaculty proposals.

The appointment of external examiners is an area where there is still significant variation across the sector in terms of devolution of authority. In practice external examiners are approached, nominated and approved at school or faculty level before being confirmed by the quality unit under powers delegated to it by academic board or senate, either directly or through an academic standards committee.

All of these arrangements are in principle satisfactory. The issue is to ensure that the arrangements are clearly documented and widely understood. They must also be shown to be working effectively in practice, with evidence that there are systems for monitoring their effectiveness, and safety nets are in place should things go seriously wrong. Irrespective of the extent and form of devolution the role of the central quality unit is fundamental. Not only will it be closely involved in supporting (even if not servicing) the work of the local units, it will be required to report to the sovereign body on the effectiveness of the current arrangements and make proposals for alterations to any schedule for further devolution. And of course the unit will be directly involved in effecting those aspects of AMR not devolved.

It should not be forgotten that in some institutions, as is the case with some HEIs which lack their own degree awarding powers (or choose to use devolved powers from others), the sovereign body within the institution is not the sovereign body for quality, but the senate or academic board of a different institution. Issues of further devolution within the institution will of course not only have to be handled carefully but will almost certainly be subject to the approval of the degree awarding institution. In such cases the college academic board will need to reassure itself that the devolved arrangements are meeting its own QA needs.

As will be discussed in more detail later it is clearly important that whatever the arrangements are for devolution of AMR authority, the sovereign body needs to have a system in place for monitoring that devolution. This system will need to include some view on what successful devolution actually looks like. Is a system in which all proposals are successfully validated successful or not?

## *Externality*

*Precept 3: Institutions should ensure that the approval and review of programmes involves appropriate persons who are external to the design and delivery of the programme. Such contributions should be sought in a way that will promote confidence that the standards and quality of the programmes are appropriate.*

The principle of externality in universities is almost as old as the idea of the university itself. University visitors, often from the Church, and latterly external examiners, have one way or another made contributions to institutional judgements on standards. The new university sector had the benefit of compulsory externality under the arrangements for polytechnics and their relationship with the CNAA for degree awarding powers, and with local authorities, until the 1988 Act made them independent corporate bodies. The precept here explicitly identifies academic peers, external advisors, any programme partners (for example in the case of collaborative provision) and any relevant PSB as potential points of external consultation.

The contribution of academic peers from within the institution but outside the discipline is often underestimated. They will have knowledge of institutional mission and contexts generally but will normally be disinterested parties. They will of course have some degree of insider knowledge on the potential limitations of an area, being familiar possibly with the track record of the sponsoring department. Counterbalancing this of course is the fact that these peers will themselves be studied through the quality lens at some future date. Rather than draw upon internal academic peers in an *ad hoc* fashion, often at the 11th hour, some institutions have established approval and review panel members who commit to a number of such events over the course of the academic year.

Academic external advisors from other disciplines are an important part of the general assurance that programmes are of comparable standard and maintain an appropriate level of currency. We have discussed in the introduction to this chapter the tensions and contradictions that can exist in the role of the external academic advisor. The role is an attractive one to many academics as the description on the CV takes up about as much space as an entry for an external examinership but the external advisor role involves considerably less work. It is a simple way of finding out what other departments are doing, developing professional relationships and picking up examples of good practice. For those in the market for such roles, external panel membership offers opportunities to acquire external examining responsibilities. However, most institutions officially frown on the idea that external panelists are potential external examiners, for the simple reason that panelists should have no vested interest in the outcome of the validation. But many panelists do not see it this way and course teams and institutions are happy to collude in the practice.

The contribution of POs (such as FECs or overseas universities) to approval or review in the context of proposed collaborative provision is important and distinctive. Where there is a proposal for collaborative provision the collaborating institution (the PO) accepts that it has to reassure the host university (the AI) that it will operate according to the systems and standards specified. While there is in some cases significant value that can be added to the scrutiny process through examples of good practice, the role of potential collaboration must inevitably remain one where the PO is answering questions about the provision rather than posing them. We must distinguish here of course between franchise proposals and joint validation proposals. In joint validation proposals (where a proposal is being jointly validated by two institutions) there will be a role for both partners to scrutinize the nature of collaboration and how quality will be protected.

Participation of PSBs in validation and review has become increasingly well specified since the advent of the QAA. Different PSBs take different roles in validation in ways which reflect their relationship with the discipline. In medicine, nursing and other professions allied to medicine, the statutory responsibility of professional bodies means that the programme has to be approved by them in order for successful completion of the programme to confer the relevant professional recognition. In law the Law Society will visit provision over a set period of time and review resources and the student experience. Recently the British Psychological Society has developed its recognition procedures to move away from a once-and-for-all, paper-based approval of curriculum and resources at the launch of a programme, and towards a rolling programme of visits. Often PSB representatives will sit on approval panels in order that the one approval event and process can serve both needs and to avoid duplication and unnecessary burden. It is rare for the institution and the PSB not to agree on the outcome. This is unfortunate since the scope for high drama and teeth gnashing is considerable. As mentioned earlier, PSBs often find themselves seeking to outdo the HEI in terms of standards since they wish to maintain their credibility in a period of QA reform, but also because they recognize that institutions have a vested interest in ensuring that often high demand, lucrative, professionally recognized programmes get through.

## Transparency

*Precept 4: Approval and review processes should be clearly described and communicated to those who are involved with them.*

The aim of this precept is to ensure that there is no mystery or mystique to the processes of AMR. This is particularly true when stakeholders such as employers and students are involved in the process in a partial way; they do have a right to know how their contribution fits into the overall picture. One issue however, is that making principles and procedures clear to the wide range of stakeholders involved in AMR will mean different kinds of explanations. A single set of guidelines may not be enough.

Clearly identified roles and responsibilities for approval and review is an important part of any QA system that seeks to be robust and effective. However, there are hidden problems in some areas related to role descriptions, diverse provision and programme structures. First, key academic roles often have different descriptions in different areas of an institution, especially if the institution is large and if subunits are not of uniform size and structure. Second, academic regulations are usually drawn up often implicitly and inadvertently to reflect undergraduate single honours provision wholly located within a single department. Even where all provision is modular the difference between single honours provision and combined honours provision can lead to ambiguities, duplication or gaps. This can cause problems for AMR when insufficient attention is paid to the different kinds of responsibilities that occur in combined honours schemes. A common issue is that combined honours do not have course leaders but rather subject leaders who are not always responsible for the students' overall programme. Similarly, responsibilities for QA often fall particularly on the relevant head of department or dean even though a student's programme may stretch across two or three departments or faculties. (Similar issues can arise in relation to student complaints and discipline procedures.)

A further problem can arise when programme approval and review documentation assumes that all proposals for new provision are for the establishment of new awards. In combined honours programmes new areas may be set up as joint or minor subjects which do not in themselves create a new award, but rather offer new elements which can be incorporated with other subject elements already validated into existing awards. Institutions with sizeable and growing combined honours programmes almost certainly need to have separate though comparable documentation for such provision. Difficulties which can arise otherwise include panels struggling to know what to do with institutional injunctions that 'all new undergraduate provision must reflect relevant QAA benchmark statements' – a requirement that a new minor subject designed to offer only one third of a degree programme will be hard pressed to meet. Similarly, in combined honours schemes, annual monitoring reports tend to be at the subject or overall programme level, with no review or monitoring of the experience of students on specific combinations. This is a perennial and widespread problem because issues of overlap and inconsistencies of expectation between areas are rarely explicitly addressed in monitoring even though they can be significant issues for the students pursuing particular combinations.

It has always been clear, to the providers at least, that combined honours programmes do not attempt to offer curricular integration of two or more areas of study (even if prospectuses do nothing to disabuse students of that misconception). However, it does not follow from this that there is not a responsibility to monitor the overall student experience, an experience which is more than the sum of its modular parts. In combined honours the programme is the scheme which encompasses theoretically many hundreds if not thousands of combinations. It is impossible for each of these combinations to be separately monitored but some recognition of the QA issues needs to be addressed within the monitoring arrangements. Often the experience of 'subject' students in a discipline can be lost within the larger cohort of combined honours students and their experience of working across two or more departments is not regularly monitored. As institutional audit increasingly incorporates direct evaluations of the learning experience by students themselves, institutions are going to face queries, comments and complaints about issues about which their QA systems know almost nothing – the experience of students on combined modular programmes.

The final note of guidance here – that institutions should consider 'how staff development strategies and activities may include the dissemination of good practice in relation to programme design, approval and review' – seeks to ensure that AMR is seen as a set of professional skills which can be developed, and may be effectively developed through peer discussion. Here as elsewhere in discussions of staff development however there is an assumption that there exists a consensus on basic principles of course design, approval and review and that good practice is self-evidently identifiable. In truth many claims about assessment load, attendance requirements, scope of student support and for that matter basic academic standards in higher education are contentious.

## Programme design

*Precept 5: Institutions should publish guidance, for use within the institution, on principles to be considered when programmes are designed.*

As with many precepts, the meaning of this is made clearer when the guidance notes are considered. Here the meaning is that institutions should be unambiguous about what needs to be submitted for scrutiny by validation and review panels. The guidelines here almost spell out the sections for a validation document. It is worth considering in some detail how the precept and guidance here relate to current and potential institutional practice in the area of approval.

Most of the areas covered by the guidance under the programme design precept are aspects already covered by institutions in their approval and monitoring policies. Few institutions if any would fail to specify that validation panels should see reference to the institution's mission, information on the aims, level, qualifications of the programme, completion opportunities, and resource needs. However, the emphasis now given to progression, curricular coherence and to learning outcomes is probably more than most institutions have given to this area in the past. The explicit guidance on negotiated programmes, by which is meant both combined modular programmes and open content masters programmes, is new and demands particular attention.

The guidance in appendix 2 of the Code is provided as general outline guidance of the parameters for effective programme design. However, it is also designed to serve as a set of principles for guidance given to students on negotiated programmes. The same set of principles therefore is seeking to achieve the same end through two very different routes. Given that the process of approval is very different from the process of academic counselling for students, we will have to look carefully to see how effective these principles are likely to be in these two very different contexts. As well as referring to 'negotiated' programmes, the appendix refers to 'interdisciplinary' and 'innovative' programmes. These are of course by no means co-extensive categories so it is important that we consider these principles in each of these contexts separately. Table 12.1 lays out in detail what some of the implications of the criteria are for negotiated, interdisciplinary and 'innovative' programmes.

*Precept 6: Institutions should ensure that programme approval decisions are informed by full consideration of academic standards and the quality of the learning opportunities. The final decision to approve a programme should be taken by the academic authority, or a body acting on its behalf. The body should be independent of the academic department, or other unit that will offer the programme, and have access to any necessary specialist advice.*

The areas identified in the guidance as important for any approval process to engage with are not controversial and reflect what the vast majority of validation panels would normally consider and have been covering for many years. However, the way in which these areas are now considered very much reflects the emergence of the 'quality infrastructure' that has recently emerged. The design principles outlined above, the FHEQ, the SBSs and the Code itself all figure prominently in addressing the issues raised at validation. It is interesting that one of the areas foregrounded here is the anticipated demand for the programme, which in a sense is not directly a quality issue at all. Of course problems can arise where demand for a programme is so low that there is insufficient income for the programme to pay for the resources required and therefore the programme requires subsidy from other areas, a situation not conducive to the maintenance of standards in the longer term.

The precept seeks to identify the core considerations, which the approval process needs to take into account when validating a programme of study. However, not all approval events involve new programmes. Some involve the approval of additional subjects within modular programmes, which are not in themselves programmes.

## *Monitoring and review*

*Precept 7: Institutions should monitor the effectiveness of their programmes:*

- *to ensure that programmes remain current and valid in the light of developing knowledge in the discipline, and practice in its application;*
- *to evaluate the extent to which the intended learning outcomes are being attained by students;*
- *to evaluate the continuing effectiveness of the curriculum and of assessment in relation to the intended learning outcomes;*
- *to ensure that appropriate actions are taken to remedy any identified shortcomings.*

**Table 12.1** Relationship between negotiated, interdisciplinary and 'innovative' programmes and QAA criteria for programme design

| QAA Criterion | Negotiated (eg combined honours) | Interdisciplinary | Innovative |
|---|---|---|---|
| Level | The constraints of the scheme will specify that modules must be drawn from those available at a certain level. This will be built into the structure of the subject provision | Given that a level is 'an indicator of the relative demand, complexity, depth of study and learner autonomy involved in a programme' consideration should be given to ways in which interdisciplinarity makes greater demands intellectually than comparable intradisciplinary programmes at ostensibly the same level. There may be here also a lack of accessible learning materials covering the interrelationship between disciplines | If genuinely innovative it may be the case that the level of intellectual demand is underestimated. Tutors themselves may in the early periods of delivery need time to revise pedagogic strategies. Additionally, there may be here also a lack of accessible learning materials, such as textbooks, at the right level for students. This may mean that learning outcomes may be more challenging than initially assumed |
| Progression | Progression in terms of curricular content will be built into modules in terms of prerequisites. There may be issues on skills progression since the skill development strategy for two subjects may be quite different | Progression in interdisciplinary programmes should address the staged intellectual challenge of developing a mastery of the interdisciplinarity itself, including deeper appreciation of the relationship between disciplinary perspectives, complementary epistemologies and methodologies and how this relates to progression in terms of content *per se* | Programmes which offer genuine curricular innovation face the challenge of identifying the necessary skills, knowledge and methods required as adequate *preparation* for any given stage. There is a risk that the preparedness required will be underestimated because the challenge at higher levels is itself underestimated. Progression then is seen as less problematic than is in fact the case |
| Balance | Modular schemes in general and combined programmes in particular offer students the chance to create personalized balanced programmes. The academic/ practical and the personal/outcomes balances are important to students. Breadth/depth is less important while interest/employability is a further area of balance | The key balance for interdisciplinary programmes is between breadth and depth: eg area studies requires careful consideration of the relative emphasis on economic, cultural and historical dimensions and thematic coverage. Ways of managing the balance include breadth in core and depth in options, and offering and requiring depth in the final year dissertation | Innovative programmes tend to be in the vocational and personal development areas rather than the academic. It might be important therefore that the innovation is counter-balanced by core academic knowledge and traditional transferable skills |

**Table 12.1** continued

| QAA Criterion | Negotiated (eg combined honours) | Interdisciplinary | Innovative |
|---|---|---|---|
| Flexibility | Clearly modular schemes and highly flexible – that is their strength and their weakness. Quite apart from the difficult issue of balancing flexibility with coherence (below) is the issue of flexibility constrained not by coherence or other academic considerations, but through pragmatism reflected in artificial prerequisites and timetabling to keep numbers down and exclude combined honours students | Interdisciplinary programmes are often themed around a single topic (eg American studies, Victorian studies, peace studies, women's studies) or vocational focus (occupational therapy, speech therapy). Students needs in the former are more diverse than in the latter. PSBs constrain the amount of flexibility in some cases | Innovative programmes will want to be flexible as the area of study will itself be likely to be fluid and with little history of research or curriculum development. There is unlikely to be a benchmark statement. Programmes such as entrepreneurship, computer games, development or surfing studies will in any case draw on a core of common traditional foundational modules in business studies, programming and engineering |
| Coherence | Coherence within constituent components is managed through subject level prerequisites and core-option structures. Coherence across subjects is not necessarily desirable or possible. Coherence should not be confused with complementarity which while elective could be both desirable and feasible | Coherence in interdisciplinary studies is in one sense almost guaranteed through the common focus on a particular topic or vocation. The challenge is to ensure that the contribution of contributing disciplines is presented in a coherent fashion. While conflicting interpretations are to be welcomed in many cases in the humanities this may be less welcome in the sciences. The extent to which ontological, epistemological and methodological assumptions are divergent is an important part of an interdisciplinary programme | Innovative programmes can run the danger of bringing together what is available rather than what is ideal. The contributions from different existing courses or modules, existing staff and existing learning resources, designed, hired and bought for different programmes while in many ways often worthy of support and encouragement, needs to be set in a framework of a coherent educational experience for students |

**Table 12.1** continued

| QAA Criterion | Negotiated (eg combined honours) | Interdisciplinary | Innovative |
|---|---|---|---|
| Integrity | While modular and combined subject provision is promoted as being flexible, the impression can be given that any subject can be combined with any other and clearly resource limitations, timetable constraints and prerequisite stipulations mean that this can not always be the case. Students need also to have it made clear to them that combining X and Y does not mean an integrated course drawing together the insights of both disciplines. Students enrolling on combined honours law and psychology and expecting three years of illumination into the interpersonal dynamics of juries, the personality of criminals or the non-verbal behaviour of policemen are likely to be sorely disappointed. And irony upon irony, where such genuinely psychology of law or legal psychology modules do exist they are likely to exist as option modules which for timetable and prerequisite reasons are available to single honours students only | The promotion of interdisciplinary programmes is not particularly problematic. Students will be attracted by the opportunity to study an interesting topic from a number of disciplines and will normally get the chance to do just that. The threat to integrity comes only where the need to develop a basic competence in the underlying disciplines is understated: eg science interdisciplinary programmes are sometimes attractive to students who are uncomfortable with the perceived mathematical nature of traditional science subjects, but those students may not fully realize there is still a need for numerical skills (such as in forensic science or food technology) | The danger with innovative programmes is that they will oversell themselves. There is probably a need to advise applicants that although the programme may have been developed directly to meet the emerging needs of employers, that the programme will have not yet established its credibility in the market place. As always this can be offset by emphasizing the key transferable skills which the programme provides as well as any additional skills or knowledge which characterizes the programme as distinctive |
| Reference points | Curricular reference points from benchmark statements should be built in the subject module structure. Attempts to address benchmarks by selecting combinations of subjects is misguided and should be avoided. Special considerations may have to be borne in mind. Students who wish to pursue teacher training will want to ensure that their programme has adequate coverage in the core national curriculum subjects | The reference point for interdisciplinary programmes may well include benchmark statements since many interdisciplinary programmes do have a benchmark statement (eg area studies, communication studies). Interdisciplinary subject associations also publish outline syllabi partly to promote the development of the area. Comparison with other successful programmes can also be beneficial | In a sense a truly and entirely innovative programme would have very limited reference points. In reality it can be useful for a new type of programme to reference itself to cognate areas if only simply to show what it is not. Typically a programme might be innovative in one or two aspects and can still reference itself in terms of those elements which are less radical. Of particular interest is the (critical) referencing of programmes from overseas |

*Precept 8: Institutions should periodically review the continuing validity and relevance of programme aims and intended learning outcomes.*

Programme monitoring, sometimes referred to at programme level in different institutions as an 'annual course report' or 'annual monitoring report' typically involves a review of the previous 12 months of the programme incorporating external examiners' comments, student feedback and consideration of statistical data such as progress from year 1 to year 2 and final degree classifications. Progress on the action plan from the previous year will be reviewed and new actions will be identified to address any threats to QA and to bring opportunities for enhancement. The process will normally involve a report for each named award or cluster of cognate awards, a synoptic departmental or discipline report and a discussion with a departmental, school, or faculty quality committee. The action points can include actions for the course team in relation to amending assessments of the curriculum, staff development, organizational matters or referral of an issue to a university-wide quality committee. The danger here is that issues referred up to institutional committees or to central services get lost, or are perceived as getting lost, down some bottomless institutional bureaucratic pit. It is essential therefore that some kind of response is made when issues are referred forward in this way.

Programme review is often thought of as a form of revalidation and often takes place over five-year cycles (hence the name quinquennial review in some institutions). Much of what has been outlined above in relation to validation is relevant here, except of course that there will now be significant experience of running the programme to draw upon. As institutions have come to take the annual monitoring process more seriously there are often very few changes made at review. However, by the same token as implied by the guidance, if annual monitoring has led to incremental change to the programme and its organization, the review process provides a valuable opportunity to consider and reflect on how the programme has changed since validation. In some pre-1992 institutions initial validation was considered to be effectively permanent approval for the programme and so the need for formal review or revalidation did not technically arise. This has however been identified as an area where practice needs to be revisited and most institutions now have some system in place. In post-1992 institutions, partly as a legacy of CNAA practice, initial validations were limited to five or seven years and so the need for review was built in to the process.

*Precept 9: Institutions should evaluate the effectiveness of programme approval, monitoring and review practices.*

The guidance notes here suggest that institutions should consider the benefits for staff and students of the AMR process, the impact on enhancement and opportunities to improve the efficiency and effectiveness of the processes. However, it may be appropriate for institutions to assess the burdens as well as the benefits, the impact on QA as well as on QE and what the criteria are for effective processes in this area. In reviewing AMR procedures there are probably two specific additional considerations which institutions might wish to bear in mind. First, approval and review should probably be separated from monitoring in terms of any overall evaluation of the processes (though of course there are links). Second, an evaluation needs to be part of an overall strategy and resultant priorities for AMR in the institution. Is the institution determined to avoid any kind of quality disaster? Is the institution trying to reduce bureaucracy? Is the institution seeking greater participation in quality issues by more staff?

## QA ISSUES WITH AMR

The area of AMR is designed to establish, monitor and maintain academic quality at the programme level. Nevertheless, as a process itself it is also liable to quality failures. These can be difficult to pin down in specific terms but the following problems can arise:

- failure to manage the participation of external stakeholders in the approval or review process, either in terms of timely administration management, identifying the distinctive contribution different external stakeholders can make or engaging them in the process, rather than just the event;
- failure to ensure that conditions set by validations panels are met or monitored;
- failure to apply to combined, interdisciplinary or innovative programmes the same level of scrutiny in approval or monitoring as traditional programmes;
- failure to support combined, interdisciplinary or innovative programmes in ways which acknowledge their distinctiveness;
- failure to ensure baseline consistency in AMR in the context of devolution;
- failure to provide sufficient staff development or administrative support for chairs of approval panels;
- failure to manage the issues referred centrally by programmes of departments;
- failure to maintain the credibility of the monitoring process in the context of overly detailed report requirements and a lack of transparency of audiences and response responsibilities.

## QE ISSUES WITH AMR

Although identified as an aspect of the monitoring of AMR itself in the guidance, this area is not normally thought of as one that contributes to enhancement. However, there are several ways in which the process can contribute to programmes based on generic developments if managed and supported appropriately. In order to facilitate enhancement through the AMR arrangements, institutions might wish to consider the following:

- proactively treating internal staff participation in approvals and review events as staff development, with in-house support for learning for validations, support for personal learning targets, mentoring and reflexive development;
- ensuring that good practice for approval or monitoring activities is widely circulated, possibly in an annual publication to all staff, rather than burying the information in extended overview reports;
- raising the status of AMR activities and recognizing that different levels of quality exist in AMR activities;
- making provision for new or less experienced members of staff to attend approval and review events as observers;
- making provision for potential chairs of AMR processes to discuss good practice with experienced chairs in an occasional forum;
- ensuring that AMR is seen as a corporate priority with clear standards, strategies and outcomes. The vice principal or pro vice chancellor with responsibility for this area should make an annual report to staff on progress and developments in this area, such as might be done for research, estates, finance, ICT or teaching and learning.

---

## Reflecting on AMR

How does your institution draw on employers and employers' organizations as part of approval and monitoring? How does your institution evaluate the benefits of this input? How are differences in opinion amongst employers or between employers and academics managed within the process?

How can potential tensions between programme design criteria be reconciled? Which criteria are more important than others? How adequately do the criteria capture the curriculum and associated issues for negotiated, interdisciplinary and innovative programmes? Would you add any additional criteria for these areas?

How is devolution of approval managed in your institution? How well does it balance the autonomy of the school or faculty with accountability?

How effective as a staff development opportunity is participation as an internal panel member in the approval or review process? In what ways could this development opportunity be improved?

Does your institution make provision for students to be members of validation or review panels? Is this opportunity often taken up? What kinds of briefing or training would be appropriate for this role and to what extent is this provided?

Would it be possible to approve a programme purely over the Internet without a validation event? If not, why not?

# 13 | Career education information and guidance (CEIG)

Ask any student on any programme of study to explain his or her motivation and there is a fair chance that the answer will be to get a good or better job.

## FROM GUIDANCE TO EMPLOYABILITY

In the past, career education, information and guidance (CEIG) for most graduates sat outside the curriculum and was given little attention until the final year of study. Participation was often limited to collecting a schedule for the annual 'milk round'. Today however 'employability' is a central concept for students, employers and universities themselves. Universities know that applicants, parents and employers all pay particular attention to the graduate employment column in newspaper league tables. In parallel with the increased public information on employment indicators, CEIG has grown more complex and has become more closely integrated with programme content. Key skills, curricular focus and teaching input will all reflect the consensus on the need for students to enter the world of work with something useful to offer. Additionally, issues around student access to customized information that is relevant and up to date have been revolutionized with developments in IT that have changed the whole practice of CEIG. With this shift from narrow, extracurricular, reactive CEIG arrangements to a complex, integrated, proactive and student-centred and more strategic approach, the focus on QA and QE have been in the foreground.

---

### Quality issues in CEIG

Key quality questions in this area might include: How can we be sure that students are getting the right kind of advice at the right time? How does a

---

prospective student know how relevant to his or her career aspirations a particular course of study might be? How effective is a university at ensuring that all students are able to take useful skills to the workplace? How are students with disabilities catered for?

Section 8 of the Code, which covers CEIG, recognizes that the nature of student employability and the sector's understanding of it has changed radically over the last decade or so. No longer is employability seen in the narrow terms of simply doing a vocational rather than non-vocational programme of study, or even mapping graduate skills onto employers' needs. Increasingly there is the realization that employability is something that students and graduates need to actively manage and construct throughout a programme of study and over the course of their active working lifetime. Specifically, according to the Code they need to 'develop the skills to manage their own career including the abilities to reflect and review, to plan and make decisions, to use information resources effectively, to create and take opportunities, and to make provision for lifelong learning' (para 8). Given this more dynamic model of employability, effective management of CEIG requires a much greater awareness by institutions of the need to plan CEIG provision holistically and coordinate support mechanisms to integrate the different locations and processes.

## ORGANIZATIONAL ISSUES IN SUPPORTING CEIG

It is important in understanding CEIG to understand how it is institutionally organized. The relationship between the institution's departments and its careers service is particularly crucial of course and can be fraught. There are at least two types of problem in this area. The first is the relationship between the careers service and departments with strongly vocational or employer-led programmes. The department may feel that CEIG is superfluous as the students are clear in their minds about what they want to do and in any event the 'real' expertise is in the departments. While there is often some truth in this, there are other considerations. For example, effective CEIG can help graduates get the post they want within the career they have chosen. In reviews of vocational provision the most penetrating question is not *how many* of your students in nursing/teacher training/occupational therapy eventually get jobs in the profession but rather – *how long* did it take them to find a post, *how far* do they travel to work etc?

Additionally, in terms of lifelong learning, students in areas with high employability do not necessarily stay in the profession permanently, as any PGCE graduate will confirm. A further issue is that in some courses with clear links to specific professions students sometimes have a poor sense of the labour market demand. This is particularly true in law, psychology, journalism, media studies and forensic science where high levels of student interest in the highly competitive related professions can sometimes be counterproductive in terms of CEIG.

The second type of issue is in those areas where the programme of study in curricular terms has no obvious specific vocational dimension at all – particularly in the humanities. In the past, students of these subjects, when they thought about employment, if they thought about it much at all, would think in terms of teaching or public sector administration. More recently there has been a recognition that even in traditional humanities programmes graduates possess a wide range of key skills in relation to document management, communication, evidence evaluation, judgement and time management. To this has been added opportunities to develop ICT, interpersonal and project skills. Consideration of the SBSs in these areas highlights the changes in expectations of academic communities about the employability of its graduates in recent years. Nevertheless, the challenge in this area can be in relation to skills such as numeracy, which few humanities students would develop significantly in the normal course of events. Some academic departments take the view that numeracy is not an essential skill in humanities programmes and therefore there is no need to make provision for it. This has to be assessed in the context of institutional commitments that all graduates will possess a certain skill set.

A further issue, and one on which departments and careers services can work on together, is helping students realize what skills they actually possess and presenting evidence of these to potential employers. Managing quality in this area involves ensuring that student expectations, tutor advice, curriculum design and specialist careers services are able to work together to achieve aims which reflect the needs of students.

## PROGRESS FILES

Students' own sense of skill development will be helped with the introduction of progress files. Most institutions have taken some time to make any progress with progress files. This initiative needs to be integrated into the curriculum and therefore needs to be built into validation and review processes. Updating course developers' 'toolkits' and guidance, and institutional briefings for validation and review panel chairs need to be revised. The development of effective progress files requires some staff development, as these are a relatively new initiative in higher education.

A progress file contains an academic transcript and a personal record of learning and achievement, and of the planning for those achievements, all of which are created and supported by personal development planning (PDP) systems. While the transcript element has been in place since 2002–03, the PDP element is expected to be in place by 2005–06. The aim of the transcript is 'to improve the quality and consistency of information on the learning and achievement of individual students in higher education for the benefit of everyone who has an interest in such information' (Guidelines for HE Progress Files, Appendix 3). 'The progress file is an important element of the new policy framework being created to help make the outcomes or results of learning in higher education more explicit. In doing so, it is argued, the quality of learning will be improved (because students are clearer about what is expected of them and what they, in turn, might expect), and the basis for academic standards will be clearer' (Guidelines for HE Progress Files, Introduction ).

## SCOPE AND FOCUS OF CEIG – ENHANCEMENT ISSUES

Careers services are more flexible in their approaches to differentiated student constituencies than they have been in the past. However, the culture, structure and internal university management expectations for CEIG are such that much policy development and assessments of the quality of service are based around the following assumption – the principal client for CEIG services is a young, white, able-bodied, full-time, campus-based student who is following a degree programme with a view to securing a long-term position immediately with a large company. Many aspects of this assumption are reflected in the Code despite the precepts relating to inclusivity. Systems and institutional developments further assume that securing employment is essentially a process of acquiring key transferable skills which match well developed, carefully researched and impeccably applied transparent selection criteria of stable companies. Few careers services seek to support, for example, graduate applicants who might face discrimination in selection procedures and show them how to respond if they suspect this is an issue.

The Code and most service statements by university careers services will, quite rightly and understandably, emphasize that they should be 'client-focused'. However, the issue in some ways is not so much that CEIG should be *client*-orientated but that it should not be exclusively *supply*-orientated. In other words, university careers services seek to help graduates match their skills with the labour market. However, much work can be done, and in some areas is being done, to help create a more informed demand-side of the equation. For example, not all businesses understand exactly what skills graduates of different disciplines can offer, nor might they be clear about what combination of skills they might need in certain new roles (particularly in the area of new technology but in other areas too). Sometimes small businesses in particular fail to appreciate the skills provided by graduates and having hired graduates lose disproportionate numbers of them rapidly, possibly because the organizations fail to provide further development and training. While there may be some resource issues this can be caused by a misplaced sense that a graduate is 'the finished article' and needs no further significant skills development.

The precepts direct HEIs to develop systems for the 'monitoring, feedback, evaluation and improvement' of CEIG services but it is important that this is done in a holistic and inclusive fashion. In addition to these mechanisms for incremental enhancement, more radical innovation and development in this area is likely to focus on addressing the needs of non-traditional students, deconstructing the hiring process and working with employers to review their assumptions about recruitment and retention of graduates.

## REFLECTIVE PRACTICE POINT

In assessing the effectiveness of CEIG for all students it is important that the careers advice is not just focused on getting the institution's graduates their first job, but also on helping:

- mature students get their first graduate job;
- students going through retraining to get back into the workforce;
- international students secure employment in their home country or elsewhere;
- students already in employment advance their career with their current employer or otherwise;
- students start up their own businesses.

To what extent does CEIG at your institution address these issues? To what extent does your department, or the department you are currently working with most closely, work closely with your careers service in these areas? What percentage of your students fall into the categories outlined above?

In our review of the precepts and the associated guidance we will attempt to keep these points in focus.

## IMPLEMENTING THE PRECEPTS

### General principles

The general principles here essentially highlight the need for quality assured, documented CEIG strategies that are delivered in a professional and targeted manner.

*Precept 1: The institution should have a clear, documented and accessible policy for career education, information and guidance (CEIG), including statements of the institution's objectives and of students' entitlements and responsibilities.*

*Precept 2: CEIG provision should be impartial, client-focused, confidential, collaborative, accessible and in accordance with the institution's equal opportunities policy.*

*Precept 3: CEIG provision should be subject to the institution's quality assurance procedures.*

*Precept 4: The institution should seek to identify and cater for the special needs of students who may be disadvantaged in the labour market.*

The guidance emphasizes the need for clarity of roles and relationships, equal opportunities, support for students who are not in full-time mode, inter-service strategies, AGCAS or GC standards and the law.

## Institutional context

*Precept 5: The institution should ensure that its CEIG provision is designed to prepare its students for a successful transition to employment or further study and for effective management of their career thereafter.*

*Precept 6: The institution should ensure that CEIG interests are represented in appropriate internal decision-making forums.*

*Precept 7: CEIG should be promoted internally, with mechanisms in place to support and encourage collaboration with academic and other appropriate departments for the benefit of students.*

The recommendations inherent in the notes of guidance should not present difficulties for most HEIs. Evidence that a university takes CEIG seriously may be found in the person specification of lecturer posts that emphasize the desirability of recent experience in a relevant industry or profession. Programme specifications which reflect skills relevant to a particular industry or profession will have more credibility if they have been drawn up on the basis of discussions with local companies or practitioners and explicitly draw on information from professional body or trade organizations. Similarly, referral to internal sources of advice is unlikely to be problematic, but reference to external sources may be difficult due to resource implications. Smaller institutions may wish to make arrangements with larger HEIs to provide specialist guidance as appropriate.

**REFLECTIVE PRACTICE POINT**

In your institution, on what main university committees do representatives of the following groups sit?

- careers service;
- student counselling service;
- library;
- academic computing service;
- academic registrar's office.

Is the pattern indicative of the relative importance the university places on each of these functions or can nothing be inferred from the pattern? What principles are used at your university to determine representation on key policy groups?

## Students

*Precept 8: Students should be provided with information on the services available to them while registered at the institution and those which will continue to be available to them when they have left.*

*Precept 9: The institution should make clear in its information to prospective and present students how the skills and knowledge acquired during study are intended to be of use to them in the development of their careers.*

This part of section 8 of the Code seeks to ensure that all students reflect on transferable skills, know-how and where they are located in the curriculum, and are supported up to and including references. Although referred to in the precepts, the guidance does not however propose how HEIs should continue to support students after they have left the institutions. This is arguably unfortunate since although most universities will provide support for any student (whether from their HEI or not) for normally up to 12 months after graduation, there is still a lot that universities can and should do to promote lifelong learning and employability in its graduates. Students should be able to contact their university careers service when they are ready to move on from their first job and universities should be keen to help them. On purely business terms universities might wish to maintain supportive contact with potential future 'repeat clients'. The post-graduation contact most universities have with their students is through alumni associations but these mostly focus on donation and reunion activities rather than continuing mentoring and support.

## REFLECTIVE PRACTICE POINT

*CEIG and ICT*
Given the information intensive nature of CEIG it is widely recognized that ICT in general and the Internet in particular is changing the nature of the work of careers services.

Offer, Sampson, and Watts (2001) have highlighted the need for CEIG planners to think strategically about how best to harness and exploit ICT for client needs. They argue that careers services need to develop and review their own Web sites as this is now the main form of the relationship between students and services, that national sources of information on careers such as the prospects.ac.uk site needs to be better integrated with university and other sites in order to develop a coherent network of sites and that regional Web sites can play a positive role in the middle ground between local and national sites. They further argue that careers services should go beyond simple content-based sites and develop more interactive process-led sites including chatrooms and discussion forums and that online portfolios should be supported.

How ICT-focused is your university's CEIG strategy?

### External relations

*Precept 10: The institution should promote close collaboration between employers and CEIG providers to maximise the benefits to both students and employers.*

*Precept 11: The institution should ensure that its CEIG provision takes account of developments in the employment market and work opportunities in the community at large.*

The careers area has many national organizations sometimes with overlapping missions and functions. The guidance encourages HEIs to allow 'employers and other opportunity providers' to publicize their companies and related opportunities, but states that this must be done in such a way so as to not undermine impartiality. The CEIG network can incorporate alumni, local businesses and regional employers' organizations. One example of good practice in the area of providing opportunities for employers' views to be shared is through employers' forums. While most HEIs have these for industry specific areas such as engineering, manufacturing or healthcare, they are less common in areas such as humanities or social science. Similarly it is sometimes difficult for small businesses to be represented.

## *Staff*

*Precept 12: The institution should ensure that all members of its staff involved with CEIG provision, including academic staff, have the skills, knowledge and training appropriate to the role they are undertaking.*

The need for staff development in this area is of paramount importance. This is particularly true in relation to labour market intelligence, the role of ICT in the CEIG matrix and the need for supportive work in relation to equal opportunities. In addition to students with disabilities, careful consideration needs to be given to the needs of distance learning, part-time and international students.

## *Monitoring, feedback, evaluation and improvement*

*Precept 13: Providers of CEIG services should be required to account formally and regularly for the quality and standards of their services with the objective of promoting continuous improvement.*

*Precept 14: The institution should ensure that data collected by the institution on graduate destinations informs its CEIG provision.*

This section of the Code seeks to encourage institutions to reflect and improve their CEIG provision. Traditionally, the quality of CEIG services was assessed only by the first destination data and word of mouth. If target setting is to be pursued, as encouraged by the guidance, this needs to be carefully located in the context of the profile of students, the mix of programmes offered by the institution, the local as well as national job markets and the mix of undergraduates and postgraduate students. Ensuring a client-focused approach to CEIG can be helped through asking students to identify what targets should be set and not just by asking students to rate the service following use.

## QA ISSUES WITH CEIG

The effectiveness of CEIG in many senses cannot be genuinely assessed until many years after students' involvement with it. There has been widespread dissatisfaction with the traditional first destination statistics, which measures the number of full-time graduates in paid employment and further study. Universities are as yet reluctant to pursue US systems where graduate earnings are researched and reported – a system that lends itself to an assessment of the value added to the career progression of part-time students. In either case it is the capability for long-term job choice, satisfaction, earnings and career development that is the real aim of most CEIG strategies. Nevertheless, the slow fuse effect should not be used as an excuse not to monitor the quality and standards of a CEIG policy. In that context the main quality risks may be said to be as follows, on the grounds that they typically involve more than one unit in an institution and might have disproportionately damaging consequences if allowed to occur unchecked:

- failure to consult with careers services or other providers of the CEIG strategy when making curriculum policy changes;
- failure to adapt advice and information in the light of regional, national or international labour market intelligence data;
- failure to ensure effective communication and reciprocal understanding between academic departments and an institution's careers service;
- failure to provide effective support to students on the high volume final year application to graduate entry schemes for large employers;
- failure to coordinate print-based advisory materials with online materials;
- failure to provide staff development for specialist careers staff in relation to students with special needs;
- failure to meet the needs of part-time employed students in relation to career progression.

# QE ISSUES WITH CEIG

There are several ways in which institutions can improve and develop their CEIG activities. These include basic inputs into QE from standard QA activities on an incremental basis such as monitoring and review, staff development and learning from complaints. In addition, institutions may want to explore options for enhancement and innovation in a more holistic and possibly step-change manner by taking some or all of the following approaches. Some universities already take many of the following measures:

- Ensure that the production of the CEIG policy is shared across the whole university and that the final policy is owned by the key stakeholders. The responsibility for enhancing employability needs to be seen as a partnership amongst a range of internal stakeholders including careers service, library, student services, academic departments and of course students.
- Ensure that service standards for careers service advice are clearly spelt out and publicized. This needs to go beyond a simple target for how long a student should have to wait for an appointment with a careers advisor to more relevant issues such as interviews secured. The areas for service standards should be negotiated with student representatives.

- Ensure that further study and careers are equally well provided for.
- Ensure that the careers service works in partnership with other university careers services regionally and nationally both to support students who relocate or return, and to ensure that specialist expertise or information is available to as many students as possible.
- Ensure that a member of senior management at directorate and board/senate level has CEIG as a clear part of his or her portfolio of responsibilities.
- Establish a cross-university CEIG group that brings together careers service, local employers, academic representatives, student groups and academic planning officers.
- Ensure that a member of the CEIG team has a responsibility for disseminating workforce needs and planning intelligence.
- Ensure that there is a specialist advisor for students with special needs or a clear commitment to regular staff development in this area.
- Assign a member of careers staff to have responsibility for identified groups such as part-time or distance learning students (and to run this alongside any department or faculty liaison).
- Help students to tackle discriminatory, inconsistent, opaque or non-inclusive recruitment practices by employers both in terms of training and support.
- Consider post-graduation mentoring networking, post-recruitment and refresher support for students.

---

### Reflecting on CEIG

To what extent does your institution have a CEIG strategy that includes but goes beyond the aims and service agreement of the university careers service?

Does your careers service collate statistics on students' ratings of the objectivity, transparency and consistency of recruitment interviews? How could such information be used?

If you are attached to a small institution what arrangements are in place to refer students to CEIG expertise regionally? If you are in a large institution do you encourage smaller institutions to make referrals to your specialist staff?

If asked to summarize your department's strategy on CEIG on one side of A4 what would be the main points? If your main contact with the careers service was asked to guess what you would write how accurate would he or she be? Where would the main differences in the two accounts lie? Would you be more concerned if there were areas of overlap or gaps?

How familiar are your careers service staff with the final year optional modules in your programmes? How could knowledge of such modules be useful to careers staff advising students? Do you experience or anticipate any problems if students are receiving advice on final year option modules from both the department and the careers service?

# 14 Placement learning

## FROM INDUSTRIAL SANDWICH TO SME CONSULTANCY

For many years vocationally orientated degrees have operated a variety of schemes designed to ensure that students get first hand experience of the workplace. In particular sandwich courses involving up to a year or more in the workplace, particularly in the technology and manufacturing sectors, have been successfully organized and delivered for many years. While students certainly develop specific skills on these sorts of programme there has always been an additional curricular aim of exposure to the realities of the industrial or marketplace setting. Additionally, for some students, the placement will be their main opportunity for independent learning.

Employers often value placements since the system allows them to maintain links with universities, acquire some expertise and labour at relatively limited cost and occasionally access a source of potential high quality recruits. More recently business courses have seen the value of placements not necessarily for the opportunities they might provide to acquire any specific technical skills, but as a means of providing experience for students to reflect on and analyse in relation to the dynamics of organizational decision making, marketing or human resource development. These placements last less than a year, and usually operate in parallel with other taught courses or modules. They have also proved popular with employers, especially where the student's engagement with the company is organized around some kind of time focused project with tangible (if modest) outcomes for the company. While for many years industrial and business placements were restricted to larger companies, more recently many universities have successfully explored the opportunities for placement learning in small to medium enterprises (SMEs). Although these companies, typically of less than 150 employees, may not be able to provide the extensive support or variety of experience of larger firms, this can be more than compensated for with opportunities for the student to have a real impact on the company and get a overall feel for the entire operation in a way that would not be possible in a large and complex multi-site concern. Additionally, there has been a greater emphasis also on the benefits for learners of working in public sector or charitable organizations with students developing marketing strategies and internal business information systems.

Recent government funded initiatives have taken the concept of placements one step further, seeking to help students on programmes not normally associated with business gain some kind of exposure to the marketplace and how companies operate within it. With the increasing focus on transferable skills humanities students are now seen as capable of working within small and large companies in ways which not only help students rethink their view of the private sector operations, but help companies see the skills set beyond the degree title.

We should not forget that in this context 'work placements' also includes the teaching practice of PGCE students and the overseas placements of modern language students. While the precise issues and most effective way to protect quality and support enhancement in these cases will be different, the underlying principles remain essentially the same. While such placements tend to be to other public sector teaching institutions, and to that extent there is some degree of cultural similarity, this also means that the placement providers will have their own bureaucratic agenda.

Broadly, placements and related learning from the workplace, be it in the industrial or business context, in large or small organizations, in the private or public sector, can be seen as one of the successes of UK higher education since the Second World War. Any initial scepticism and elitism which looked down upon the grubbiness of the real world diluting the quality and focus of the academic experience has largely dissolved, to be replaced with a general expectation that most programmes will make some kind of provision for placements to occur. Students, employers and academics all recognize the value of a relevant placement for the training, personal and career development and liaison opportunities they can offer. Such concerns as remain relate principally to the impact on the core curriculum in areas where the placement is not seen as central. Universities and companies are understandably keen to hail new initiatives and agreements to further extend placement opportunities often figure prominently in the corporate literature of both. Students too of course rightly emphasize in CVs and job interviews the experience and skills they have acquired while working in companies as part of a placement arrangement within their programme. Students often identify their period on placement as the most enjoyable and useful part of their programme.

However, there is and always has been a less successful side of placements, and it is to these areas that we must look if the quality of the student experience is to be maintained and enhanced. Effectively managed placements need careful planning and involve considerable administrative burden to match the student to the placement opportunity, and then to ensure that the student is receiving adequate support and is making progress. Companies inevitably have their own schedules and priorities and cannot always respond to placement officers' requests in a timely fashion. Where placements are an essential part of a curriculum there is always the temptation on the part of universities to accept an inferior placement rather than no placement at all. Indeed such is the burden of identifying and assigning placements that many programmes now require students to seek out and initiate their own placements. Changes of personnel in companies can mean a lack of continuity of support, administrative understanding and liaison. For the universities' part there is always the danger of a lack of support, guidance or communication with students on placements. Additionally, as universities try to structure the kind of local, company-based input students can expect to receive, there is the danger that agreements, while struck in good faith, are not implemented as the exigencies of running, say, a million pound concern get in the way of supporting the learning of a mere student.

## REFLECTIVE PRACTICE POINT

Does your institution have a central policy of work placements and their management? Are there briefing notes for panels at approval and review events? Are there specific issues which annual monitoring reports must address where the provision includes work placements? Taking these issues into account, to what extent is QA in this area actively managed in your institution?

The challenges and resource implications of managing effective, credible and academically beneficial placements are now widely recognized across the sector.

Section 9 of the Code, on placement learning, is broad in scope in that it seeks to address all learning that occurs outside the institution in partnership with an external company or organization (the 'placement provider'). However, the Code does not cover learning which occurs outside a placement agreement. This is understandable as by its very nature such learning is in many ways difficult to plan, and therefore support or quality assure. However, many universities recognizing that many students do work part-time but outside any placement arrangement, and yet wanting to 'annex' that experience to the student's overall personal and learning development, have established modules which in principle confer academic credit for this casual employment and related experience including volunteering. Based on support for students' reflection, skill development and personal planning, such modules can play a part in the overall learning experience.

The Code emphasizes that planning and transparency of the intended learning outcomes, and the relative responsibilities in relation to the achievement of those outcomes, lies at the heart of the QA processes in this area. Crucially the Code makes clear that the university must take responsibility for making sure all the parts fit.

## BALANCING QA AND QE IN PLACEMENT MANAGEMENT

As is the case with many other aspects of effective quality management, the challenge in the planning and support of placement learning is to ensure that in the drive to manage QA, QE is not undermined. It is probably true in the past that although all parties recognized whether a particular placement was valuable or not, there was occasionally a lack of clarity about what it was *specifically* that made one placement better than another in learning terms, what *specifically* a student was expected to learn and how that learning *fitted* into the overall curricular aims.

However, in specifying the precise intended learning outcomes of a placement, and in organizing the academic and administrative input to ensure that those outcomes are documented, promoted, assessed and reviewed, there is a danger that the opportunity for spontaneous, unplanned serendipitous learning in a productively chaotic environment will be diminished. One of the key and defining qualities of a genuinely engaging and worthwhile placement is precisely that at the outset it is not clear *what it is that needs to be learnt*. This is related in part to the project-structured nature of many placements, which, for successful completion of the brief, require flexibility, and the picking up or combining of new skills along the way. Work-based learning is promoted as an excellent opportunity for using problem-solving skills, however, the solution to many problems in the workplace is not always 'do X' but sometimes 'learn X'. It is important that placements have clear learning outcomes, and it is important that students know what those outcomes are, but it is also important that in being focused on those outcomes only that they do not 'tune out' the dynamics and developments of the rich and exciting learning environment that will surround them. Thus attention might be given to consideration of whether or not the placement, in being subjected to careful QA standards of specification and structure, does not lose the very learning opportunities that give it its distinctive curricular function.

### REFLECTIVE PRACTICE POINT

How is feedback elicited from work placement stakeholders? If students' views are elicited only once in what way if any does the timing of the feedback affect their perspective?

# IMPLEMENTING THE PRECEPTS

## General principles

*Precept 1: Where placement learning is an intended part of a programme of study, institutions should ensure that:*

- *their responsibilities for placement learning are clearly defined;*
- *the intended learning outcomes contribute to the overall aims of the programme; and*
- *any assessment of placement learning is part of a coherent assessment strategy.*

Overall the Code attempts to ensure that placements are a coherent part of the curriculum for a named programme of study, with clear learning outcomes that articulate with and contribute to the overall intended learning outcomes of the programme specification.

Assessment of placement learning can be an area of particular complexity and sensitivity. There is always a danger that there will be an undue focus on product rather than process. The academic, possibly remote from the placement on a day-to-day basis, may sometimes be able to review only output summary documents of the project report, while in the business culture getting from A to B is sometimes seen as more important than how you got there or what you learnt along the way. While this may be an issue in only a minority of placements it is important that these considerations are explicitly addressed as part of an overall assessment strategy for placements. If placement organization staff are involved in assessment it is essential that they understand the assessment criteria that go along with the intended learning outcomes. From the academic point of view it is useful to have logbooks or placement diaries running alongside the substantive project in order to ensure that skill- and personal development-based outcomes are fully and appropriately assessed.

## Institutional policies and procedures

*Precept 2: Institutions should have in place policies and procedures to ensure that their responsibilities for placement learning are met and that learning opportunities during a placement are appropriate.*

The guidance rightly encourages institutions to lay out how placements will be allocated and, crucially, what happens when, for whatever reason, a student is unable to have a placement secured for him or her. However, it is unclear why this responsibility is emphasized as an *institutional* one since it is unlikely that one system will be equally appropriate across all programmes and placements. Indeed, given the variety of placements, their differing curricular function and status, their size and complexity, it is likely that effective procedures are likely to be local ones, sensitive to the context and implications of different contingencies. As in other parts of the Code, and in QAA documentation generally, the term 'institutional' is slightly ambiguous, sometimes equivocating between 'university rather than some other external agency' or 'the corporate body centrally rather than local departments'. To the extent that what is intended here is the latter, the emphasis on centralization would appear to be unnecessary and overstated.

Nevertheless, while the function of institutional policies on selection and approval of placements is unclear, there can be no doubting the need for institutional policies on health and safety, even if there are additional details added at local departmental level and even if most of the risk assessments are done departmentally. Additionally, given the rapid change in workplace legislation and codes of practice, it is essential that any guidance on health and safety, regulatory requirements generally, or equal opportunities policies, are regularly reviewed, updated and disseminated.

From the QA perspective a placement is essentially a learning opportunity and as such must above all else enable the intended learning outcomes to be achieved. The challenge for the academic administrator in this area however is not assessing simply whether a placement provides the learning opportunities required but in matching the opportunity to the student, acknowledging that different students will perhaps seek to achieve the outcomes in slightly different ways. Indeed it could be argued that placements provide an almost unique opportunity within academic programmes of study for tutors to reflect on the learning style and interim achievements of individual students and assign them to the learning environments that are most likely to be productive for them: reflection, it is fair to say, that the timetable rush at the beginning of the academic year to allocate students to seminar or laboratory groups rarely affords.

Supporting students on placement is at the heart of effective placement management. Non-academic support will relate to basic health and safety checks of the placement provider, ensuring that the student feels comfortable in what will be a different workplace and possibly culture, that any special needs are being adequately met, and that morale and enthusiasm is kept high. Academic support will focus on ensuring that the learning outcomes are kept in mind (without missing other learning opportunities), to facilitate reflection on the learning process and to provide guidance on the submission of relevant assessments. Prosaically, where students are pursuing a placement in parallel with other programmes academic support may include ensuring that the demands of the placement are neither being neglected nor overshadowing other programme-related requirements. Much of this kind of support is difficult to outline in advance and the support needs to be flexible, reflecting the atypical dynamic nature of the curriculum and learning which placements involve. Nevertheless, for QA purposes it is wise for academic staff to be supported with a handbook that identifies, as a minimum, key interim points during the placement period when specific issues need to be checked, confirmed and reviewed. Equally it is important that the academic supervisor or equivalent keeps his or her own logbook of process and progress, both to maintain continuity of support and to facilitate QE at the end of the academic year or semester when the effectiveness of placements and the support offered to students can be reviewed.

## REFLECTIVE PRACTICE POINT

To what extent do work placements in your department or institution focus on fixed end-product learning outcomes rather than dynamic process-orientated learning outcomes? What are the advantages and disadvantages of this orientation?

### Placement providers

*Precept 3: Institutions should be able to assure themselves that placement providers know what their responsibilities are during the period of placement learning.*

Perhaps surprisingly, the guidance here for what is in fact one of the key aspects of placement management is rather limited. It is indeed important that placement providers are aware of their responsibilities for the provision of learning opportunities and their role, if any, in the assessment of students, but achieving this awareness can be a mammoth task. Such is the variety of placement providers that it is important to consider the precise issues with each individual case. However, there are some general issues that need to be taken into account when considering how to ensure that providers are aware of their responsibilities, which are worth reviewing in detail.

### Placement providers and strategic QA

Precept 3 urges institutions to reassure themselves that the placement organization is aware of its responsibilities. In order to ensure that this is done there is likely to be a need for a formal placement agreement which lays out responsibilities and schedules, but if the placement is to be of decent quality this piece of paper needs to be supported by a clear *strategy* for securing buy-in from the placement organization, a strategy which must begin from consideration of what is best for the student and how organizations perceive placements. There are different ways of approaching this but some of the key elements are motivation, political context, key players, documentation, and induction. Additionally, there should be a clear sense of how the placement relationship can be developed as part of a QE strategy of the provision generally.

## Motivation

Placement providers must be motivated to know what their responsibilities are and how to implement them. It is important that placement providers see what the value of the placement is to them both in terms of the specific student or students involved, but also the potential longer term benefits of the relationship with the university.

## Politics

Not all constituencies in the placement provider organization are necessarily going to be in favour of placements at any given point in time. Management and the local department may not see eye to eye on some matters such as support, training, office space or equipment support. Some departmental staff might see placements as a low priority, some may have had bad experiences in the past and still others may be threatened by the presence of a student with 'up-to-date' technical knowledge. Alternatively, the department may have been 'fighting' to gain approval for a placement student for some time and management (or organizational bureaucracy) may have delayed the process. In either case, or in any of the many other configurations of organizational or office politics, some of the gatekeepers, managers, administrators or supervisors involved in the placement may have a vested interest or expectation in the placement succeeding, or failing, as the case may be. Knowledge of these political dynamics will help ensure that the right information is going to the right people, at the right time in the placement organization, with the right message. In this context it is not enough to know that the placement organization understands its responsibilities but to know *who* in the organization has the responsibility and for what.

## Gatekeepers and champions

It is necessary at an early stage to identify who the key gatekeepers are to placement opportunities in the placement organization. These can be the local departmental managers, the human resource section of larger concerns, or site training officers. Securing the support and trust of these decision-makers is crucial in the early stages of a programme. Champions are those within the placement organization who are placed to speak at key meetings about the benefits of the arrangements. These are often the line managers of gatekeepers, a relationship that can be a key dynamic in placement politics.

## Documentation

Businesses are used to dealing in agreements and will welcome a printed statement of the reciprocal rights and obligations of all parties. It is important that *students* are aware of the existence of such agreements and that they are happy with the content.

## Briefing, induction and training

Ideally the placement organization would simply send everyone who is going to be significantly involved in managing the placement along to the university for a two-day training programme or equivalent. Clearly the likelihood of this happening is very low indeed. Even nowadays, when most businesses recognize that induction and training at the beginning of an enterprise is much more effective than disaster recovery half-way through, they cannot spare the time or the people for extensive induction activities. Even where human resources staff take responsibility in larger organizations for the efficient management of placements, there is rarely the opportunity to provide extensive briefings. There are, however, several ways in which this situation can be managed (see Box 14.1).

---

**Box 14.1**

Good Practice – ensuring placement providers get the briefing:

- Consider running induction events in business location rather than the university.
- Combine briefing events with 'what's in it for the company' activities.
- Make a video outlining the course and the role of the placement in it.
- Make a CD ROM, or set up a Web site which explains the basics of the expectations of the university and any inputs in the assessment process. Key documents can be placed on the Web site for downloading.
- Cascade the briefing process year on year with key placement provider personnel carrying out some of the briefings.
- Combine briefings for placement providers with network meetings and speakers. Students can usefully be involved at these events.
- Establish and circulate good stories of successful placements elsewhere.

All of the above emphasizes how typically and ideally the placement is itself part of a much broader relationship between the placement providers and the university.

---

Strategic QE

Once placement organizations feel that the system is basically working and is providing some benefit for them (and that the costs are not high) it is possible then, but not before, to introduce enhancements to the placement programme. Attempts to introduce enhancements or innovation before a placement organization feels it has a good sense of what is involved may backfire. Once confidence and trust is established, there is considerable scope for enhancements to be rolled out in order to improve the quality of the learning experience and cement the placement relationship. A sure sign that a genuine partnership for enhancement has been established is of course when the placement organization spontaneously proposes new developments which seek to enhance the student experience.

## Student responsibilities and rights

*Precept 4: Prior to placements, institutions should ensure that students are made aware of their responsibilities and rights.*

Students' rights and responsibilities are the 'hygiene' factors for any successful placement. The guidance provides a very basic outline of what is relevant here (and it is interesting here that students' responsibilities outweigh their rights). Their responsibilities are seen as relating to their role as university ambassador, pseudo-employee, learner and quality monitor. It is important that information given to students about their responsibilities, especially in the areas of responsibilities to the placement provider, are drawn up following full consultation with the placement provider. A further quality risk here is that students become reluctant to inform the university about difficulties with the placement for fear that they will have to start a new placement from scratch, or will be implicated in the failure of the placement as a learning opportunity. It is important therefore that students are clear about what the implications of such 'whistle-blowing' are and are given appropriate reassurance. It also is important that institutions do not rely solely on students to monitor the extent to which placement providers offer learning opportunities in the manner laid out in the agreements before the placement starts.

### REFLECTIVE PRACTICE POINT

To what extent does your institution have a general policy on the responsibilities and rights for students on placements? To what extent do these link to or reflect the legal obligations of the university? Are they linked to issues around student complaints?

## Student support and information

*Precept 5: Institutions should ensure that students are provided with appropriate guidance and support in preparation for, during, and after their placements.*

The guidance here ranges from the very necessary and practical ('the need for personal insurance cover particularly when on placement abroad') to the areas often neglected ('cultural orientation and work expectations' and 'appropriate re-orientation on students' return to institutions'). In any event the section here does not provide a complete list of all areas of support that need to be provided for students, nor is it intended to. Of particular importance here is the use of progress files. These are a requirement for all programmes from 2005 and their role in placement learning is particularly significant.

## GOOD PRACTICE POINT

In drawing up strategies for students in support of placements institutions might want to consider thinking about:

- what information students need to have in a placement handbook;
- what relationships students will have with teaching and support staff at the institution;
- how crises and emergencies will be handled;
- whether and how students can get confidential advice on practical, personal and academic matters when on placement;
- how visits to the placement site where relevant and appropriate will be managed and what their function is.

More generally placement support is an area where the World Wide Web comes into its own and some institutions are already exploiting this area effectively. Some of the *basic* ways in which the Internet can support placement learning include:

- allowing students access to definitive documents remotely (such as placement handbook and student services information);
- allowing students to keep informed on course or departmental developments while away from the institution;
- through e-mail, keeping in close contact with supervisor/other academic contacts throughout the placement.

Some of the more advanced uses of the Internet (albeit with resource implications) include:

- enabling peer-to-peer bulletin boards and chat rooms for students to both share experiences on current placements and to receive advice from other students on past experiences in placements;

- enabling online logbooks to be completed so that students have a central location for daily or weekly updates – in some cases tutors can have access to these logbooks in real time so that monitoring and support is timely and effective;
- enabling students to remain and feel part of their host institution even while in another part of the country or overseas through for example voting in students' union elections, booking tickets for social events on their return, or conceivably making contributions to student submissions for QAA institutional audit.

With or without Web support, access to reliable, accessible and relevant information before, during and after a placement is at the heart of effective support for students in this area.

## Staff development

*Precept 6: Institutions should ensure that their staff who are involved in placement learning are competent to fulfil their role.*

Staff development is a key part of effective QE for placements. The guidance however is again sparse and focuses on generalities. The emphasis is on identifying and developing placement opportunities but no further detail is offered. Possible staff development priorities in this area might involve support for the following skills:

- In the context of the intended learning outcomes of the programme specification, staff need to be able proactively and strategically to define the characteristics of types of placements, understood as complex learning opportunities, which would enable those outcomes to be met. Staff should be able then to seek or create those opportunities in collaboration with placement organizations or their parent bodies.
- Staff need to be able to assess the extent to which placements, however identified or proposed, are *in principle* capable of being managed within the context of a declared framework of learning outcomes for the placement as a learning opportunity, such that the intended learning outcomes of the programme specification are met.
- Staff need to be able to understand and develop the placement partnership with placement organizations such that a foundation of confidence and trust is established to support QA and to provide a basis for development and innovation for QE.
- Staff have to be able to maintain a balance between the QA needs of well specified learning outcomes and their achievement on the one hand and the support for serendipitous learning in the placement on the other.

## Dealing with complaints

*Precept 7: Institutions should ensure that there are procedures in place for dealing with complaints and that all parties (higher education institutions, students and placement providers) are aware of, and can make use of them.*

We have discussed earlier some of the thorny issues of student complaints in the context of placements. While complaints about the placement as a practical place of work or about a lack of support by the HEI are usually taken seriously, complaints about the learning value of the placement are less frequent but equally significant. Institutions need to ensure that there are mechanisms for identifying the extent to which any given placement, or set of placements, actually do provide the learning opportunities they were designed to offer. As always the QA agenda here anticipates recording of complaints and investigating them, but the QE agenda, more subtle, must involve exploring the cultural and communication systems which underpin the student experience and how the placement may have promoted expectations that were not met. The QE agenda of learning from complaints to enhance delivery can of course be difficult to focus on when complaints are urgent and personal, but in the longer term it is attention to the QE agenda which is likely to diminish the grounds for complaints, rather than the ever more formal application of a QA complaints framework.

## Monitoring and evaluation of placement learning opportunities

*Precept 8: Institutions should monitor and review the effectiveness of their policies and procedures in securing effective placement learning opportunities.*

Where placements amount to a significant part of the curriculum for a named award it is likely that it will be a prominent part of the AMR agenda. In order to monitor and review effectiveness of placements the guidance places heavy emphasis on feedback. This is wholly appropriate and is a process which all parties are likely to see as legitimate and credible. However, even more than usual the time at which the feedback is solicited will have an effect on the response received. Most placements have a steep learning and orientation curve for the student (and sometimes for the placement provider) and early feedback may be negative or inconsistent. Occasionally, first impressions of buildings, equipment, facilities and key contacts are very positive but subsequently, as the student gets deeper into the organization and has to deal with a broader range of people, and realizes the level of expectations in ambitious companies, the initial sheen can wear off. These fluctuations are particularly important with overseas language placements where real-world language levels, cultural disorientation and isolation can conspire to demoralize the most committed and prepared of students. However, it can be further argued that such is the nature of placements, particularly longer term ones which are well managed and stretching for the student, that the true impact of the learning and the raising of awareness is not evident until some considerable time afterwards, possibly even after graduation when the student has returned to a workplace environment.

It is important to provide the right forum and vehicle for feedback from placement organizations. Crucial too is ensuring that the right person is providing the feedback. While it may be useful in some circumstances to get the corporate view from the human resources department of a large company on the effectiveness of a placement or set of placements, the feedback from those most closely involved with the placement is likely to be much more valuable. However, it is necessary in organizations to keep track of how placement is really perceived by those who, while remote from the placement itself, are influential in determining whether and how the placement arrangements will continue. Clearly, any misunderstandings or unrealistic expectations need to be addressed sooner rather than later.

One important issue in evaluating placements on the basis of feedback and one which is directly related to the understanding of QE and QA in this area, is that generally students have little to compare their own placement experience with. Thus student feedback and evaluation is usually likely to be more useful in assessing the extent to which the placement met the student's expectations and needs (and these should be informed by the intended learning outcomes) than assessing how the placement could be developed in the context of QE. Although students will be able to identify ways in which placement could be improved beyond the narrow consideration of how it could better meet the learning outcomes, one way of dealing with this is to provide opportunities for students to meet as a group and share experiences of different placements, allowing them to consider whether the arrangements in another placement could be usefully applied to theirs.

## QA ISSUES WITH PLACEMENT LEARNING

Effective management of quality in this area, then, is principally an issue of ensuring that the placement has clear learning outcomes which contribute to the overall intended learning outcomes of the programme noted in the programme specification, and that the placements do in fact in practice provide the learning opportunities required for those outcomes. The major risks to quality in this context then are:

- poor articulation between placement outcomes and programme outcomes (which may include poorly expressed or inconsistent placement outcomes);
- lack of effective support by academic staff for students during placement;
- under-briefing or under-commitment of placement providers;
- failure to brief students on issues around insurance, liability, data protection;
- poor record keeping by academic supervisors.

Ways of addressing these issues have been highlighted earlier in this chapter.

# QE ISSUES WITH PLACEMENT LEARNING

A coherent approach to improvement of the student learning experience in this area is likely to involve the committed participation of the university, the placement provider and of course the students. The need for effective collaboration between the university central services and local departments should not be underestimated. Since by definition the learning takes place off campus in liaison with an external body, corporate issues will arise for the HEI as an organization. Equally, however, since the placement by definition is a personalized learning opportunity supporting independent learning in the context of a programme specification, departmental involvement is obviously central. In this context the key issues for QE in this area are likely to be:

- ensuring the careful nurturing of placement partnerships with placement providers that acknowledge their agenda and priorities;
- appropriate staff development for managing the distinctive challenges and opportunities of placement learning;
- ensuring that the focus on the learning outcomes framework does not exclude the opportunity for learning from a complex and dynamic organizational environment;
- harnessing the opportunities afforded by the Internet to support the information intensive and distributed multi-site nature of placement programmes.

---

### Reflecting on placement learning

In what ways do long and short private sector work placements, teacher training placements, overseas language placements and any other placement types with which you are familiar differ in terms of the QA issues they raise? In what ways do they differ in terms of QE of the provision?

In what ways do PSBs provide a resource, framework and set of constraints for the effective management of the quality of placements?

To what extent have the provisions of the Data Protection Act, health and safety legislation and SENDA affected your institution's approach to work placements, if at all? Who takes responsibility for ensuring lawful practice in relation to these areas in your institution? How are course leaders and work placement coordinators briefed on these issues?

Partly due to a lack of work placement opportunities and partly due to staffing limitations in some areas, some universities offer work placements to their own students. What are the general advantages and disadvantages of this system? What are the opportunities and threats for QA and QE resulting from this system?

What arrangements are there in your institution for respecting the cultural or religious concerns students might have for certain types of placements? What expertise is there in your department or unit for supporting students in such situations?

Identify five programmes in your institution where there are currently no compulsory or recommended work placement opportunities. In what ways might students on these programmes benefit from a work placement? In what ways would it not be beneficial? What scope is there in your institution for students to take a generic elective module which is based on a placement? If there is such an opportunity is it well promoted, and is there significant uptake?

What is the role of work placements or equivalents for masters programmes? In what ways from the point of view of QA and QE do they raise additional issues?

What particular quality issues are raised in the context of mature part-time students taking up work placements? Who might these issues affect? What should a university's position be where a company has an (implicit) under-30s rule for placements?

# 15 Recruitment and admission of students

## FROM ELITISM TO DIVERSITY

In an era of mass participation in higher education the issues around admissions are not about accessing higher education, but about accessing a particular course at a particular institution. Over the last few years university admissions have become a hot political issue both in terms of 'dumbing down' of access to higher education in general and in terms of equal opportunities in relation to access to 'elite' institutions.

The key issues covered by the Code here (in section 10) are not about what criteria universities should use in selecting applicants but rather that whatever criteria and selection processes universities adopt, those processes are fair, documented, available to applicants and implemented by staff who know what they are doing – and crucially that they are able to reassure those who enquire about admissions with robust evidence that this is so. The underlying issues here which form the foundation for the precepts are generally that:

- The public should have faith in the recruitment systems.
- Universities should see recruitment and admission as the beginning of the extended relationship with the applicant as a student.
- While universities have a right to exercise judgements about a candidate's achievement and potential, such judgements need to be systematic.

In the UK access to higher education has been seen historically as an important microcosm of progressive reform and in the movement towards social inclusion and meritocracy, university admissions are expected by governments, the media and schools to reflect that progress.

In common with other sections of the Code this section places heavy emphasis on review, staff development and the management of complaints, reflecting a greater awareness of the relationship between QA and QE.

> ## REFLECTIVE PRACTICE POINT
>
> What do you remember of your own experience in applying for university (if you did)? Was it a positive or negative experience? Did you feel there was too much information or too little? What were your first impressions of your university as an organization? To what extent do you feel your experience is similar and different to that of students applying today?

## IMPLEMENTING THE PRECEPTS

### *General principles*

*Precept 1: Institutions should ensure that they establish policies and procedures for the recruitment and admission of students that are fair, clear and explicit and are implemented consistently. Transparent entry requirements, both academic and non-academic, should be used to underpin judgements that are made during the selection process for entry.*

The guidance here inevitably raises many more questions than answers – which is of course exactly what it is intended to do. Nevertheless, we need to consider how *exactly* does an institution (as given in the guidance): 'recognize the diversity of background, experience and age of applicants to higher education and the different modes of study available'; What precisely is meant by 'recognize' in this context? Does it mean simply 'acknowledge' or does it mean 'make specific provision for'?

The guidance note on responsibility is interesting. It is self-evident that someone somewhere needs to be responsible for 'each part of the recruitment and admissions process, such as determining the number of offers to be made relative to the number of places available, the setting of criteria against which applicants will be considered, and the selection of applicants'. This will not of course be the same person, and it may be different people at different times for the year for different programmes. In the context of a stable, high demand programme which looks for 360 points at A-level for a single honours BSc route there might be little ambiguity about who is responsible for setting what and who is responsible for implementing it. However, in a franchised, combined honours programme which has different A-level points entry for different subject combinations, going through a period of administrative and staffing transitions in the first few days of clearing, responsibilities and their implementation may be a littler rougher around the edges. Institutions need to face up to the fact that however marginal or atypical a particular mode of entry to a specific programme might be to the institution, it will always be of fundamental importance to the applicant.

## Recruitment

*Precept 2: Institutions should ensure that promotional materials are relevant, accurate at the time of publication, not misleading, accessible, and provide information that will enable applicants to make informed decisions about their options.*

The importance of accurate information is widely recognized in the process of recruitment. However, students come to know about particular courses in many different ways. While UCAS information on the availability of courses and the entry criteria (provided by the institutions themselves) is of distinctive importance other sources include the university prospectus, information from teachers and careers advisors, leaflets picked up from open/visit days, and the press.

Overshadowing all of these sources now and in the future is of course the Internet. Most students now access UCAS and university prospectuses online. The Web is also a major source of information for university league tables, bad press about a university, HEFCE performance indicators and of course dedicated Web sites devoted to advising students which university is likely to be right for them.

Clearly the area of fees and associated costs and the availability of financial support is likely to become more significant as institutions seek to move to differential fees combined with 'blind to financial need' admissions processes.

Universities of course are required to publish a wide range of items of information as a consequence of the Cooke report (HEFCE 02/15) ranging from external examiners' reports to progression rates. All of these have a important impact on students' perceptions of universities and on the views of those that advise students. The relative impact of such information on student choices is difficult to assess however (see Box 15.1).

---

**Box 15.1**

*Programmes of study*

As laudable as it is to provide information to students to help them make choices over courses, such research as there has been into what kinds of information students are influenced by in their choice of institution or discipline makes sobering reading.

HEIST (Higher Education Information Services Trust) found in 1996 that students were influenced by:

- city brand names (such as Manchester in the early 1990s and Leeds in the late 1990s);
- whether or not the name would impress friends;

- success of local soccer club;
- reputation of the local shopping, music and the dance scene.

More recently there have been dramatic increases in forensic science, culinary science and history programmes, rises which are seen as directly related to high profile television programmes.

Also important for students are Web sites such as Prospects (www.prospects.ac.uk) which covers postgraduate programmes and HERO, both of which are used extensively by overseas students.

## *Selection*

*Precept 3: Institutions should ensure that selection policies and procedures are transparent and are followed fairly, courteously, consistently and expeditiously; that information concerning applicants remains confidential between designated parties, and that decisions are made by those equipped to make the required judgements.*

Although institutions are clearer now that they have been before on the admissions criteria for individual programmes there is still probably much work to be done. Programme specifications do not, as yet, attempt to define the skills and experiences of students that would make them more likely to succeed on the programme. Few universities carry out retrospective research to explore the correlation between the entry skills (as distinct from the qualifications) of new entrants and their eventual achievement on the programme. Since universities no longer carry out their own entrance examinations and are generally reluctant to introduce them, the only evidence they will have is from examinations or the reports of others, which may not be using the same skill definition. Thus admissions tutors need to assess skills not directly but at second hand. Interviews provide an opportunity for applicants to present more information about themselves but as a showcase for demonstration of skills they are highly problematic. Interviews have a high face credibility with applicants but much research indicates that these have limited validity and reliability. The individualized nature of applications and the sensitivity of judgements about that information raises difficult issues for QA in this area. The need for maintaining a paper trail for the purposes of audit (and for that matter legal process) needs to be placed in the context of the Data Protection Act and related legislation. While the approach taken by UCAS to manage this tension is effective, it will not cover institutions' own documentation procedures.

*Precept 4: Institutions should ensure that applicants are made aware of the obligations placed on prospective students at the time the offer of a place is made.*

Students normally have little difficulty in understanding what is expected of them in the normal course of events if they wish to decline or defer the offer or if they fail to meet its conditions. However, students can become unclear when they appeal against the examining boards grading or if they were ill at the time of the examinations. The key here is to ensure that the lines of communication are kept open with students and that they feel comfortable with contacting the university about matters relating to their application.

## Information to successful applicants

*Precept 5: Institutions should ensure that prospective students are informed of any significant changes to a programme between the time the offer of a place on that programme is made and registration is complete, and that they are advised of the options available in the circumstances.*

It is important that significant changes are communicated to applicants in good time. Ideally there should be no significant changes. Accreditation should not be withdrawn and courses should not be located to other campuses but these things do happen. Possibly the most common serious issue is the deferral of accreditation or recognition by the relevant body such that guidance given in good faith by course tutors turns out to be inaccurate. The dilemma facing course leaders or admissions tutors in this situation is not that the application for approval has decisively failed, but that it remains unresolved. Convincing students that approval will be forthcoming may not be straightforward even if the course team has a well-founded expectation that everything will be resolved rapidly. Similarly, where departments have been relocated to a different campus at short notice heads of departments find themselves phoning or writing to students reassuring them that this relocation will have no impact on their programme, words spoken perhaps through gritted teeth.

Informing students prior to arrival on changes to assessment would be seen by most institutions as something of an overreaction (though much hinges on what one might mean exactly by the precept's term 'significant changes'). Contacting students in this way is likely to cause anxiety and confusion amongst many applicants as they assume that the changes must be serious to warrant a letter about it. Thus the desire to communicate openly with applicants must be balanced with a recognition that students generally trust universities to manage the implementation of a programme as necessary. If mishandled, attempts to appraise students of changes in course delivery, which in some cases they would not even be aware of as changes, can backfire. Realistically, only major shifts from coursework to examination, additional compulsory placements or rules for progression to subsequent years of the programme might genuinely count as significant changes where students would appreciate that the fact of communication did not amount to a nervous defensive measure by the institution.

*Precept 6: Institutions should explain to successful applicants their arrangements for the enrolment, registration, induction and orientation of new students and ensure that these promote efficient and effective means of integrating the entrants fully as students.*

The guidance here outlines the different kinds of students' needs and the different kinds of information that might be important to students. All of this will come as no surprise to admissions tutors or academic registrars. The main message here is the focus on enrolment, registration, induction and orientation as four stages in one process.

In QA terms, there should be a procedure appropriate to students' circumstances for sending information and effecting students' initial academic and administrative engagement with the programme. This is fundamentally a cross-functional organizational issue. If left on their own departments, the registry, finance, the library, academic computing systems and the students' union will merrily send students the same information several times over, with, it is hoped, only a handful of inconsistencies and erroneous cross references. Organizing efficient supply of information requires a project team focused on delivery and a seamless set of initial contacts with the applicant/student.

## Monitoring and review of recruitment, admission and enrolment

*Precept 7: Policies and procedures related to admissions and enrolment should be kept under regular review to ensure that they continue to support the mission and strategic objectives of the institution, and that they remain current and valid in the light of changing circumstances.*

Realistically, reviews of admissions procedures in most universities are going to be at least as focused on whether recruitment targets have been hit as much as on whether policies and best practice guidelines have been scrupulously adhered to. Yet of course these two concerns should not necessarily be seen as entirely separate. While thorough, fair and transparent applications procedures are unlikely to attract extra applicants, deficient ones are likely to deter better applicants or applicants who are unsure about their own suitability. Most damagingly, if applicants with special needs, or those from ethnic minorities, or the networks and communities of advice, lose faith in the integrity of admissions procedures at particular universities they are unlikely to recommend applications to those institutions. (Quite apart from whatever other course of action they might rightly wish to pursue.)

More generally many universities find that attracting applications to courses is one thing but actually converting those applications to acceptances is quite another. Students who are prepared to travel, and in the larger cities even those who intend to stay put, have a reasonable choice of institutions available to them. In these contexts, the more coherent, efficient and fair the admissions procedures are seen as being, the less likely applicants are going to be put off. All of these needs have to be put in the context of service standards for applicants and the application process. The precepts only refer to dealing with applications 'courteously'. In the new millennium applicants are looking for slightly more than 'courtesy' especially in postgraduate or overseas applications.

## Staff development and training

*Precept 8: Institutions should ensure that all those involved in recruitment and admissions are competent to undertake their roles and responsibilities.*

Staff development for recruitment and admissions is becoming more of a priority for institutions as the political and legal stakes for selection procedures are raised. Areas where QA effort is required to ensure provision meets its objectives include interviews, making decisions on applicants with special needs, and issues around gender and ethnic discrimination. One of the key areas for consideration, where recruitment policies can usefully spell out institutional expectations, relates to where in the selection procedure the decision of one individual can have an effect on the overall outcome. Whether it is in the initial processing of application, forms, taking a telephone enquiry, answering an e-mail, single interviewer arrangements or provision of advice on special needs, where there is no opportunity for a second opinion or review there is correspondingly greater possibility of an ill-judged decision.

To some extent the key issues are not simply staff expertise, cultural awareness and knowledge of routes into higher education but how these skills and knowledge are organized and deployed in relation to specific types of applications. Ultimately, admissions procedures will always involve some degree of subjective albeit expert judgement. It is important that there are staff development opportunities to enhance and inform such judgements. However, too much emphasis on individual expertise and experience amounts to a threat to quality if that emphasis is at the expense of considerations around effective team and cross-institutional liaison, and, above all, coherent and transparent *systems* for managing applications.

## Complaints

*Precept 9: Institutions should have policies and procedures in place for responding to applicants' complaints about the operation of their admissions process and should ensure that all staff involved with admissions are familiar with the policies and procedures.*

While it is possible to have a request for an appeal without a concomitant complaint about the process *per se*, the reverse is much less frequent. Complaints about the admissions system are typically and understandably built on the back of experience of an unsuccessful application.

Arguably the most important distinction that institutions might wish to keep clear in the minds of their applicants is not so much that between complaints and appeals, but between complaints and litigation. In terms of QA, complete and detailed recording is inevitably a central part to the whole process.

Grey areas such as records of interview need to be carefully considered. Every interview should have a criterion referenced output record but it must be remembered that it will be difficult to explain to unsuccessful applicants why they were not offered a place while someone with lower ratings was. Weightings for criteria within interviews, and the contribution of the interview or other distinctive part of the selection procedure need to be clearly documented and consistently applied. In complex admissions arrangements, including those involving portfolio of work, reference, application form and interview (as used for many art and design courses) the challenge is not so much to be clear about the criteria used in each element of the selection procedure, but rather to provide convincing accounts of how these different types of information are *integrated*. From the QA point of view there should not be ambiguity about what each of these activities is for, or a lack of transparency about how these elements are combined in a final overall decision. Any rationale which looks like retrospective justification for essentially unexamined preferences for what kind of candidate 'fits' is likely to be treated with little sympathy by quality auditors, the courts or students themselves – and rightly so.

## QA ISSUES WITH RECRUITMENT AND ADMISSIONS

Effective management of quality of recruitment and admissions is tied up with effective marketing and revenue issues. However, in terms of academic QA the central issues relate to clear institutional policies, demarcation of departmental authority, the deployment of properly trained and experienced individuals and effective coordination across the institution of clear admissions strategy. Common threats to quality in this area fall into three areas as follows.

Threats to quality related to characteristics of the *provision*:

- new provision where experience of recruitment is limited, and where marketing has occurred before validation;
- established provision where inconsistent or out-of-date information is still in circulation, or where a degree of complacency may be in evidence;
- rapidly expanding provision which oversells or overreaches itself;
- declining provision which abandons its admissions procedures or standards through desperation.

Threats to quality related to characteristics of *staff*:

- overburdened staff serving as admissions tutors alongside other responsibilities;
- lack of effective staff development reflecting external developments.

Threats to quality related to characteristics of *systems*:

- too many decisions left to individuals without review or second option opportunities;
- failure to specify how individual elements of the selection process come together;
- failure of systems integration at institutional level (marketing, admissions, the registry, academic departments, the library).

All of these threats to quality are amplified when dealing with students from under-represented groups.

## QE ISSUES WITH RECRUITMENT AND ADMISSIONS

It can be argued that staff development and systems monitoring is the key to enhancing the quality of the admissions process. Providing there is also a degree of risk management so that the implications and impact of any radical innovations are carefully assessed beforehand, there is no reason why recruitment and admissions management cannot be an area of continuing improvement. Feedback from schools, colleges, schools' careers advisors, tutors, applicants and parents can all help identify where the areas for improvement might be. Successful applicants can provide useful information on how the process hangs together from the client side, or not, as the case may be. There is also scope in the system for 'mystery shoppers' who contact institutions on the pretext of being genuine applicants. While this can provide useful preliminary information, it is unlikely to be appropriate for interview or portfolio assessment procedures. Such an arrangement does not necessarily help build up trust between the marketing section and academic departments.

### Reflecting on admissions and recruitment

If your department or institution were to face a legal challenge over the fairness of its selection procedures, what aspect of those procedures would it most likely focus on?

What do you consider the role of interviews in the selection process to be? Are they used widely in your institution? Is there a university policy on the conduct, function and record keeping of interviews? In your view what skills in principle can interviews assess?

At what point in the selection process for postgraduate students are special needs first picked up? What are the procedures for assessing students' needs at that point?

What are the elements of good practice which characterize the recruitment and admissions procedures at your institution? Are these elements institution-wide or limited to certain departments?

At what point if any do admission tutors in your institution see the text for their subject in the university prospectus? Or the photographs which illustrate the subject and the captions for the illustrations?

At what points, if any, in your institution or department's selection procedures is just one person involved in processing applications?

What do you know about selection procedures in other parts of your institution? Is there a forum for discussion of challenges or dissemination of good practice?

Approximately how many person hours are devoted in your department to selection of applicants? Do you feel this is too many or too little, or just right?

To what extent if any does your institution discuss the potential tensions between the need to recruit sufficient students and the need for QA in recruitment and selection procedures?

To what extent are lecturers and course leaders involved in the recruitment of overseas students? What training if any do admissions tutors receive in your institution in assessing applications from overseas students?

Does your institution or department solicit information from students on their experience of recruitment and selection? If so is this review carried out by the marketing unit, academic departments, the quality unit or by someone else? In what ways does this research filter back to admissions tutors?

# 16 Distance learning

## DISTANCE LEARNING AND ACADEMIC STANDARDS

Distance learning has often been identified as a solution for the various challenges of widening participation, learning for continuing professional development, resource reductions and internationalization. Distance learning however splits academics in a way that very few other developments in the last 25 years have managed to. Despite the success of the UK's Open University in delivering what are widely regarded as high quality accessible programmes of study, the idea of learning at a distance, remote from libraries, support structures and, crucially, other students – all seen as essential parts of the university experience – is treated with scepticism by many UK academics. In contrast to the generally positive attitude to *campus*-located resource-based learning, the remoteness of the *distance* learning student from the tutor, the campus and other students has not received widespread approval.

QA in relation to distance learning has thrown up issues that reflect these fundamental concerns. How can students be effectively supported if there is no regular face-to-face contact? How can the quality of the learning materials be guaranteed? How can we be sure that the students registered on the programme have actually submitted the coursework? Underpinning this is the recognition that degrees offered on a distance learning basis must reflect the same academic standards as those from equivalent campus-based programmes offered by the same institution.

Some of the quality issues around distance learning are related to the inherently distinctive characteristics that define remote learning. Others however are more historical, reflecting the context of the emergence of this new form of delivery. This is particularly true in the area of resource planning for the development and delivery of distance learning programmes. Consistent underestimation of the costs of distance learning production, which has much higher start-up costs than traditional provision, has led to premature programme launches of inferior quality material. Similarly, the high costs of production have meant slow cycles of review and development as print runs are used up. More generally, particularly in the context of e-learning, the highly visible and user-friendly interface and content features have been afforded significantly more resources than the less attractive but equally important student support activities. As a business activity universities have sometimes struggled to define the parameters of relevant market research let alone carry it out. Projections for volume are often out of line with actual enrolments, undermining the credibility of distance learning as a product or as an educational solution. As a consequence distance learning has been seen as a high-risk activity in cost, revenue and planning terms. Since all these areas affect quality it is unsurprising that the AMR of distance learning provision has been particularly demanding.

The QAA guidelines on distance learning do not have the status of a section of the Code. However, the Code does reflect the advice and support for good practice contained in earlier publications and serves as a useful point of reference for review in this area. Additionally, section 2 of the QAA report on institutional audit explicitly specifies that a subsection of the report must cover 'Assurance of quality of teaching delivered through distributed and distance methods' (*Handbook for Institutional Audit*, p 34).

## TYPES OF DISTANCE LEARNING AND IMPLICATIONS FOR QA AND QE

As we shall see, many of the precepts exhort providers of distance education to do things which are no less necessary for providers of campus-based programmes. It is the case that whatever the state of students' expectations and skills for campus-based learning, they are likely to be no more conducive for distance-based learning. Generally speaking, outside the Open University, distance learning students tend to be postgraduate students and are, in some senses at least, more capable and discriminating learners than the average new undergraduate.

The first distinction that needs to be drawn is between print-based and e-learning distance programmes. Print-based programmes typically involve the production of course units accompanied by study guides. These will be supplemented by set texts and course textbooks which are compulsory for the programme. E-learning programmes on the other hand rely heavily on electronic documents available through the Internet. Until recently such programmes were based on detailed electronic handouts which were simply uploaded to the Web as linked HTML documents. With a few notable exceptions such programmes typically lacked interactivity and impact. Indeed, despite the much vaunted hyperlink structure of Web documents, such learning materials were highly linear in nature leading to a crass reproduction of the worst kind of print-based distance learning, with the only difference being that the page of text now sat vertically on a screen rather than horizontally on a desk. In such circumstances some students simply print out scores of pages of Web documents.

More recently however there has been widespread adoption in UK HEIs of e-learning platforms such as WebCT or Blackboard. These systems enable academics to upload material easily in a Web-ready format, attach formative online assessments and, crucially, manage the timing of student access to learning materials and monitor student interaction online. These systems come with built in bulletin board and chatroom facilities. While these systems reduce the amount of creative input from academics in terms of structural layout and functionality, this is compensated for by the ease with which interactive courses can be put online. In terms of QA there should be fewer concerns in this platform approach since not only is the inter-relationship between the e-learning components stable, consistent and coherent, students' engagement and progress can be carefully monitored, both by academic staff and the students themselves. Indeed the level of monitoring that is possible in such programmes is greater than that which would normally be possible in traditional campus-based programmes since almost every student engagement with the learning materials, the tutor and other students is automatically logged by the system.

The Open University has used a print-based distance learning model extensively and successfully since its inception in 1969. Although the print-based materials are traditionally supported by optional face-to-face seminar classes at UK regional centres, these are not usually seen by students or staff as a central part of the course in the way that seminars are in campus-based programmes. However, the Open University is moving more into e-learning provision with almost 178 of its 360 courses in 2002 requiring students to have Internet access. It is important to note that the Open University has three levels of e-learning incorporated into courses:

- *Web-enhanced:* courses in which students choose to use basic 'e-services', including digital resources, course Web site, and computer conferencing. Use of these services while taking these courses is not obligatory.
- *Web-focused:* courses in which the use of ICT is a required element of teaching support; and some teaching and student support is delivered online to all students.
- *Web-intensive:* courses in which all teaching and student support is delivered online. (Adapted from E-learning at the Open University)

What are the implications of these different types and subtypes of distance learning for QA? One way of assessing this is by considering the ways in which different modes of study pose different kinds of risk to academic quality and standards. It should go without saying that there will be much variation within each mode in relation to each risk as a function of local institutional factors. Additionally, each risk can be unpacked in different ways (for example some students with mobility difficulties prefer distance learning, but by no means all). Table 16.1 attempts to highlight a 'risk profile' for each mode.

The principal function of Table 16.1 is to stimulate debate and awareness on the challenges and opportunities inherent in different modes of study. More generally, looking at the overall pattern of risks by mode should help to unfreeze the assumption held by some that campus-based provision is invariably impeccably managed

**Table 16.1** Potential risks to quality and standards mode of delivery

| Potential Risks to Quality | Mode of Study | | |
|---|---|---|---|
| | Distance e-learning | Print-based distance learning | Campus-based learning |
| Failure to manage recruitment and admissions effectively | Medium – if managed online i) test systems in advance with dummy students; ii) have paper back-up system | Low – providing initial counselling as to suitability is pivotal | Medium – due to unregulated face-to-face element |
| Failure to induct students into learning arrangements | Medium – high learning curve of students, technical complexity of arrangements i) clear documentation; ii) gradual provision of additional information to manage curve | Low – students are generally experienced with reading to learn | Medium – due to large number of students, spoken briefings, complexity of campus arrangements |
| Failure to monitor student progress | Low – built into e-learning systems | Medium – if monitoring of engagement dependent on monitoring of submission of assessments i) establish weekly or monthly 'touchbase' telephone contact; ii) where appropriate assign mentor in workplace or identified by student | Medium – dependent on attendance monitoring |
| Failure to provide appropriate student support | Medium – due to novelty of learning environment | Medium – due to ease of keeping low profile and diverse needs | Medium |
| Failure to guarantee integrity of assessment | Low – digital submissions subject to textual analysis/limited access to student experts | Medium – no digital fingerprint but no access to student experts | Medium – high access to student experts and 'copyable' resources – but visible social and institutional monitoring |
| Failure to protect academic standards (in relation to assessing achievement) | Low – ease of moderation | Low | Low |

Table 16.1 continued

| Potential Risks to Quality | Mode of Study | | |
|---|---|---|---|
| Failure to provide appropriate staff development for academic staff | High – technical specificity, limited relevant pedagogical expertise. Help tutors access national or international dedicated Web sites | Medium – low technical specification, relatively widespread expertise | Low |
| Failure to make adequate provision for students with disabilities | Medium – difficulty of some screen accessibility issues/uncontrollable external sites | Low – alternative formats available | Low – alternative formats and recording devices |
| Failure to include students in departmental decision-making representative process | Low – electronic consultation | High – disengagement and difficulties of rapid consultation. Ensure major issues have sufficient consultation periods | Medium – representatives may have limited mandate/cannot communicate with all students (personal experience and anecdote driven) i) training; ii) electronic communication on campus |
| Failure to update learning materials in a timely fashion | Low – material needs changing in one location (relatively cheap) | High – materials needs changing for all students (high cost) | Medium – lecture updating cheap and easy (but other resources, eg handouts and reading lists low priority) |

and enjoys little or no threat to quality, while distance learning programmes are simply quality disasters waiting to happen. Table 16.1 attempts to assess the risk level of each mode on the basis of a hypothetical pure e-learning, print-based or campus-based programme. Alongside each assessment is a brief explanation where relevant for the level of risk assessment given, and a brief indication of the kinds of 'risk controls' which anyone planning provision in any of these modes might wish to consider.

---

The Open University has been awarding degrees since its incorporation in 1969 and has had over 2 million students since then. In 2001 it had almost 200,000 students worldwide enrolled on its courses. Around 80 per cent of its students are in paid employment while studying and many are sponsored by their employers. The University claims that about a third of its students since 1973 who were able to obtain first class degrees on entry held less than the minimum entry requirements for traditional university entry.

Source: *Open University Media Office Background Information Fact Sheet*

---

In what ways do the different modes of study shown in Table 16.1 relate to QE considerations? In terms of the basic elements of monitoring, staff development and managed innovation there is superficially little to separate the three modes since they all lend themselves to review and development in ways which are familiar. However, if we are looking for more subtle differences across these modes we can find them.

In terms of *monitoring*, the e-learning environment will tend to provide more relevant information about the *process* of learning than the other two modes. Campus-based tutors (c-tutors) do not typically know how often their students visit the library, while e-tutors will know how often and when their students log on and access online materials. C-tutors do not normally make a transcript of their seminars, but online seminars can be automatically archived if required.

In terms of staff development however, normally there is not a great deal available locally for e-tutors because the experience and expertise is not widespread. However, e-tutors have the benefit of international forums with other e-tutors operating in the same learning environment with whom they can share problems and good practice.

In terms of delivery development the e-tutor can change some fairly significant aspects of delivery from within the platform quite easily, unlike a c-based tutor who might need to liaise with the room bookings office or prepare additional handouts for 200 students before a new learning activity can be delivered. In all of this the print-based tutor (p-tutor) is squeezed out, lacking both the ease of communication with students and the ease of amending learning materials, yet also lacking the immediacy of the campus-based programme. Generally speaking, the enhancement implementation cycle for print-based programmes is typically slower than that for either the e-tutor or the c-tutor. This can lead to the loss of any focus on enhancement in print-based distance learning since the costs for implementing even minor changes can be prohibitive.

## IMPLEMENTING THE GUIDELINES

We turn now to consideration of the QAA distance learning guidelines, continuing to draw distinctions around the e-learning and print-based approaches.

*Guideline 1: System design – the development of an integrated approach.*

Guideline 1 emphasizes the need to integrate, explicitly, arrangements for distance learning provision with the institution's overall systems for QA and programme delivery. Interestingly the guidelines suggest that there should be a test of systems before offering the programme itself. Whatever the merit of this advice it is interesting that the testing before delivery principle, common in other non-educational quality systems, does not appear anywhere else in the Code.

As noted in Chapter 7, covering section 2 of the Code on collaborative provision, the need to underwrite programmes in their entirety is emphasized here. This is to ensure that the quality of the provision is not dependent on the revenue streams. This is particularly important in relation to fixed costs that are directly relevant to QA, such as the resourcing of staff development opportunities and of assessment systems.

*Guideline 2: The establishment of academic standards and quality in programme design, approval and review procedures.*

It can be seen that the underlying concern that the guidelines are keen to address is that the distance learning programme will comprise the integrity of the presumably already established and successful campus-based awards. Where an institution offers an award in distance learning mode only, the comparison, in QA terms at least, needs to be first and foremost with other awards from the same institution rather than with distance learning awards from other institutions since it is the integrity of the awarding institution which is at stake.

The need to take into account the specific requirement of distance learning programmes extends to the concept of outline and final approval, with the former relating principally to the overall curricular structure, assessment and support systems and so on, and the latter relating to the specific content of the learning materials. This kind of conditional approval prior to peer review of the primary teaching materials is not something which is typically applied to campus-based provision.

There is nothing distinctive about learning materials used in distance learning compared to campus-based programmes, but the concern is that since these materials are in the public domain and theoretically widely circulated, there is a risk of damage to the reputation of the institution. Additionally, there is a perception, not always well founded, that in distance learning programmes the learning materials carry a bigger burden of the learning than, say, lecture handouts would for a campus-based programme.

Precept 11 emphasizes that learning materials in a distance learning programme should be regularly reviewed. The costs of large production runs for print-based learning units have meant that in order to be economical, they can only be replaced infrequently. In the Open University's case such review periods can be eight years or more. Often, however, the primary teaching materials are accompanied by study guides that are cheaper to produce and are more easily re-issued. In the case of e-learning it is cheaper to update Web materials than it is to update material associated with campus-based programmes. It can be argued that the organizational issues around monitoring and updating e-learning materials are more significant than the technical issues of simply uploading a new set of Web pages, but this is also the case for traditional modes of delivery.

The direction of Precept 11, while laudable, does not seem to be identifying anything which is particularly important for distance learning:

*An institution should ensure that programmes of study and component modules once designed, and in use, are monitored, reviewed and subject to re-approval regularly; in particular an institution should ensure that the content of all learning materials remains current and relevant and that learning materials, teaching strategies and forms of assessment are enhanced in the light of findings from feedback.*

It is not made clear how much more regularly it is being suggested in Precept 11 that distance learning programmes should be updated compared to traditional programmes. Similarly the advice in the notes of guidance here do not appear to be any more relevant for distance-based learning as opposed to campus-based provision in relation to currency of teaching materials:

*[Institutions should have] a procedure through which learning materials are verified as to their continued effectiveness, accessibility and currency, and action taken to effect necessary modifications and updating before a new intake of students begins work on a programme, or on a component module.*

It is not clear whether it is assumed that campus programmes will be routinely updated (and therefore need no special exhortation to do so); or that distance learning tutors are particularly negligent or forgetful in this area; or that campus modules do not need such regular updating (which is unlikely); or that if they are not updated the tutors will in some way be able to muddle through regardless. There is nothing distinctive about distance learning programmes that requires them to display more currency than campus-based programmes.

*Guideline 3: The assurance of quality and standards in the management of programme delivery.*

The precepts in this area relate primarily to those situations where the awarding institution is delivering provision in collaboration with some other party. This is the case for some overseas provision and the boundaries between the two forms of provision (franchise and distance learning) are blurred. The QA principles for these forms of provision start to blend together also, however the message remains the same: the university has a 'strict liability' responsibility for academic quality, and it is a responsibility which cannot be delegated to a third party.

*Precept 12: The providing institution is responsible for managing the delivery of each distance learning programme of study in a manner that safeguards the academic standards of the award.*

*Precept 13: The providing institution is responsible for ensuring that each distance learning programme of study is delivered in a manner that provides, in practice, a learning opportunity which gives students a fair and reasonable chance of achieving the academic standards required for successful completion.*

The guidelines emphasize that if universities hire agents or tutors to delivery some of the administrative or learning support at a remote site they cannot delegate responsibility for quality to those third parties. Agreements need to be in place with agents and local teachers need to be properly recruited and trained. Similarly precept 14 highlights the important role in QE of feedback from all involved in delivery including students.

*Guideline 4: Student development and support.*

*In respect of students taught at a distance, a providing institution should give explicit attention to its responsibility for supporting and promoting autonomous learning and enabling learners to take personal control of their own development. An institution should set realistic aims, devise practical methods for achieving them, and monitor its practice.*

This raises the complex issue of student support. This extends beyond academic support and into vocational and personal guidance. As noted in section 8 of the Code on CEIG, the revolution in digital information means that many of the guidance needs of students are more than adequately met by online sources and these are generally as available to distance students as to campus students. Face-to-face interviews are clearly less realistic, but the dialogue of question and answer can be supported online or through structured telephone arrangements. Personal support is more complex. While a minority of students may sometimes prefer the relative emotional distance of e-mail or the telephone, the role of face-to-face contact to support cannot be underestimated or easily implemented when preferred. In practice however this issue is much less of a problem as most distance learning students are at the postgraduate level and are thus traditionally less heavy users of university-based personal support services. Nevertheless this is a challenging area with no clear answers. The most effective and realistic approach is to make clear to applicants prior to enrolment what level of support and guidance service they are likely to be able to receive and how that will be managed so that students do not experience frustration or disappointment.

*Guideline 5: Student communication and representation.*

Effective systems for communication with students and the provision of clear and consistent information about operational matters cannot be underestimated. In particular, students will need particular support for dealing with university bureaucracy on everything from paying library fines, suspending studies and submitting medical documentation for extenuating circumstances, and with departmental administrative policies for submission of assessments and module selection procedures.

## GOOD PRACTICE POINT

Where programmes run both on campus and remotely, pairing up a campus and remote student as buddies can provide useful means of practical support.

Precept 16 lays out information which while important for campus-based students may need reinforcing for distance learning students. Many of the issues covered in relation to academic credit and progress are theoretically spelt out in university regulations and course validation documents, neither of which are known for their clarity of expression or 'student friendliness'. On campus such issues can quickly be resolved in face-to-face consultation. For distance learning students there is no such opportunity and there is no chance to catch the tutor after the lecture. More generally, distance learning students, although they have in principle considerable flexibility in terms of which modules to study when, are often keen to accelerate their progress by studying several modules in parallel often in excess of recommended maximum loads. In such cases time must be taken by the relevant academic member of staff to advise and / or veto as necessary.

An additional point to bear in mind in reviewing the quality of communication with distance learning students is that in on-campus provision the proximity of students on the same programme of study and their social interactions means that where one student has discovered a problem affecting, say, his or her enrolled status, module combination or relationship with the library, the speed with which the issue is circulated to others can be rapid. This can lead to several queries from students at the same time about the same issue. Academic tutors can then issue reassurance or advice as appropriate and the programme continues. By contrast distance learning students lacking this everyday social interaction with other students (at least in the traditional sense) may not be alerted as rapidly to local emerging issues as campus-based students.

Precept 18 encourages institutions to consider how students will be represented at course meetings or equivalent. Where there is a campus-based version of the programme, distance learning students should have their own course representative able to convey concerns or issues from distance learning students in writing via the campus-based representatives. Where there is no campus-based programme, and the programme is electronically delivered, one system is simply to designate all students as representatives and establish a forum rather than a delegate system.

*Guideline 6: Student assessment.*

All the precepts listed in guidance for section 6, on assessment, are areas which all programmes, whatever their mode of delivery, need to adhere to. As is often the case however distance learning requires that providers are more explicit about how these and similar objectives are achieved than would be the case for campus-based provision. Complications around assessment are most likely to occur when, because of the remoteness of the learner or because the programme is being offered in collaboration with another provider, some aspects of the assessment are delegated to a third party. The level of confidence in the 'security of locally-administered and assessed summative course-work assignments' relates to both the scope for post-submission amendments by any party and, of course, impersonation. Where the local agent or tutor group has a conflict of interest in relation to QA on the one hand, and student achievement on the other, particular care needs to be taken in the moderation and validation of student work. Of course the problem should not be overstated – there cannot be a *prima facie* assumption that tampering will occur otherwise the level of trust for effective partnerships will never develop. Equally, academics unfamiliar with agency agreements with overseas students seeking to obtain UK degrees should not shy away from ensuring that mechanisms are in place to reassure all parties that students achieve their award on merit. In relation to the authentication of coursework it is difficult to see why the problem might be considered more of an issue in distance learning contexts.

## GOOD PRACTICE POINT

The Joint Information Systems Committee (JISC) has recently funded a plagiarism advisory service hosted by the University of Northumbria. The service offers:

- generic advice for institutions, academic staff and students;
- educational tools for students in the area of plagiarism;

- a portal to external online resources on the issue of plagiarism;
- guidance on copyright and data protection issues relating to plagiarism;
- a link to an electronic plagiarism detection service and training on its use.

http://www.jiscpas.ac.uk

Examining how this service could help programmes or modules at risk from high levels of plagiarism could help improve prevention and detection.

The Internet enables access to a wide range of sources, and in some cases sites, dedicated to the sale of pre-written or bespoke essays on a range of topics. Several systems are now in place to assess the probability of a student's submission being his or her own work or that of someone else. Of course all students, distance learning and campus-based, have access to the Internet and there is no particular reason why distance learning students would be more, or less, likely to use it to cheat. In some senses campus-based students are more likely to be in position to impersonate or plagiarize. Campus students are part of a cohort of peers tackling the same coursework at the same time in the same place with easy access to extensive print-based resources and, as is easily forgotten, to a cohort of students who are likely to have passed the same module and possibly its assessments the previous year. Distance learning students do not always have access to comparable library facilities or a group of individuals who are doing or who have recently completed similar assessments.

In terms of reducing the motivation by students in whatever mode to plagiarize from print or electronic documents the simplest system is to demonstrate the many different ways the ideas and findings of others can be incorporated into a piece of work and still attract significant credit. This is one of the aims of the JISC Plagiarism Advisory Service (PAS).

## GOOD PRACTICE POINT

It is increasingly common for universities to publish some anonymized details of students caught plagiarizing or otherwise violating academic regulations. While this is a legitimate approach to take, more effective, and more educational, is at the start of a distance learning programme to invite students to exchange views on the severity of sanctions that should be used when an individual is caught cheating. This will not only reinforce the assumption that cheats will be caught, but it gives the group a collective sense of owning the norms which informally police the boundary of fair and unfair practice.

## QA ISSUES WITH DISTANCE LEARNING

The main risks to quality in the area of distance learning are likely to be:

- failure to provide or facilitate access to learning resources such as texts and journal articles in print or electronic format;
- failure to provide adequate support for students in relation to preparation for assessment;
- failure to manage enrolment, registration or progression issues;
- failure to manage students' access to CEIG, complaints or pastoral support;
- failure to apply pedagogical principles to presentation of learning materials;
- failure to take reasonable steps to prevent, detect and respond to plagiarism and impersonation;
- failure to make print, electronic or other learning materials fully accessible for all students or to provide alternatives.

## QE ISSUES WITH DISTANCE LEARNING

Although the print or electronic nature of materials affects the ways in which and the regularity with which some aspects of distance learning are provided, there are other characteristics of provision which are likely to support enhancements to the student experience:

- regular review of the effectiveness of student support arrangements;
- providing opportunities for peer-to-peer communication for students on academic and non-academic matters;
- ensuring reasonably rapid response to e-mail, fax or other queries to compensate for lack of face-to-face communication;
- providing where feasible and appropriate the optional opportunity for students and staff to meet at weekend or summer schools;
- ensuring that there are regular staff development opportunities for e-tutors and support staff on e-learning programmes;
- ensuring close liaison between academic staff and support staff in relation to access to learning materials.

## Reflecting on distance learning provision

What skills are required of a distance learning tutor above and beyond those required for one involved in campus-based delivery? How could staff development programmes seek to develop and enhance those skills?

To what extent is it an advantage for tutors to have themselves been distance learning students? How many tutors teaching on any distance learning programme at your university have been distance learning students?

Does your institution have particular guidelines for validation and review for distance learning programmes? In your experience what issues are given a high priority during the process?

It is sometimes said that since much distance learning is at the postgraduate level students will have developed good ICT and independent learning skills as part of their undergraduate programme. Do you find this to be true on the distance learning programmes at your institution? How are students inducted in the process of distance learning at the beginning of their distance learning programmes?

Assuming that distance learning programmes increasingly have a 'blend' of electronic, print-based, face-to-face and other modes of communication how should these different modes of delivery be effectively integrated?

Many e-learning platforms, such as Blackboard or WebCT, have multiple choice question (MCQ) formats built into the delivery template as an option. What are the advantages and disadvantages of MCQs for summative, and for formative, assessment in the context of e-learning?

What decisions will institutions need to address in relation to the working patterns for tutors implied by distance learning? What are the implications of these issues for QA and QE in your view?

What kind of support do different kinds of students need on e-learning and print-based distance learning programmes? Are these different from the learning support needs of campus-based students?

# Appendix: Useful contacts

## ORGANIZATIONS

HEIST
The Coach House
184 Otley Road
Leeds LS16 5LW
Tel: (0113) 226 5858
Fax: (0113) 226 7878
www.heist.co.uk
e-mail: enquiries@heist.co.uk

HERO
Higher Education and Research Opportunities in the UK
Registered Office
Dickinson Dees
St Ann's Wharf
112 Quayside
Newcastle upon Tyne NE99 1SB
Tel: (0191) 279 9000
www.hero.ac.uk

Higher Education Funding Council for England
Northavon House
Coldharbour Lane
Bristol BS16 1QD
Tel: (0117) 931 7317
Fax: (0117) 931 7203
www.hefce.ac.uk

The Institute for Learning and Teaching in Higher Education
(formerly Institute for Learning and Teaching)
Genesis 3
Innovation Way
York Science Park
Heslington
York YO10 5DQ
Tel: (01904) 434222
Fax: (01904) 434241
www.ilt.ac.uk

Learning and Skills Council
Cheylesmore House
Quinton Road
Coventry CV1 2WT
Tel: (0845) 019 4170
Fax:(02476) 49 3600
www.lsc.gov.uk/contactus.cfm

Quality Assurance Agency (QAA)
Head Office
Southgate House
Southgate Street
Gloucester GL1 1UB
Tel: (01452) 557000
Fax: (01452) 557070
www.qaa.ac.uk

QAA Glasgow Office
183 St Vincent Street
Glasgow G2 5QD
Tel: (0141) 572 3420
Fax: (0141) 572 3421

UCAS
Rosehill
New Barn Lane
Cheltenham
Gloucestershire GL52 3LZ
General enquiries:
Tel: (01242) 222444
Minicom:
Tel: (01242) 544942
www.ucas.com

# WEB SITES

AGCAS
http://www.agcas.org.uk/

Careers Research and Advisory Centre (CRAC)
The mission of lifelong learning and career development was augmented via careers education, research, courses, conferences and resource materials for learning about jobs.
www.crac.org.uk
Department for Education and Skills
www.dfes.gov.uk/index.htm

Centre for Recording Achievement (CRA)
Originally established as an Employment Department Project in 1991 the CRA now supports good practice and the sharing of experience in recording achievement and personal development planning on a national basis, not only in initial education but also in lifelong learning in employment and through professional bodies.
www.recordingachievement.org

Disability Rights Commission
The Disability Rights Commission (DRC) is an independent body set up by the government to help secure civil rights for disabled people. It works to eliminate discrimination, promote equal opportunities, encourage good practice and advise the government on disability legislation.
www.drc-gb.org

Guidance Council
www.guidancecouncil.com/provider/qual_stand/index.asp

National Institute for Careers Education and Counselling (NICEC)
A network sponsored by CRAC
http://www.crac.org.uk/nicec/nicec.htm
Open University Media Office Background Information Fact Sheets
www3.open.ac.uk/media/factsheets/index.asp

Scottish Higher Education Funding Council
www.shefc.ac.uk

SKILL: National Bureau for Students with Disabilities
Skill promotes opportunities for young people and adults with any kind of disability
in post-16 education, training and employment across the UK.
http://www.skill.org.uk/

Society for Research in Higher Education
www.srhe.ac.uk

Staff and Educational Development Agency
www.seda.ac.uk

TechDis(JISC)
www.techdis.ac.uk
TechDis, in conjunction with ALT (the Association for Learning Technology), has
produced *Access All Areas: Disability, technology and learning*. This book is aimed at all
staff in further and higher education and contains advice and case studies relating to
many aspects of the learning process in relation to disabled people and students
with learning difficulties.

# References

Akoojee, S (2002) Access and quality in South African higher education: the challenge for transformation, *HERDSA Conference Proceedings*

Gordon (2002) The roles of leadership and ownership in building an effective quality culture, *Quality in Higher Education*, **8**, pp 97–106

HEFCE 02/15 (2002), *Information on Quality and Standards in Higher Education* (*The Cooke Report*), HEFCE, Bristol

Houghton, W (2002) Using QAA subject benchmark information: an academic teacher's perspective, *Quality Assurance in Education*, **3**, pp 172–86

Huitema, D, Jeliazkova, M and Westerheijden, D F (2002) Phases, levels and circles in policy development: the cases of higher education and environmental quality assurance, *Higher Education Policy*, **15**, pp 197–215

Jackson, N (2002) Growing knowledge about QAA subject benchmarking, *Quality Assurance in Education*, **3**, pp 139–54

Knight, P T (2002) The Achilles' heel of quality: the assessment of student learning, *Quality in Higher Education*, **8**, pp 107–15

Larrington, C and Lindsay, R (2002) Equal among firsts: reviewing quality in higher education, *Psychology Learning and Teaching*, **2**, pp 6–11

Laugharne, M (2002) Benchmarking academic standards, *Quality Assurance in Education*, **3** (3), pp 134–38

Mehrez, A and Mizrahi, S (2000) Quality requirements in rapidly growing higher education systems: the Israeli example, *Higher Education Policy*, **13**, pp 151–71

NCIHE (1997) *Higher Education in the Learning Society (The Dearing Report)*, NCIHE, London

Newby, P (1999) Culture and quality in higher education, *Higher Education Policy*, **12**, 261–75

Newton, J (2002) From policy to reality: enhancing quality is a messy business, LTSN Generic Centre, October 2002

Offer, M, Sampson, J and Watts, A G (2001) *Careers Services: Technology and the future*, CSU/NICEC, Manchester

Pond, W K (2002) Twenty-first century education and training: implications for quality assurance, *Internet and Higher Education*, **4**, pp 185–92

Rakic, V (2001) Converge or not converge: the European Union and higher education policies in the Netherlands, Belgium/Flanders and Germany, *Higher Education Policy*, **14**, pp 225–40

Scott, P (2002) The future of general education in mass higher education systems, *Higher Education Policy*, **15**, pp 61–75

Smeby, J-C and Stensaker, B (1999) National quality assessment systems in Nordic coun-tries: developing a balance between external and internal needs, *Higher Education Policy*, **12**, pp 3–14

Smith, A and Webster, F (eds) (1997) *The Postmodern University? Contested visions of higher education in society*, SRHE and Open University, Buckingham

Tovey, P (2002) Teaching at the edge of chaos: complexity theory, learning systems and the idea of enhancement, LTSN Generic Centre, Quality Enhancement Debate, June 2002, available at www.ltsn.ac.uk/genericcentre

Universities UK (2002) *Quality: Report of the teaching Quality Enhancement Committee to the Main Committee of Universities UK*, MC/02/21, 28 August 2002

van der Wende, M and Westerheijden, D (2002) *Report of the Conference 'Working on the European Dimension of Quality' of the Joint Quality Initiative*, Amsterdam, 12–13 March 2002

# Further reading

Correa, H (2001) A game theoretic analysis of faculty competition and academic standards, *Higher Education Policy*, **14**, pp 175–82

Damme, D V (2001) Quality issues in the internationalisation of higher education, *Higher Education*, **41** (4), pp 415–41

Franke, S (2002) From audit to assessment: a national perspective on an international issue, *Quality in Higher Education*, **8**, pp23–28

Gordon, G (2002) The roles of leadership and ownership in building an effective quality culture, *Quality in Higher Education*, **8**, pp 97–106

Gowan, M *et al* (2001) Service quality in a public agency: same expectations but different perceptions by employees, managers and customers, *Journal of Quality Management*, **6**, pp 275–91

Harvey, L and Green, D (1993) Defining quality assessment and evaluation in higher education, *Higher Education Policy*, **8**, pp 9–34

Lawless, C J and Richardson, J T E (2002) Approaches to studying and perceptions of academic quality in distance education, *Higher Education*, **44**, pp 257–82

Leeuw, F L (2002) Reciprocity and educational evaluations by European Inspectorates: assumptions and reality checks, *Quality in Higher Education*, **8**, pp 137–49

Lemaitre, M J (2002) Quality as politics, *Quality in Higher Education* **8**, pp 29–37

Lomas, L (2002) Does the development of mass education necessarily mean the end of quality? *Quality in Higher Education*, **8** (1), pp 71–79

Ramsden, P (1998) Managing the effective university, *Higher Education Research and Development*, **17** (3), pp 347–70

Robinson, B (1995) The management of quality in open and distance learning, in *Structure and Management of Open Learning Systems, Proceedings of the Eighth Annual Conference of the Asian Association of Open Universities*, New Dehli, February, **1**, pp 95–109

Smout, M and Stephenson, S (2002) Quality assurance in South African higher education: a new beginning, *Quality in Higher Education*, **8**, pp 197–206

THES (2001) Worthy project or just a game? THES, 30 March, 2001

Warn, J and Tranter, P (2001) Measuring quality in higher education: a competency approach, *Quality in Higher Education*, **7**, pp 191–98

Wiers-Jenssen, J, Stensaker, B and Grøgaard J B (2002) Student satisfaction: towards an empirical deconstruction of the concept, *Quality in Higher Education*, **8**, pp 183–95

Yonezawa, A (2002) The quality assurance system and market forces in Japanese higher education, *Higher Education*, **43** (1), pp 127–39

# Index